It Was Fun
While It Lasted

It Was Fun
While It Lasted

BY
ARTHUR H. LEWIS

Trident Press : New York

SBN 671–27106–7
Library of Congress Catalog Card Number: 72-88943
Designed by Irving Perkins
Manufactured in the United States of America
By American Book–Stratford Press, New York, N.Y.

1 2 3 4 5 6 7 8 9 10

ACKNOWLEDGMENTS

Special Credits: Herbert L. Golden; Dore Schary; Ray Crossett; George Cukor; Helen Strauss; Arthur Knight; Margaret Herrick; Florence Collis; Carl C. Curtiss; Charlotte Leigh-Taylor.

General Credits: Art Arthur; Harrison Carroll; Dave Friedman; Gloria Safier; George Glass; Bill Golden; Abel Green; E. T. "Buck" Harris; Bob Thomas; Al Horwits; Harry Kleiner; Harry Harris; Howard W. Koch; Chris Michon; Ken Murray; Tom Pryor; Harold Robbins; Hank Frankel; Linda Brent; Roy Newquist; Hal Mohr; John Springer; Irving Wallace; Herb Davis, Newspaper Department chief, Free Library of Philadelphia; Rosalie J. Coyle and Elaine V. Ebo, Theater Collection, Free Library of Philadelphia.

ARTHUR H. LEWIS
Virginia Center for the Creative Arts
Wavertree Farm,
Virginia
May, 1972

For my daughter,
Suzy, with love

Chapter One

"IF YOU want to find out what the ———'s happened to Hollywood, the best ———in' way to start is to come to my New Year's Eve party," advised Mr. Harold Robbins. "Whoever the ———'s left in that ———in' town will be there. It's going to be the last ———in' one I'll ever give."

I was aware that Mr. Robbins indeed spoke the truth about the near demise of Hollywood parties. Only recently I had read an interview the peripatetic partygoer, Cesar Romero, granted to UPI.

"The only big parties given today," Romero declared, "are for benefits or following premieres. Tax deductible, you know. Nobody can afford to give a huge, lavish party anymore. The closest thing these days are some of Liberace's costume parties. I went to one where he was dressed in a gold Santa Claus suit."

Eeech!

And so I accepted Mr. Robbins' invitation and spent the next four months in Hollywood. The man who conceived this junket is Herb Alexander, my editor. He gave me a few leads, a general idea of what I should look for, then waved good-bye to me at Kennedy where I stepped into one of TWA's 747s,

9

there to be ingurgitated by the usual assortment of haughty, stiff-necked, tight-assed hostesses.

This would not be my first trip to the onetime capital of the movie world. A few years back I spent several months there trying to grind out a script from one of my books Joe Levine bought and was in a desperate hurry to make into a movie. My colleague in this ill-fated venture was Jeremy Lloyd, a tall, skinny, funny (at least when he arrived) English actor-writer. After three weeks of utter frustration, Jeremy smashed his guitar against the wall, screamed "——— you, Hollywood!" and forthwith flew to London.

That movie, incidentally, has yet to be made, although over the years I read Joe's ads in trade publications wherein he claims the picture is currently "scripting," whatever this might mean. It would be the height of egotism for me to assume Mr. Levine's purchase of *The Day They Shook the Plum Tree* had anything to do with cooling the once passionate romance between *The Graduate*'s producer and the Aviation Corporation of America. I recall during a very early stage in their torrid, albeit truncated affair, the couple modestly announced to the world via sixty full-page ads in *Variety* that they would give birth to sixty motion pictures after breathtakingly brief periods of gestation.

This bedding down of Little Joe, the virile groom, and big Aviation Corporation of America (AVCO), the rich bride, somewhere on Paramount's huge lot, empty except for a lone company producing bad TV Westerns, was to be the start of Hollywood's comeback. It didn't work out that way. What was left of the "Industry" cocked a collective snook at its pigheaded, self-destructive unions and its anachronistic star system, and got the hell out of Hollywood. It fled to England, Spain, Italy, Yugoslavia, Mexico, and other lands to make a different kind of picture with a different kind of actor, for a different kind of audience.

To all of us for whom the movies still mean Garbo, Gable, Crawford, and Davis, and the gaudy moving picture cathedrals which once stretched cross-country from the Roxy to Sid Grauman's Chinese, this was indeed a bitter blow. However, we ourselves long ago switched allegiance from movies to television. Ergo, we couldn't reasonably expect the new generation for whom *our* American dream was cancelled out by the H bomb, Haight-Ashbury, Kent, Vietnam, and pot, to buy Doris Day, Betty Grable, Gregory Peck, Charlton Heston, and the other faded hams.

Most of the silver screen heroes and heroines of my youth and early middle-age, the twenties, thirties, forties, and fifties, either died or melted away into oblivion, although, surprisingly enough, quite a few survive both physically and professionally. For some inexplicable reason these hardy residuals still appeal to the only group—the eighteens to twenty-eights —willing to fork over three bucks to see a movie.

Why such a self-admitted anachronism as John Wayne, for example, can still draw bigger box-office receipts than Elliot Gould, or why college crowds cheer Lillian Gish and George Cukor, is as much a puzzle to members of this trio of rugged old-timers, or so they averred, as it is to me.

My first trip to Hollywood was made eleven years ago and to hell with *de mortuis nil nisi bonum.* The purpose of my short stay there was to begin a lawsuit against the late Charles K. Feldman, an unscrupulous talent-agent-turned-producer who took an option on one of my books and refused to pay for it despite a contract he couldn't wait to sign. Feldman tried to weasel out of the deal on a technicality but finally paid in full, not because of any change in his character, but because I had a good lawyer.

To get back to Harold Robbins' New Year's Eve party and the start of my hegira which ended only after interviewing several scores of Hollywood legends, and falling in love with Barbara Stanwyck, Joan Crawford, Lana Turner, Sylvia Sidney, possibly a half-dozen others whose names will come to me as I go along, and finally Zsa Zsa Gabor.

I'm usually first to arrive every place I go because I'm literal-minded. When an invitation says be there at eight o'clock I'm there on the dot of eight, often before my host has finished dressing and while my hostess is still in the shower.

I did it again, almost but not quite, at the Robbins' party. The invitation I fingered nervously and dropped twice on my way through the Beverly Hills Hotel lobby said "ten o'clock." Conscious of my propensity for being on time, I waited until five after ten before walking into the grand ballroom and presenting my credentials to a couple of Pinkertons all dressed up in fancy tuxedos but, to an old-time police reporter such as I, they were clearly recognizable as fuzz.

They finally cleared me but only after a sergeant scrutinized my invitation with care, even holding it up against the light to check possible forgery. I attribute this caution to the facts that (a) I was at least fifty-five minutes ahead of all but one of the expected guests, and (b) in contrast to the resplendent fuchsia, green, crimson, and beige garments worn even by the cops, my dinner jacket was plain, old-fashioned black, and my shirt was white, starched, and pleated. I suppose nothing like this had been seen in Hollywood since the days of D. W. Griffith.

Harold and his wife Grace, an attractive, dark-haired young woman, were there of course and so were the bands, one of them on the dais tuning up, the other unpacking instruments. A not-so-old (by my standards at any rate) actress named Lizabeth Scott had gotten to the party ahead of me, I think because she'd spent that afternoon with Grace Robbins, her friend. Miss Scott hails, as I do, from the hard-coal regions of Pennsylvania; she's a native of Scranton, home of the International Correspondence School. I toss in this last fact for the benefit of those who, like myself, go through life compiling thousands of utterly useless tidbits of information.

The first time I saw Miss Scott she was playing ingenue roles in Mae Desmond's Philadelphia repertory company and the last time, since I rarely go to the movies and then only under extreme pressure from my wife, was about 1946 when she had the lead in a Hal Wallis production called *The*

12

Strange Love of Martha Iver. My agent, Paul Gitlin, warned me never to ask members of the profession what their last picture was (or the first one either), so I kept silent on this score. Miss Scott volunteered nothing along those lines and our conversation was restricted to generalities. For me, this was a pretty bad start for an in-depth study of Hollywood.

Gradually the room began to fill and by eleven-thirty it was jammed. This may be a likely spot to do some name-dropping and show the importance of the people an internationally famous writer like Harold Robbins associates with. So I'll mention that among those present were Liza Minelli and father, Vincente, Sidney Poitier, Irving and Sylvia Wallace, Eva Gabor, Lana Turner, Anita Louise, Ernest Borgnine (I would run into him frequently during the coming months in our neighborhood A&P), Lawrence Harvey, Joanna Shimkus, Burt Bacharach and his wife Angie Dickinson, Bob Newhart, Vince Edwards, Connie Stevens, Rona Barrett, Carolyn Jones, and Jill St. John.

A columnist had reported recently that this last named attractive young lady claimed she was "dying" to play the lead in a book I wrote about a ten-thousand-dollar-a-night prostitute, *La Belle Otero.* Keeping in mind La Belle's vital statistics—42–32–38—I carefully scrutinized Miss St. John when we were introduced and without seeming to pry I asked Miss St. John if she could meet these specifications. The actress gave me a noncommittal shrug and we let it go at that.

I'm sorry to report that even though there was a plethora of celebrities, a couple of bands blasting away (one at a time, thank God!) with utter contempt for decibels, and dozens of waiters scurrying about wildly pushing drinks and hors d'oeuvres, the party was dead. Actually, I'd had more fun at the strawberry festivals they gave on the lawn of the German Lutheran Church across the street from our house in Mahanoy City.

I danced once, a fox trot, with Helen Strauss who used to be with the William Morris Agency. Except for Helen, I couldn't find another young lady who even *heard* of the fox trot. Besides, what the bands kept playing called for Terpsichorean skills I never did possess.

In one corner of the room, a well-known (or so I was told) television comedian named Marty Allen tried to liven the affair by removing all of his clothes except a diaper and then giving his famous interpretation of an infant. I tried to encourage Mr. Allen by applauding vigorously, as did Miss Scott, who was standing next to me. I think the comedian appreciated our little volunteer claque; no one else seemed to care.

A guy to my right muttered he'd heard Joe Levine was coming around to do card tricks. I didn't want to dash that wishful thinker's hopes by telling him I'd read only recently Joe was planning to spend this New Year's Eve in Monaco as a house guest of the Princess Grace. So I backed off and wandered around listening to the subdued chit-chat of all the Beautiful People quietly sipping cocktails and munching the elegant hors d'oeuvres our hosts thoughtfully provided.

I sneaked a look at my watch; it was only quarter to twelve. I hate to be a party pooper and although my own frail poop probably would have gone unnoticed, I was afraid that if I left then, a few husbands just might happen to see me and say to their wives, "O.K., can we go? We won't be the first to leave." Could be my act of self-indulgence would start a stampede for the exit and, since the Robbinses were gracious enough to invite me to their party, this would have been extremely rude. I figured I might as well stick it out at least until we all saw the New Year in together. So I retreated. It may have been only my imagination but I could have sworn that one gentleman, who had been eyeing me with hope as I edged my way toward the door, now regarded me with contempt. A girl who introduced herself as Barbara Eden stifled a yawn and propped herself into a vacant space along the wall beside me.

I finished a martini and was sucking on the olive stone wondering where to dispose of it when there came, without warning, first a ripple, then a wave, of excitement which started where the fuzz stood, then swept throughout the ball-

14

room. In its path it aroused even the most somnolent guest into a veritable tizzy of anticipation.

I am forced to mix a few metaphors to arrive at a reasonably accurate description of the phenomenon, something or someone—at the moment I didn't know which. I'm sure that when it happened, I myself was shocked out of my lethargy and gave little thought to the rhetorical potentials of the scene. I'd like to compare the reaction of Grace and Harold Robbins' guests to that of a vast field of wheat (corn, if you prefer), tall but listless under a soporific sun, suddenly twisted into wild undulating action by the unexpected presence of a strong fresh breeze sweeping out of nowhere.

I do not wish to prolong the suspense more than necessary to give it a proper buildup. The phenomenon turned out to be Zsa Zsa Gabor, and from the moment of her breathtaking arrival, Grace and Harold's party came to life. Zsa Zsa's no classic beauty; I think Mama and Eva are prettier. But this one's got something the others have not. I can't even tell you what she wore but when Zsa Zsa worked her way through the wildly enthusiastic crowd, calling out "Hello, dahlink" to each of the ladies and occasionally bussing one of the gentlemen, she was Madame Bovary, Lady Hamilton, Helen of Troy, Cleopatra, and Santa Claus.

How lucky can a man be? Just as Zsa Zsa got within a few feet of me the lights grew dim and both bands struck up "Auld Lang Syne." The moment arrived; Zsa Zsa reached out, threw her arms around me, and gave me a kiss. When I recovered my breath I wished the lady a Happy New Year and told her I couldn't think of a better way to start one.

Zsa Zsa glanced up at me.

"I can," she said.

Chapter Two

EVEN THOUGH I'm cursed with the obnoxious habit of waking up at six A.M. no matter what time I go to bed, I was perfectly willing to forgive others for sleeping that morning after. Naturally, at seventy-five bucks a day, which is what it cost me to live in Los Angeles, I was anxious to get going.

I have several old Hollywood acquaintances directly or indirectly connected with the Industry but I didn't dare telephone them until at least noon. So I spent the morning of January 1 examining resources and outlining my "campaign," although the truth is that at this moment I had no idea it would be necessary to conduct a campaign to see the men and women I wanted to.

In my innocence I assumed I'd have no more trouble reaching Hollywood personalities than I, or members of the working press, ever had getting to talk to almost anybody once objectives were clearly understood. During my lifetime I have interviewed senators, witch doctors, billionaires, murderers, Supreme Court justices, scientists, Miss Americas, and even one President of the United States. None of these, including a mass killer in the shadow of the electric chair, was running scared. In Hollywood, everyone is—and with good reason.

Figures change rapidly and conditions are getting worse all

the time, so I haven't any idea how many members of the Industry are out of work today. The last time I looked, eighty-five out of every hundred were jobless. Not long ago Jack Valenti, president of the Motion Picture Association, informed President Nixon, to whom he was appealing for tax relief, that the Industry "is in a state of collapse."

However, since I've neither the inclination nor the ability to write a report on the economics of the movies *vis à vis* Hollywood (or *vis à vis* anywhere for that matter), I'm not going to permit statistics to get in my way. Instead I'll concentrate on those comparatively few durable souls who, because of either peculiar abilities, philosophies, staying power, or cash reserve, face the future with equanimity.

Maybe I even ought to apologize for my remarkable inexpertise re the Movies, which factor, Herb Alexander assured me, is why he asked me to do this book.

"You don't know a goddamned thing about what's going on out there," he said, "and so you won't have any preconceived notions. This ought to give us a fresh point of view."

The expression on my face obviously troubled Herb. He shook his head.

"Look, my boy," he went on, "think of me as your mother [an impossible task; I loved my mother, *olav hasholem!*]. I packed your lunchbox with sandwiches, an apple, and a piece of homemade chocolate cake. You're off to the Fair; here's a quarter, enough for a ticket to the freak show, a ride on the roller coaster, and a bottle of Moxie. All you have to do is tell what you saw when you come back."

It may be that I'm acting unduly modest about my knowledge of the Industry and its products. Once, some time back it's true, I played the fiddle for a solid week in the augmented pit orchestra of the Victoria Theater in Mahanoy City, Pennsylvania, where Betty Blythe was making a personal appearance to promote *The Queen of Sheba* in which she starred. Even Louie Edwards, my classmate, who played at the rival Family Theater where they had five acts of vaudeville, was envious of my proximity to the luscious Miss Blythe.

Of course I developed a grand passion for Miss Blythe but kept it a secret for nearly half a century, finally making my confession to the star, whom I visited in her room at Hollywood's Country House. There retired members of the profession who are short of cash spend what are contradictorily known as the "Golden Years," and you can have them!

Furthermore, for the past two years, ever since my youngest grandchild developed an interest in the cinema, I've been accompanying him and his older sister to Saturday matinees, where amidst six inches of spilled popcorn and discarded candy wrappers we have seen *King Kong, Son of King Kong, King Kong vs. Godzilla,* and variations on the theme, plus one hour of Woody Woodpecker and Friends.

I should also point out that I am an expert on one film, *High Noon,* for which I am willing to sacrifice sleep whenever it appears on the Late, Late Show. Naturally everybody knows Gary Cooper and Grace Kelly played the leads and a few people are aware that Fred Zinneman was the director. But I defy even the most rabid aficionado of this 1952 Stanley Kramer classic to list the rest of the cast—Katy Jurado, Thomas Mitchell, Lloyd Bridges, Otto Kruger, Henry Morgan, Lucien Prival, William Newell, Howland Chamberlain, Ian MacDonald, William Phillips, and James Millican. And how many others are aware that the hit song, "Do Not Forsake Me, Oh My Darling," came from the pens of Dmitri Tiomkin and Ned Washington and was sung by John W. Cunningham?

Besides this encyclopedic knowledge of the Industry, I have two old friends who, for a goodly portion of their lives, have been connected with motion pictures. Each assured me I could count on him if I needed help; a telephone call to their New York homes or offices would suffice. The first of these is Dore Schary, who used to run M-G-M, and Herb Golden, for many years *Variety's* movie editor and critic and later vice-president of United Artists.

A few weeks before I left the East, I talked to Dore. We met on the stage of the Golden Theater where his play,

Brightower, was in rehearsal. The cast had just been dismissed for lunch and we had a half-hour or so. Schary sat on one chair and I was about to draw up another.

"For God's sake, don't touch it," he almost shouted. "You want to have the stagehands' union strike us?"

So hastily I obeyed and sat on the proscenium, legs dangling over the edge while I briefed Dore on my objective. That was, at the time, to have informal conversations with as many of Hollywood's great and near-great as I could arrange within the time limit I set—three to four months—and emerge with an unstructured history of the Industry based solely upon personal reminiscences. From this compilation I said I hoped to come out with the reasons for the death of Hollywood and find out if the body was too cold for artificial resuscitation.

Dore thought the idea sound, gave me a couple of hints on what to look for and what to avoid, suggested a few key people to see, and gave me his promise that if I needed help I could count on him. I scarcely mentioned the problem of arranging those interviews I planned because I didn't really think there'd be any problem. But Dore brought it up.

"I don't know how you're figuring on reaching some of the stars you want to see; you might have a bit of trouble on that end. A lot of them are in hiding; they can't face realities and won't admit they've had it. And they *don't* want to be interviewed. You saw *Sunset Boulevard,* didn't you?"

I nodded.

"Well, that's really true, today even more so than in 1950 when it was released. Hollywood was dying then but nobody believed it. At any rate, in some quarters mention of my name could be useful and you're welcome to it. A small number of people still remember me kindly."

He smiled.

"And a larger number don't. If you get to Lana Turner, for example, you'll find she's not one of my admirers, though I like her."

(This, as I discovered during a pleasantly productive afternoon and evening session with the indestructible star, was an understatement. Miss Turner, only occasionally given to profanity, at least in my presence, really let go when Dore's name came up, albeit merely in passing.)

Dore added that when I completed my research and returned to New York he'd be happy to tell me about his own experience making films on the M-G-M and other lots, and would give me his predictions for Hollywood's future. Then, when we were about to shake hands and say good-bye as his cast came back to work, Dore gave me an odd look.

"You wrote a book about witchcraft and witches once, didn't you?" he asked.

I nodded. In the book I explored the potency of warlocks and lady witches who thrive in Pennsylvania's hex belt.

"Want one of them to make a few incantations on *Brightower*'s behalf, Dore?"

He grinned and nodded.

"O.K.," I promised. "I'll get in touch with the most powerful *brager* I know."

Brightower, starring Robert Lansing and Geraldine Brooks, folded after a single performance. I was in Hollywood then and Dore sent me the following telegram:

> Your witch turned out to be a fagot. The play and I got clobbered.

If only to keep the record straight I am compelled to set forth these facts. *Brightower* opened and closed on January 29; the witch upon whom I relied died the night of January 28.

My friendship with Herb Golden dates back to the mid-1930s when we were both police reporters in Philadelphia; he on the ill-fated *Record* and I on the *Inquirer*. Herb, who now heads a corporation which finances movies, and I discussed my project in his office. After listening to me for a little while he threw up his hands in disgust.

"Jesus Christ! How do you expect to write a book about Hollywood when the last film you saw was *The Birth of a Nation?*"

This, I protested, was a gross exaggeration. I told him about my weekly pilgrimages to the lands of Godzilla and King Kong; that I'd seen not only *It Happened One Night* but also *True Grit* and that I never missed a Chaplin or Bogart revival.

"Not enough," he said sadly. "You'd better get with it so they won't toss you to hell out of the first studio you get into for asking stupid questions. Come over to the apartment for dinner tonight and I'll bring you up to date. There's a revolution going on out in Hollywood, kid, and you're talking about the Pleistocene age of films. I'll even give you the names of some people you ought to see before you disgrace yourself."

It is true, I suppose, that I *was* rather proud of my cinematic ignorance. But, as my friend Herb Golden correctly emphasized, such ignorance is not necessarily a prerequisite for doing an objective book on the subject. I spent most of that evening listening to Herb's synopsized version of major changes in the Industry.

"The thing to remember," he said, "is that they don't make movies out there anymore. Well, not many at any rate. Hollywood's no longer a center for film production; it's now merely a generic term for the entire Industry."

(I thought of this when Joan Blondell told me one of the most depressing experiences in her life was a stroll she took over the vast, lonely, empty Warners lot, the first time she'd been there in twenty years.)

Herb continued.

"Don't be fooled by what you see at Universal; that action bears little relation to the Industry. Much of the noise there comes from a big hotel they built on the lot and the bustle you'll hear is for yokels taking two-dollar studio tours to see other yokels taking two-dollar studio tours. And once in a while they might get a glimpse of Robert Stack making a TV series. Recently, there's been considerable stirring on this lot, but it's almost all for television.

21

"They did make *Airport,* and put everybody in it. It did great business, but I think this one'll be the last of Universal's, or anybody else's, ten-million-dollar gambles. Nobody has that kind of dough to risk anymore. Talk to my friend, George Seaton, *Airport's* producer, and you'll find he'll agree."

Airport did make money; I did talk to George Seaton, and he did agree.

The evening wound up with Herb's promise to send me a list of his Industry contacts and permission to use his name for introductions. But the following day he was leaving for Spain where his firm was financing a film and the letter wouldn't be sent until his return some time in January.

Actually, as I planned my strategy that New Year's day, I was confident that I wouldn't need anyone to pave my way. After all, I'reasoned, it was the stars I wanted to interview and, since most of them apparently had little to do, I was sure they'd be delighted to spend time with me. This would be as good a day as any, I felt, to start listing names of those I intended to see. I assumed I'd be able to handle at least three three-hour interviews per day. So, if I excluded weekends and deducted a small percentage of last-minute cancellations, I ought to talk to an average of a dozen men and women a week.

I'd brought with me the *International Motion Picture Almanac* which devotes almost three hundred fifty pages to brief biographies of Hollywood's Who's Who. The edition was only three years old but I figured this wouldn't make much difference. The criteria for their appearance on my list of the Chosen would be my familiarity, even if vague, with their names. While I could hardly be classified as a fan, I am a regular reader of the New York *Times,* several weekly news magazines, and all three Philadelphia dailies. So I have better than a cursory knowledge of what goes on in the world, including the portion of it known as Hollywood.

Four hours after I began combing the *Almanac* I was surprised to discover that between "Abel, Walter," and "Zukor,

Adolph," I'd amassed exactly four hundred prospects. A bug for the appearance of progress, if not progress itself, I carefully transferred each name to a five-by-eight index card, intending to fill therein what the *Almanac* left out, i.e., the address and telephone number of each of the Chosen.

Just for the hell of it I blindly pulled one card out of the pack, Ida Lupino, matched it in the telephone directory I had in my apartment, West Los Angeles, and there she was. This would be a snap. All I had to do now was look up the other three hundred ninety-nine, call only the pick of the litter, give them my pitch, make dates, and probably head for home by mid-February at the latest. I simply could not understand why several of my colleagues who'd worked the Hollywood beat on previous assignments kept trying to impress me with the logistical problems they were sure I'd encounter.

I might as well do this systematically, I told myself, so I extracted the first card, that of Abel, Walter. There was "Abel, Edward," "Abel, Richard," "Abel, Mrs. Russell," but no "Abel, Walter." Probably lives in Beverly Hills, or one of the other suburbs, I consoled myself. I'll check him later. So I went to the apartment office and borrowed three more L.A. area telephone directories. "Abel, Walter" wasn't in any of them. Nor was "Adler, Luther," "Ayres, Lou," "Crawford, Joan," "Cukor, George," "Davis, Bette," all the way through to "Robinson, Edward," "Stanwyck, Barbara," "Wayne, John," and "West, Mae."

What in the hell is this? I wondered. How can I be expected to reach these people if they haven't the decency to list their phone numbers? So I put aside my five-by-eights and walked out into the smog. I crossed over Fairfax to Sunset, had a milkshake at Schwab's Drugstore, but the only celebrity I saw there was Sid Skolsky oozing out of a telephone booth. It was still only a little past noon. I strolled past Grauman's Chinese, kept twisting my head to look at the names of Hollywood's famous embedded in bronze stars on the pavement, and wound up at Hollywood and Vine.

I haven't an iota of sentiment for this spot which a large

portion of surviving members of my generation regard as sacred. Now, at this fabled intersection, not so long ago mecca for believers in the Dream, there are only a couple of chain shoe stores, a pharmacy, and a bank. *Sic transit gloria mundi!*

Chapter Three

A FEW doubts about the ease of making contacts crept into my thoughts and I had a troubled sleep the night of January 1. I cheered myself up with the knowledge that at least I had Miss Lupino's telephone number. I figured she must know a lot of people in the Industry and that, after my interview with her, I'd wind up with a list of names, addresses, and permission from Miss Lupino to use her as a reference. That's the way it always worked out for me in the past.

I really didn't know much about Miss Lupino; as a matter of fact, I couldn't recall ever seeing her on stage or in the movies. But her uncle, Lupino Lane, was a great vaudeville favorite of mine and I planned to mention his name if only to prove I was an authority on family history. Before I placed the call, however, I checked the actress's biography in the *Almanac* and among her credits I discovered she'd appeared in *High Sierra*. I'd seen the picture, so I must have seen *her*. This gave me another point of reference. Of all the females on my list, she was one of the very few with the courage to give her date of birth (February 4, 1918). I wasn't sure just how I'd bring this into our conversation; as a matter of fact, I determined it might be best to ignore it.

It turned out all this advance planning was for naught. The

telephone number listed was Miss Lupino's answering service and all I could do was leave word. Miss Lupino eventually did call—she'd been out of the country—and sounded charming and cooperative. However, by that time I'd finished my research and was leaving for home the following day.

I kept trying to think of any Hollywood people I knew or at least interviewed in the past. Many years before I did a magazine piece about Cornel Wilde and since I'd spoken favorably of him, I thought he might remember me. But I hadn't the slightest idea where he lived or what *his* telephone number was. The last time I saw him was when I was working on the Paramount lot during the *Plum Tree* script for Joe Levine. Wilde was coming out of old Adolph Zukor's office one morning and he said hello in a friendly fashion although I'm sure he didn't remember me or the dinner we had together in 1953 at State College, Pennsylvania.

I remembered a former actress, Linda Brent, who'd become one of Paramount's story editors. We used to take coffee breaks together almost every day during the period I was on that lot. She, too, had an answering service number, but she did call me back the same day. Linda no longer worked for Paramount—practically no one else did either, she said sadly —but she knew Cornel Wilde was currently producing a film in England and probably wouldn't return to the United States for at least six months. I told her my problems and she said she'd try to dig up a few telephone numbers for me from her agent. "Don't call me," she said. "I'll call you in a week or so."

It occurred to me that I'd once done a TV documentary for CBS. Jack Palance was the narrator for this hour-long show; we'd worked together on location and he, our producer Al Hollander, and I won an Honorable Mention at the Emmy Awards for it. In addition to all this, Palance and I were born and raised within a few miles of each other and had a number of mutual friends in the hard-coal regions of Pennsylvania.

I'm not sure why Jack hadn't made my original list, perhaps because I didn't think he'd been around Hollywood long enough to have memories of the good old days. But now I hastily filled out his five-by-eight. He'd given me both his address and unlisted telephone number but naturally I'd left them at home. I thought it about time to call my wife anyway and let her know I'd survived the Robbins' New Year's Eve party.

I got the information I needed and as soon as we hung up I called Palance and of course reached his answering service. Mr. Palance was in Mexico making a film; they had no idea when he'd return. I racked my brain for other possible leads and dredged up two potentials. One, Harry Kleiner, a former Philadelphia newspaperman I used to know, has been in Hollywood these past twenty-five years writing scripts. The second was W. R. Burnett, author of *Little Caesar*, *Scarface*, *High Sierra*, and half a hundred other novels. His studio on the Paramount lot was next to mine, he was friendly and helpful, and, what was more important, I had his telephone number with me.

Both Kleiner and Burnett, I was positive, would know *everyone* and exactly how to reach them; I couldn't understand why I hadn't thought of them sooner. Since I already had his number I called Burnett first. A very gracious voice answered, wife, daughter, or friend, I didn't ask. "Sorry, but Mr. Burnett is in Peru, working on a script for a film being shot there." When was he expected back in Hollywood? "Oh, certainly not for at least three more months."

Kleiner wasn't even listed in the telephone directory. But I recalled he had a brother, a practicing psychiatrist, and he *was* listed, but for all the good it did the physician might as well have remained anonymous. I slashed my way through answering service, receptionist, nurse, wife, and finally the doctor, himself. "You say you're a friend of Harry? Too bad; he's in Australia making a picture and we haven't *any* idea when he's coming home."

Harold Robbins' office was only a few blocks from my apartment. I knew Harold wouldn't be there—he'd left for New York the morning after his party—but I had to discuss my problem with somebody and thought maybe one of his secretaries or his assistant, Ray Crossett, would be around. I drove my rented car up Sunset and found the office open, although it was, by that time, three P.M. and I recalled that Hollywood observes long weekends, Friday noon till Monday noon.

Unless you're aware that the writing of books is only one of Robbins' major activities (the minors include collecting the works of unknown artists and yachting), you might wonder why in the hell he needs a suite of offices, a couple of secretaries, and an assistant. I haven't any idea how many other projects Robbins is involved in at any given time, but I know he has something to do with recording popular musicians and is connected with the production of several successful TV shows and one which bombed—*The Survivors*, starring Lana Turner.

Beneath a façade of toughness—four-letter words stream from his mouth—Robbins is a soft touch. I suspect that if it weren't for Crossett who culls the list of prospective visitors and eliminates those who have no legitimate business there, Robbins wouldn't have time for much besides listening to propositions, collecting unsolicited manuscripts, and giving interviews.

Except for a brief stint in New York where he was executive story editor at CBS, Crossett's been in Hollywood ever since his graduation from the Yale School of Drama. He's worked at Universal–International and most of the other major studios and is a walking compendium of detailed information about Industry personalities, except for their telephone numbers and addresses.

"*Nobody's* got them," he said emphatically. "I'm afraid that's going to be your major problem, same as it is for everybody who comes out to do interviews. There's no list; the studio won't pass out information and, besides, I'm sure most of the people you want to see haven't had studio connections for years, ever since they stopped working. All you'll get from the Screen Actors Guild is the name of the stars' agents, and a lot of them no longer have agents. They're really in hiding and have no desire to be interviewed and have their pasts dredged up."

He sighed.

"This town is dead; the ghosts don't even come out at night. They stay home to watch their earthly bodies in old films on TV."

I hardly needed anyone else to tell me what problems I faced and I wondered just what in the hell I'd gotten into. But Ray wasn't all negative.

"I'll see Helen Strauss for you when she gets back from New York next week. She's in touch with a lot of people out here. You can have dinner with us if you want. And if you'd like, I'll call Lana Turner now and see what I can do for you; she's a good friend of mine."

Naturally Miss Turner wasn't in; out of town for a few weeks. Ray left word and I left Ray. I was still unable to convince myself there wasn't some easier method of reaching the people on my list. I'd never run into anything like this in my life. The next day was Saturday and there wasn't a damned thing I could do then except berate myself.

I had dinner that night with an old Columbia U. classmate, Herman Hover, who used to own the famous Ciro's. He wasn't encouraging.

"You'll simply have to keep plugging," he said. "Years ago I knew everybody; they used to come to my restaurant. But they've all faded away. Those who invested wisely and saved their dough live in mansions in the hills or canyons. Those who're broke are out at The Country House. You can't even get to see them unless you're cleared; they protect their own and don't furnish anyone with a list of who's there. The only one I know of there is Edmund Lowe. Remember him?"

Of course I remembered Edmund Lowe. Who wouldn't recall Sergeant Quirt and his rival, Captain Flagg, played by Victor McLaglen, in *What Price Glory?* and its innumerable sequels. Their "Sez you, sez me" repartee was part of our American culture. I never did see Lowe; when I finally got to

29

The Country House, he was in the hospital and wasn't allowed visitors. The handsome, slick-mustached star who made his debut in 1923 survived the advent of sound and for two more decades played the suave rascal opposite Hollywood's most beautiful women in half a hundred films. He died broke last year at the age of eighty-one. Once married to the late Lilyan Tashman, a gorgeous blonde star of the thirties, he had no known survivors.

So much for nostalgia. The next day, Sunday, Linda Brent called to give me the address of Bette Davis and Ann Harding, both of whom are living in suburban New York and come to Hollywood only upon rare occasions. So, temporarily at least, I removed two five-by-eights from my index cards.

Before I'd left New York I'd had dinner with an old friend, Abel Green, editor of *Variety*. He knows a lot of people in the Industry but he doesn't know where they live.

"But if you ever need help on your project," he said, "try Tom Pryor. He's editor of *Daily Variety* on Sunset Boulevard. You can tell him I sent you."

I needed help all right that Monday morning and called Tom. Like most members of the working press, he was glad to do what he could for a colleague or even an ex-colleague. We spread my cards on his desk; he thumbed through them quickly, discarding dozens without saying a word. I asked him why he was tossing these aside. He looked at me very quizzically.

"These are all dead, man. Montgomery Clift, Wendell Corey, Albert Dekker, Dan Duryea, Kay Francis, Lillian Harvey, and Franchot Tone. Where'd you get the names from?"

I told him.

He shook his head and kept eliminating prospects, one by one. Then he counted what was left; it came to a total of three hundred thirty-one.

"Now let's break these down. A lot of them live in the East around New York. Walter Abel, Joan Crawford, she's with Pepsi-Cola—I thought everybody knew that—Geraldine Fitzgerald, Lillian Gish, and Colleen Moore—she's in Chicago but you can hardly ever find her there; she's traipsing around the country with her doll collection raising funds for charities.

"I'll tell you something else; quite a few on your list won't see anybody. Mary Pickford, for example. She's down in Palm Springs but you'd be wasting your time trying. I know. I get a lot of visiting firemen like you every month. Crosby takes only rare appointments and so does Harold Lloyd (who has since died).

"I notice there's a few directors and producers on your list. How come? I think you might see some of them."

I shrugged my shoulders.

"I suppose," I answered, "it's because the names of only a few are familiar to me."

"Well, you ought to go after several if you want to find out what's been going on out here. You got Cukor. What about Lewis Milestone, one of the greatest of them all? And you should speak at least to a couple of the newer breed—Delbert Mann who just finished his verson of *David Copperfield* in England. I imagine he's available and I know he lives in Beverly Hills."

I asked a leading question.

"Do you have his telephone number?"

Pryor shook his head.

"Nope. I haven't *any* addresses or telephone numbers. You're going to have to sweat your way through for these. Nobody's going to hand them out."

Here we go again, I said, but only to myself. How in the hell will I get them?

Out loud I bemoaned.

"But I've been here six days already, Tom, and I haven't a single one."

"That's always the problem. Just use up your contacts. You couldn't possibly have come out here without them, or did you?"

I told him about Herb Golden and Dore Schary, both of whom he knew but that the former was out of the country and that the latter was doing a show and I hesitated to call him.

"Telephone him anyway," Pryor advised. "He won't mind, I'm sure. You used to be a Philly newspaperman, weren't you?"

I said yes.

"Did you know a guy named Al Horwits?"

"Sure," I answered. "He used to do sports on the old *Evening Ledger*. Is *he* out here?"

"Man! You really aren't with it. Al's been around Hollywood for at least thirty years. He used to do p.r. for several of the majors. Right now he's an associate of Richard Brooks. Brooks and he did *In Cold Blood*. You saw that, didn't you?"

I was ashamed to admit I hadn't; at least I'd read the book.

"Their company's called Pax Pictures, and they've *got* to be in the directory. Al's a nice guy and he knows his way around. Not a bad place to start if he remembers you."

"I think he will. I'll call him later."

Pryor had another suggestion. He thought I should interview a few cinematographers.

"Hal Mohr, for example. He's one of the really great; won all manner of Academy Awards. Must be in his seventies now but he's still active. Then there's James Wong Howe who's just as great although considerably younger. He was director of photography for *The Molly Maguires*. I saw the screening last night. It's awful; cost Paramount nearly fifteen million dollars and my prediction is that it'll bomb. But the photography's magnificent."

(*The Mollies* did bomb, but more of that later.)

It was then I admitted I'd written the book *Lament for the Molly Maguires* which Paramount bought and upon which the film was supposedly based. Or, as phrased in the screen credits: Story suggested from a book, etc. Tom said he hoped he hadn't offended me and I answered that he hadn't.

"Mohr's easy to reach," Pryor told me. "Just call him at the American Society of Cinematographers; they're in the L.A. directory, on Orange Street, I think. If he's not in, leave word;

he'll call you back, he's very reliable. And through Mohr you ought to be able to reach James Wong Howe."

He frowned.

"Outside of Al Horwits, and he isn't in that end of the business anymore, you don't have a single press agent on your list. You surely should see Howard Strickling, the greatest of them all. Just retired after a hell of a long time with M-G-M. He's the guy who coined that phrase, 'There are more stars at M-G-M than in Heaven.' And Howard really made stars out of a lot of men and women. He's a nice guy, too, very modest."

"O.K.," I said. "Now how do I reach Howard Strickling?"

Pryor smiled.

"Sorry. That's your chore."

While we were talking Tom sorted out my five-by-eights and separated them into three neat piles.

"These are all either deceased or otherwise unavailable," he explained, pointing to the smallest pile. "And some of these live abroad, like Audrey Hepburn, David Niven, and Douglas Fairbanks, Jr., or in Africa where William Holden spends most of his time."

The prospect of foreign travel was intriguing, I confessed, but only at somebody else's expense, not mine. It was costly enough for me to work just in Hollywood. The second, and slightly larger stack, contained the names of "prospects" living in the New York area.

"You can work on these when you return east," Tom advised. "As far as I know they have neither offices, agents, nor current connections here."

The third, and by far the largest pile, bore the names of those who still lived in the Los Angeles area, at least as far as Pryor knew. I'd wasted enough of his time by then and deferred until a later date asking Tom what *he* thought had happened to Hollywood.

Chapter Four

I COULDN'T wait to get on the telephone in my apartment. I called Al Horwits first. "Out of town," his secretary informed me. "Should be back in a week or two." Hal Mohr was next. "On location," they told me at the Cinematographers Society, and I left word. I then put in a call to Dore. Kay, his secretary, said he couldn't be reached—he was at the theater —until late that evening. I told Kay my problems and she promised she'd have Dore telephone Margaret Herrick at the latter's home as soon as he could.

"Call Mrs. Herrick tomorrow afternoon; I'm sure by then Dore will have spoken to her. She should be able to give you a lift, and I think she will."

Dore had told me Mrs. Herrick ran the Academy Awards; that she was a gracious, lovely woman and probably knew more people in the Industry than anyone else. I called her the following afternoon; Dore had reached her the preceding evening as Kay had promised. Mrs. Herrick said she'd be delighted to help but, unfortunately, she was going to New York early the next day and would be gone for at least a week.

Meanwhile Ray Crossett suggested I speak to a guy named

Buck Harris, director of the Screen Actors Guild. Ray thought that if Buck opened up, he could furnish me with all the leads I'd need since practically every actor and actress belongs to S.A.G. I called Buck, his office was only a few blocks from my apartment, and he told me to come right over.

Harris was friendly enough but he wasn't much help. Ethics, he said, barred him from furnishing me with either addresses or telephone numbers of Guild members. However, if I gave him up to a total of fifty names of those I wanted to see, he'd list their talent agents. This I did while he waited. But, as I discovered after a few telephone calls, those agents either didn't know where their "star" clients were hiding or wouldn't tell. Quite a few of them said they hadn't been in touch with their "clients" for a good many years except for an occasional telephone call. One, who asked me not to use his name, was quite frank.

"We can't do a damned thing for these old-timers. They were good in their day, all right, and we did make money *for* them and *from* them. That's why our agency doesn't object when they list us as their representatives. But we really *don't* represent them; they've nothing to offer. The new breed which might last for only one picture has taken over. No stars anymore. That system is shot to hell I'm very sorry to say. We're concentrating on TV. Hollywood's finished."

I wanted to pursue this theme with the gentleman but he'd said all he intended to say. Helen Strauss returned from New York that afternoon; I had dinner with her and Ray Crossett. Each had come through for me; Helen with a date for me to see George Cukor the following morning and Ray'd talked to Lana Turner whom I was to see the next week.

I'd been "on location" for nine days, made innumerable telephone calls, used every contact I could dredge up, and until this moment I'd gotten nowhere. From here on in I'd do better and see many of the people I'd set out to see. But I never overcame the feeling that I was living in a city of ghosts.

George Cukor, I should say, is far from being spectral. He

has strong opinions about everybody and everything and confidently expects to become active in the Industry shortly although he admits his last picture, *Justine,* could hardly be classified either as a box-office or artistic success.

"*Justine* was the story of child prostitutes, but they wouldn't let us use children; so I had to substitute midgets. They weren't very convincing."

He likes Andy Warhol. "That man gives you good, strong whiffs of the gutter. He's not afraid to put whatever he smells and sees on the screen." Cukor loathes all "method schools" of acting. "The only thing those idiots do is *talk* around the subject. They can't *act* worth a damn."

Despite *Justine,* Cukor's list of screen credits, artistic achievements, and box-office successes is probably as great if not greater than any other director in Hollywood's history. After several years on Broadway where he did *The Constant Wife, The Great Gatsby,* and other successes of the twenties, he came to Hollywood to write dialogue for *All Quiet on the Western Front.*

He was co-director for the filmed version of *The Royal Family* and directed such movie classics as *Dinner at Eight, David Copperfield, Holiday, The Philadelphia Story, Winged Victory, Gaslight, Born Yesterday,* and one of the greatest money-makers of them all, *My Fair Lady.*

Among the stars he's handled are Garbo and Katharine Hepburn (two of his favorites—scores of their autographed pictures adorn his walls), James Mason, Leslie Howard, Rex Harrison, Cary Grant, W. C. Fields, Judy Garland, Wallace Beery, James Stewart, Jean Harlow, Judy Holliday, Charles Boyer, John Barrymore, Norma Shearer, in fact, the whole gamut of M-G-M stars. For it was on this lot that Cukor did most of his best work, although he directed *Little Women* (Hepburn again, with Jean Parker, Joan Bennett, Douglass Montgomery, and Frances Dee) for RKO.

"George saved his dough," Crossett had commented. "When his colleagues and the stars he made squandered theirs, Cukor didn't. He's a shrewd land speculator, too, knows exactly what to buy, what to hang onto, and what to sell. He's great on art, too, not quite in Edward G. Robinson's class, but it's still pretty damned valuable. And wait till you see his house. It's elegant, not lavish, but in superb taste."

Cukor's home, a stone structure built on several levels to take advantage of the rolling land on which it's located, stands near the summit of a rise a few hundred yards from the point where Los Angeles and Beverly Hills merge. Compared to Zsa Zsa's spectacular palace atop one of the canyons, Cukor's dwelling is indeed modest. Even so, I lost my way trying to find the main entrance after announcing my arrival into a speaking tube at the gate. By remote control the catch was lifted. Thinking the smallest of several bungalow-type buildings on the grounds was Cukor's office, I wandered up to the door but when nobody answered my knocks, I walked back to the driveway. A few moments later a short, slender man, wearing an old gray bathrobe, poked his head out of another door.

"You're knocking at the wrong place," he called out. "These are my guest houses where I put up my friends when there's an overflow."

The initial order of business was a house tour, the first level at any rate, and an introduction to his secretary, Irene Burns, an attractive, young-middle-aged woman who's been with him for years. I wish I'd taken a course in art appreciation; I would have been better able to identify the dozens of paintings all over the walls. But at least I did recognize the photographs and those I looked at more carefully were all inscribed with affectionate greetings from their subjects.

We wound up in a cheerful room, the bright morning sun streaming in through opened windows. I suppose it could be called a "den," although I'm sure my host would shudder at this classification. I asked him what he thought of the current crop of stars. He shook his head.

"There are no more stars. That system's dead as hell and any major studio that tries to revive it is doomed."

He ran his hand through a thin crop of graying hair.

"What am I talking about—major studios? There aren't any majors left. Take a walk around any of the lots and you'll see what I mean. But to get back to the stars.

"It's been said many times before, and you'll hear it again and again before you leave Hollywood, which doesn't necessarily detract from its truth, the youngsters who achieve success, even great success in a single production, aren't necessarily going on to fame. We've got to wait and find out how they make out in their next couple of pictures. Take the Fondas. Hank's a star but before you place Jane or Peter in the same category these two will have to prove themselves. To call either of them a star would be ridiculous. They're good, all right, and they may make it. But let me tell you what is one of the most important ingredients of stardom."

He paused to refill our coffee cups, then went on.

"The ability to *last*; that's what a star must possess, year after year after year, and film after film after film. I agree that today, without the backing of a major studio, it's almost impossible to achieve stardom. I'm not bemoaning the passing of the majors; their time had come; they were too shortsighted to realize that for survival they'd have to change tactics. So they died, and so did Hollywood!

"The stars of the old days were the 'property' of their studios. They were nurtured, protected, shielded, and fed to the public in just as large doses as the public would accept. And the public had to accept a great deal. The majors controlled the theaters where the films they made had to be shown. Block booking did it throughout America. The majors *made* the stars; that's something you should never forget although so many of these same stars thought they'd made it on their own. Believe me, they didn't!"

He shook his head reflectively.

"Of course, many had genuine talent—Hepburn, Ina Claire, whom I consider one of the greatest of them all, Garbo, and so on. But the majority weren't nearly as important as the studios made them. The public believed they were 'royalty' and God knows there are many members of true royal families who aren't worth as much.

"When the majors died, the stars died with them. Many of them have left town or scattered to homes in the hills or canyons, there to dream of the good old days and watch themselves on the Late, Late Show and pray they'll make a comeback. They won't. It's all over for them and they can't accept it.

"They're on their own now and will be for the rest of their days. They no longer have Howard Strickling—the great press agent—to create their romances for them, keep their peccadillos out of the newspapers, stage their grand entrances wherever they go, and make them feel wanted and important."

I asked Cukor what he thought about his contemporaries and perhaps to express an opinion about some of the newer directors. He frowned slightly for a moment.

"I suppose I'd put Billy Wyler and Henry Hathaway near the head of the class, at least of those who are still around and kicking. Billy did so many films but you might recall a few— *The Little Foxes, Wuthering Heights, Detective Story, The Desperate Hours, The Best Years of Our Lives, Mrs. Miniver, Funny Girl.* I could go on but I hope I've made my point.

"And as for Henry, he, too, has an impressive list of credits—*Trail of the Lonesome Pine, The House on 92nd Street,* 13 *Rue Madeleine, Call Northside* 777, *Rawhide, Desert Fox,* all great films and all box-office successes. You ought to try to see both of these fellows."

(I saw neither Wyler nor Hathaway; both were out of the country.)

Cukor, I noted, did not include Hathaway's last in which he was producer-director, *Nevada Smith,* a film adapted from a character in one of Harold Robbins' books. The picture, unfortunately, was both an artistic and financial failure. I further noted, although I said nothing aloud, that even I realize most of the examples of both Wyler's and Hathaway's

39

films were done in the dim past, the thirties, forties, and early fifties.

Of the current directors, Cukor considers Fellini among the best.

"The man has enormous talent and *Satyricon* is a great picture, really tremendous. He's a director who's aware of the current changes in taste and acceptability. The others just don't have it, younger men like Howard W. Koch the producer or Delbert Mann. Both second-rate talents although I must give them an 'E' for effort."

I was hardly in a position to disagree with one of Cukor's stature and experience, but I did think Koch's *The Manchurian Candidate* was a pretty good film and I must say I enjoyed Delbert Mann's *Marty* and *The Dark at the Top of the Stairs.*

A short while later I went out to what is left of the Twentieth Century-Fox lot for a screening of Mann's latest feature film, *David Copperfield,* produced in England at a cost of $1,700,000. NBC did the major financing and in turn received TV rights with Fox, expecting to release the picture in U.S. theaters. I preferred Cukor's version of the Dickens classic done in 1935, starring Freddie Bartholomew and W. C. Fields, but I still thought what Mann did was great. The critics disagreed and the movie bombed. Admittedly, my track record is not good. I recalled that after opening night of the play, *My Fair Lady,* I turned to my wife and said, "It's not a bad show, but unfortunately there's not a single hit tune in it."

Cukor has always had strong opinions of critics. His favorite was the late Robert Benchley.

"Here was a reviewer who never resorted to wisecracks to show his erudition and his wit at the expense of the show. And he didn't always like what I did. On the other hand, there's Judith Crist, a catty woman who wears her ignorance as a shining badge and has absolutely no sense of humor."

Several other matters annoy Cukor. One of these is what he

claims is the elimination of romance in the modern film.

"I'm certainly not against sex and never have been. However, in my opinion at least, before a couple climbs into bed there should be some kind of romantic buildup. Otherwise, what's the fun? The seduction of a woman, obviously itching to get laid as quickly as possible and who accomplishes her mission in the first few moments, can't be nearly as exciting or suspenseful to the audience as gradual seduction.

"I'm thinking of Shaw's *Lady Windermere's Fan* or *A Bill of Divorcement*, a film I directed in 1932, starring Hepburn— a great actress by the way, and a great lady, too—and John Barrymore. You know the plot, I'm sure, so I won't go into the fact that the heroine's virtue was vital to the plot. Today, the modern generation couldn't care less about a lady's virtue."

The coffeepot was empty by this time; one of my host's maids brought us a fresh supply, and Cukor continued.

"Let me tell you something about today's kids. I call them the 'Now' generation; they want everything right away— knowledge, sex, you name it—and they can be goddamned rude if they don't get it.

"A couple of days ago they showed *A Bill of Divorcement* to a group of students, forty or fifty of them, boys and girls, cinema majors at either U.S.C. or U.C.L.A., I don't recall which. This was in the theater where they hold the Academy Awards. Mrs. Herrick, who runs the Awards, asked me if I'd mind being present and talk to the kids afterward. I accepted.

"Now even though the audience knew I was in the house— I was introduced to them from the stage before they showed the film—they were shockingly nasty. They guffawed all through the picture and gave me what my friend Mae West calls 'the bum's laugh.' I wasn't embarrassed; I was angry; their rudeness was terribly disconcerting.

"What these young people should have done instead of laughing is to realize they were looking at a picture made nearly forty years ago. And, by the way, all three of the women in it, Maggie Albeniese, Cornell, and Hepburn went on to become stars. They were great actresses in 1932 and they're great actresses in *any* day."

My host, obviously annoyed at this unpleasant recollection, paused for a moment, shook his head, then went on.

"*This* is the generation we have to propitiate and to make movies for. A generation which acts as though it has the divine right to say what it wants to say without listening to a goddamned thing first. Furthermore, it doesn't have the slightest idea *how* to listen. Yet, with all its bad thinking and worse manners, it is 'the hope of the world.' God help us!"

Rather in agreement with Cukor is Joseph Pasternak who relates in his book *The Studio*, "You know what the real story for today's kids is? . . . It's about an eighteen-year-old girl who f———s but who's afraid to fall in love."

Since I may not get the opportunity to insert it later and because this so aptly describes what I found out, I'm going to add a few words the author himself made about Hollywood's difficulties despite the fact that these comments give aid and comfort to the enemy.

"The big problem in Hollywood today is replacement. All the big stars are on crutches. You get a young girl falling in love with Gary Grant. In real life she may sleep with him once or twice to see what it's like, then she may leave him. In Hollywood they live happily ever after."

I'll take leave of Mr. George Cukor for another brief interlude and tell you about a most unscientific poll I made on the campus of two Los Angeles area universities where they actually give credits for courses in the movies. The head of the department of one of these institutes of higher learning, the University of Southern California, is Arthur Knight, an articulate gentleman with impeccable taste who is a distinguished movie critic for *Saturday Review* and husband of a beautiful blonde.

I might add that the Knights live atop a mountain reached via a narrow road as hazardous as can be found anywhere including those winding, precipitous, narrow-gauge affairs which wander through the Italian Alps. It was only by memorizing Mr. Knight's explicit directions about turns (which, to this day, I remember), "Left, right, right, left," that guests arrive safe, albeit nervous.

"Otherwise," Mr. Knight explained, "you'll go over into the goddamned canyon, a thousand-foot drop. We lose quite a few guests that way."

"You'll frighten the man, Arthur," Mrs. Knight interjected. "You *know* that happens only when you deliberately reverse the directions."

At Professor Knight's invitation I attended not only a three-day moving picture seminar which he ran during my stay in Hollywood, but I also had the privilege of auditing several of his classes, all filled with wildly enthusiastic students. It is easy to account for the fervor Professor Knight generates among those privileged to sit at his feet. During my regrettably brief abecedarianship at U.S.C., it seemed to me that most classroom hours were spent either listening to the Professor's salty comments about the entertainment world in general or else looking at movies, some of which were old and some not yet released. It was here I saw my first full-length sexploitation film, *Trader Hornee* (the "ee"s are silent), with its producer-director-author, David Friedman, on hand to interpret his opus if anyone felt the need for an interpretation. More of Mr. Friedman and his stars later. Right now I should like to discuss my poll.

Early one morning before class I typed out a list of twenty-five stars, at least those I, in my naïve fashion, still regarded as stars. To be fair I excluded performers who were equally or even better known on Broadway than in Hollywood. I thus eliminated such members of the profession as Walter Abel, Barbara Bel Geddes, Melvyn Douglas, Deborah Kerr, Geraldine Fitzgerald, Helen Hayes, and Walter Pidgeon. There were others of similar stature.

I also excluded vintage performers whose names (which out

43

of kindness I shall not mention) might be known to men and women of my generation but, to my youthful classmates, as remote as Margaret Anglin, Sarah Bernhardt, John Drew, or Edwin Forrest. In addition I peremptorily tossed out two more stars, Steve McQueen and Paul Newman, because even if they're not quite of the Now generation, they're close to it. Nor did I include Dustin Hoffman, Elliot Gould, and Robert Redford, who haven't been around long enough.

However, I did list June Allyson, Cary Grant, Doris Day, Kirk Douglas, Charlton Heston, Burt Lancaster, Fred Mac-Murray, Maureen O'Sullivan, Gregory Peck, James Stewart, Barbara Stanwyck, Lana Turner, John Wayne, Mae West, Robert Young, and twelve others of the same ilk who, to me, represented the Hollywood I knew. The question I put to my quondam classmates at U.S.C. and to a similar congeries of students at U.C.L.A. was simply this: "Would you pay three bucks to see any of these twenty-five starred in a feature film?"

For Allyson, Day, Heston, Lancaster, MacMurray, O'Sullivan, Peck, Stewart, Young, and the other twelve there was not a single "aye." Well, that's not quite fair; I thought I detected a glint in the eyes of a pretty, long-haired blonde coed when Cary Grant's name came to her attention. On the other hand, Stanwyck, Turner, Wayne, and West came out surprisingly well, the last two garnering a high percentage of votes cast.

"How come John Wayne?" I asked one group. A bearded youth thought this over for a minute or two before answering. He finally said, rather wistfully, "Well, maybe he represents the lost American Dream. A big, strong, virile guy who knows how to use his fists and his gun to see that justice triumphs and evil is punished."

When I asked, "Why Mae West?," the answer which came from a half-dozen young ladies gathered around me was instantaneous. Almost as one they sang out, "High camp!"

Without fee, obligation, or even reimbursement for out-of-pocket expenses, I hereby offer my findings to those powers intrusted with the task of making profitable motion pictures and return to Mr. George Cukor with a promise to relate next, albeit out of chronological sequence, how I spent an afternoon with Miss Mae West.

If you recall, we left my host, Mr. Cukor, alone with a bunch of unruly members of the Now generation who, with catcalls and shrieks of disappointment, watched the presentation of A *Bill of Divorcement*. In the end, the director of that classic film came out quite well indeed. When the lights went on, Mr. Cukor once more stepped upon the stage. This time he let his audience have it. He criticized them for their arrogance, berated them for their failure to recognize great talent, and lashed into them for their display of bad manners. All in all, it was a well-deserved spanking which made up for parental permissiveness.

Then, drawing upon his vast experience as director of nearly a hundred major feature films, he touched briefly upon the details of picture-making. He wound up by pointing out that no one has ever found a satisfactory substitute for the prime ingredient of a successful movie—entertainment. When the rebuttal ended I could tell from the tapes that his audience, all of whom were Mr. Cukor's juniors by half a century, were eating out of the director's hand. The applause was tumultuous. I'm sure Mr. Cukor was just as pleased with this response as he was with the hours he stood on the same stage to receive his Academy Awards.

I visited Mr. Cukor several times more. We talked about books—he is an omnivorous reader; his favorite author and great friend was the late Aldous Huxley. We talked about Hollywood's future which he admitted was bleak, indeed, except for the hope of pay-TV which he felt was a full ten years off. (I was to hear this same opinion expressed by a great many other members of the motion picture colony.) Once, Mr. Cukor mentioned that his first mission in Hollywood was to write the dialogue for *All Quiet on the Western Front* (this was in 1929). He thought I should see Lewis Milestone, who directed the film, and Lew Ayres, who starred.

45

"It was a breakthrough in films, and an important one," he said. "For the first time American audiences were shown the enemy wasn't too different from themselves."

The last time I saw Mr. Cukor, he wondered if I might enjoy speaking to an old friend, Edward G. Robinson. When I answered, "Of course," he promptly called the star of *Scarface* and a hundred other films, and made a date for me to see him. Then, as I was about to leave, he had another thought.

"Why don't you talk to Mae West? I'll set it up for you if you'd like. It should be fun."

It was.

Chapter Five

"I SAVED Hollywood once; they brought me out here to do it again."

So says Miss Mae West, aged seventy-nine or thereabouts and who doesn't look a day over sixty.

For Hollywood's near-fatal illness ("It ain't dead yet and it won't be if they let *me* go to town."), Mae has a simple two-part explanation. The first, she claims, is her own absence from the scene for more than a quarter of a century, and the second, to quote Miss West directly, "They're makin' the titles on the pictures too long. You can't fit the names of the stars on the marquees anymore and that won't bring in the customers. If they'd oney stop this nonsense they'd be bound to make a comeback. Otherwise, all they got left is pay-TV and that's a good five years off."

I didn't know what films the star was referring to, but I hoped she wasn't counting on her latest, *Myra Breckinridge*, to resurrect the onetime movie capital which, despite Mae's good intentions, did little more than hammer a few more nails into Twentieth Century-Fox's coffin. But more of *Myra B.* later.

It was a little difficult for me to concentrate on the star's

47

words, not only because I had a feeling I was interviewing some kind of national shrine, but also because I am allergic to the scent of roses and there must have been at least three gross of American Beauties in vases scattered throughout the room in which we sat.

"From my admirers," Miss West said by way of explanation. "All that's left over from Valentine's Day. You should o' been around then; must have been at least twice as many."

I suppressed a sneeze and surreptitiously swallowed an antihistamine pill while Miss West, observing my momentary discomfort and sensing the reason for it, graciously removed a huge container of flowers from a table beside my chair and placed it on top of a grand piano several yards away.

I was glad the piano was called to my attention. It is a magnificent instrument, pure white except for gold-and-ivory trim and with a galaxy of rosy cherubs adrift and floating all over the keyboard, down the sides to the pedals. Not that this Steinway wasn't in keeping with the balance of Miss West's decor. Everything—chairs, sofas, tables, candlesticks, clocks, footstools—was pink, gold, and tasseled. Even the antimacassars, carefully placed wherever a greasy head might come to rest, were fringed and fleecy.

Without guidance I hate to venture into an unknown field, but my guess is that the decor was sort of early Louis XIV, with a smidgen of late Victorian—the antimacassars—to encourage a sense of propriety, and a weighty bronze candelabra to establish Miss West's durability.

I was a bit taken aback (disappointed might be a more apt word) not only by Miss West's own living quarters but also by the apartment house itself. This, despite the warning from my mentor, Ray Crossett, who said, "Mae lives in a big old chunk of stone and the neighborhood's not very fashionable anymore. She used to own it herself and she might *still* have a piece of the joint."

Somehow I had an idea that a star of Miss West's magnitude would live in a Beverly Hills castle or at least in a chic apartment done in the fashion of Melanie Kahane. The lobby itself is old-fashioned and with its tall, polite, liveried Negro (no "Black," this smiling anachronism) doorman, and its over-stuffed furniture might even be considered quaint. It reminded me of those aged Atlantic City hotels which have failed to keep up with the times and remain comforting reminders of a bygone era.

The hired help may have been almost as ancient as the switchboard, which I surmised was of World War I vintage, but before I was directed to Miss West's living quarters, they made damned sure it was I who was expected. I wouldn't want anyone to think Miss West is reticent about granting interviews. But before she says O.K. she wants to be reasonably certain the motives, and possibly the libidos, of would-be interrogators are above suspicion. After all, Miss West, who is convinced she is America's sex symbol, can't take any chances.

We'd agreed upon a password, Miss West and I, and about this I am not kidding one iota. The Open Sesame was "Cukor," and I first passed the magic word on to the doorman, who passed it on to the desk clerk, who passed it on to the telephone operator, who passed it on to Miss West's Japanese butler, who admitted me.

Five minutes or so later Miss West made her dazzling entrance dressed in a long pink-and-white, gold-trimmed hostess gown. I forgot to say that the star, for the past number of years at least, has refused to grant interviews to potential book writers. Whether this is because she feels members of that branch of the craft are less able to control their inhibitions than colleagues of the working press, I don't know. It also may be that the actress is trying to discourage competition for the autobiography she is in the midst of writing.

At any rate, and I do hope Miss West will forgive me for this deceit, I told her I was doing a piece about her for the Philadelphia *Evening Bulletin* and I may still do this if only to ease my conscience. I never said I was *not* going to do a book, but this is pusillanimity.

49

We got off to a good start; Miss West appeared delighted to meet a resident of the Quaker City, even though it is said she never was too fond of the late W. C. Fields, who hailed from the same place.

"Good show town, Philly," Miss West reminisced. "They've always been crazy about me in Philly. Many a time I played the Oil there."

I was puzzled, not at all certain I knew what my hostess was talking about. But then the lady cleared that up when she went on to add, "I remember the foist time I played the Oil; it was back in the twenties."

I was sorry to have to be the one to break it to Miss West that the Earle Theater, like so many of Philadelphia's vaudeville houses and movie palaces, was torn down these many years to make way for a parking lot or something. My hostess continued where we'd left off before our nostalgic digression.

"Tell you what I meant when I said once before I saved Hollywood's skin."

Although I fully anticipated reference to another section of the human epidermis, Miss West actually said "skin." She used no obscenities and, except for an occasional "damn," her language is as pure as Mrs. Shirley Temple Black's ever was.

"This was sometime ago and all the majors were in plenty trouble, just like they are today. I come out here to do a picture for Paramount. I wrote it myself. I needed a sexy leading man and they lined up about one hundred fifty guys; put 'em in bathing suits and told me to look 'em over carefully. I done this, then I shook my head.

" 'None of 'em 'll do,' I told Mr. Zukor. 'You'll have to line up some more.' This was all inside the lot. Adolph Zukor, a fellow named Al Kaufman, and another guy named Cohen—I don't remember his first name—was walking along when I spotted a man about fifty feet away on the other side of the street.

" 'See that good lookin' guy comin' this way with all his clothes on,' I said to Adolph. 'Call him over; he's for me.'

" 'O.K., Mae,' Adolph says. 'If he can talk, you can have him.'

"He could talk all right, so Adolph and the others asked me what I wanted the fellow for, a bit part? I says, 'Positively *not*, I want him for my leading man.' "

My hostess turned to me.

"Do you know who the guy was?"

I knew—Ray Crossett had given me the answer but I didn't want to spoil Miss West's tag line. I shook my head. For the dramatic effect she knew it would have, the actress paused briefly.

"Well, I'll tell you; it was Cary Grant!"

I exhaled loudly to show my astonishment. Miss West smiled quietly in appreciation, then went on.

"Up to the time I picked him out, Cary was oney playing bit parts. My picture was *She Done Him Wrong* and I give Cary the part of the Salvation Army captain. The film was a big hit; Paramount made plenty of dough and got back on their feet and Cary went on to stardom on his own."

True, indeed. In 1944, and again in 1949, Grant, according to a New York *Herald-Tribune* poll, became one of the ten best money-making stars. Whether Miss West was solely responsible for Paramount's comeback may be open to conjecture although I, for one, am in no position to contest any statement made by the star of *She Done Him Wrong, Night After Night,* and *The Heat's On.* I don't believe Miss West's fans realize this, and it may even come as a surprise to Ray Crossett, but, according to Cary Grant himself, Miss West once played Little Eva in *Uncle Tom's Cabin.* Mr. Grant didn't say when but my guess is that the historic theatrical moment occurred during the very incipience of my hostess's career.

It could be that this innocent indoctrination into the world of entertainment is responsible for the actress's contempt for dirty movies.

"I walked right out of *I Am Curious* (*Yellow*). It was disgusting. Besides, those people who play in them crudie nudies don't know a thing about sex. I got more sex appeal in my little finger than all them others have by showing their entire bodies.

"Nudity's no real attraction. I can come on the stage or walk into a room fully dressed and I know how to show 'em what sex is like. It takes more than a filthy film to get a man worked up. That's why I think feelthy films are on the way out. What counts is the way you walk, the way you shrug your shoulders, the way you move your arms. I'll show you what I mean."

Miss West arose and proceeded to give me a moving demonstration of what she'd been talking about. It was a good thing for both of us I was able to control my libido. Slightly out of breath, my hostess plumped down beside me. She'd no sooner been seated when she arose again.

"I wanna show you somethin' else," she said quietly, and this time I really didn't know *what* to expect. I hesitated.

"Come *on!* Come *on!*" my hostess urged. "Don't be afraid." And with that I stood up and almost closed the gap between us. Then Mae dramatically pulled aside the long, blonde, near-waist-length wig she wore and threw it over her slender shoulders. She thus revealed a high forehead, bright blue eyes, and a smooth ivory skin. It automatically reduced her years by another score.

"Not a wrinkle," she said with justifiable pride. "Look close at my skin and neck. I'll bet you don't see no signs of a facelift. That's somethin' very few other stars hittin' fifty can say. *Never* had one; never *needed* one, and you won't see where one was done. Am I right?"

I hastily answered, "You're right, Mae," although I have had such limited experience in these matters that I didn't think my opinion was worth very much. Somehow or other I fully expected Miss West to be tall and voluptuous. On the contrary, she's short and, at least as far as I could tell, since the gown she wore was extremely unrevealing, Nature endowed my hostess with a far less imposing bosom than She

52

bequeathed upon her current co-star, Miss Raquel Welch. According to film critics, these mammary protrusions are about the only "talent" the latter possesses.

Through the years there has been much written about Miss West and I feel pretty sure most adults, males at any rate, past the age of say forty-five, are familiar with this actress's supposedly lurid past. It is a matter of record that in the late twenties she spent time in the jug—ten days—on Welfare Island. In that era of innocence, her play *Sex*, which today I'm afraid would be rated "G," so offended those charged with keeping New York theater audiences pure that its star was found guilty of corrupting the public's morals.

Miss West took this episode in stride, even threatening to write a play on the subject of prison reform. Sometime afterward, at least according to the late O. O. McIntyre, the star of *Sex*, in a curtain speech, appealed for public sympathy.

"I hope you don't think I'm like the roles I portray. I neither smoke nor drink. . . . In fact, I'm just a campfire girl."

Upon another occasion when the Legion of Decency or some similar organization was breathing hard down Miss West's neck, she told a New York *Times* reporter that "the kiddies love me. That's because I always think of things to put in my pictures that they'll like."

These gems from the star of *Sex* and numerous other plays of a similar nature lead me to the conclusion that Miss West takes neither life nor herself too seriously. Ever since she made her professional debut some seventy-odd years ago, she has been having a hell of a lot of fun in a pretty dismal world.

Then, too, there is Mae's much-disputed (by the bride at any rate) marriage to a fellow vaudevillian in April 1911, way out in Milwaukee where the team of West & Walker was doing two a day at the Gaiety Theater. I am much indebted to Sergeant Ray Smith, pugilist-turned-journalist, for an interview he conducted with Mae's supposed spouse in 1935 when the song-and-dance man was a featured performer at Weber's

53

Hof Brau, a nightclub on the outskirts of Camden, New Jersey.

I should say a word about ex-Marine Sergeant Smith who claims—and has a scrapbook to prove it—he was the only boxer (except for Jack Dempsey) to put champion Gene Tunney on the ropes. The bout took place in Seattle, Washington, in 1919 when Tunney was champion of the A.E.F. and Smith the contender. Tunney kept his title and finally K.O.'d Smith, but it took nine rounds to do it. Ray and I were fellow reporters, he on the Camden *Courier* and I on the Philadelphia *Inquirer*. This was just after they completed construction of the Delaware River Bridge, which would make the year 1927.

Ray was a good reporter; he took his duties seriously and while he was then only a "leg man," which meant he phoned in his stories to the desk, he had ambitions and wanted, someday, to do the actual writing. Two self-admitted problems held him back. The first, an inability to type, and the second, a limited vocabulary.

There was a battered old typewriter in the reporters' room at Camden's City Hall and although more than forty-five years have since passed, I can still see the sergeant, eyes front, lips pressed tightly together in concentration, picking out with the forefinger of each hand the beginner's "A-S-D-F-G-H-J-K-L." Then, after months of diligence, but still using the same two digits, triumphantly pounding out "Now is the time . . ." using all twenty-six letters of the alphabet.

Ray handled his second problem, that of expanding a vocabulary, by pressing into service every member of the working press with whom he was then associated and asking us to teach him a new word every day. Not everyone cooperated; sometimes we'd be away on assignments, we had different days off, or we'd be too busy to be bothered. But I'd venture to state the sergeant benefited by these contacts to the extent of some twenty new words a week, far more than can be said for most of us. Ray preferred the words to be four syllables in length but since this put an intellectual strain on colleagues, he was forced to settle for three most of the time.

It would take a memory greater than mine to recall all or even a few of the words I imparted to Ray, but I do remember one that seemed to give the sergeant excessive trouble. Neither he nor I could understand the reason. The word Ray had the greatest difficulty with was "concerning," which a quick check reveals contains only three syllables. As I recall, he used to confuse it with "consorting," and you can see how the improper use of that one might result in a libel suit. All this flashed through my mind one afternoon in the Theater Collection of the Free Library of Philadelphia where I was doing some preliminary research on Miss West.

Among the hundreds of items in her file was a yellowed clipping I was ready to toss aside, sure that no one on the Camden *Courier*'s staff was likely to have inside information about the subject of my quest. But the by-line—"Sergeant Ray Smith"—caught my eye. It was an interview my old friend had had with Miss West's alleged husband in 1935.

"Is the buxom queen of the movies, otherwise Miss West, married to Frank Wallace?," asked the sarge. "And is she bringing a secret divorce action to free herself legally from the song-and-dance man?

". . . Frank showed me a certified copy of the license, obtained from the register of deeds at Milwaukee. The marriage certificate bore the number 40,533 and among other things, set forth the maiden name of Mae's mother as being Mathilda Dilken, and that she was born in France."

"Mae and I got along swell," said Frank, "but along in 1918 Mae began to get ambitions and showed me an offer she had of three hundred fifty dollars a week to appear in a stage production. She asked my advice, and I told her: 'We are married and it might interfere with your career.'

"So then we agreed we would go our separate ways, never referring to the marriage in any way. Well, I did my bit and kept my word, Mae kept hers, too, but Mae's publicity department thought of the wise idea of finding out if she at any time in her career had been married.

"They found that she was and still is and that I am her hubby."

The story went on for a half-column but, except for the fact that Mr. Wallace claimed his wife was born on August 17, 1893, I learned little I hadn't already known about my subject. I wasn't exactly sure what I was looking for but I found it anyway in the sergeant's concluding paragraph.

"Mae says, 'Come up and see me sometime,' " continued Frank. "Now I have shown you proof 'concerning' my marriage and you ask me, 'Are you her husband?' So I'll use my own saying, 'Now—what do you think?' "

Since my hostess mentioned neither her brief stint on Welfare Island nor the gentleman who claimed to be her husband, it would have been out of place for me to bring up either situation. Instead, I asked Mae how she liked the role they'd given her in *Myra Breckinridge*. She smiled broadly.

"I'm glad you asked. Would you like to see me do a few bits from the movie?"

I nodded, scarcely able to believe my good fortune. Miss West smiled, got up from her chair, and for the next hour, without props, sets, music, director, she was Letisha Van Horn, the booking agent in Gore Vidal's *Myra Breckinridge*. She was absolutely marvelous; corny but great—and I can't remember when I'd laughed as much. Of course I was impressed with the fact that I was Mae's sole audience.

Later I saw the film and I must agree with the reviewers; the movie is awful, as bad if not worse than Vidal's dreary book, and quite understandably a bomb. Even Miss West, with all her talents, couldn't pull this one out of the slime pit. It may be by now that Mae, despite good intentions and a noble effort, realizes her mission to save Twentieth Century-Fox must be regarded as less than a success. Recently, according to UPI, "The historic Twentieth Century-Fox studio is being replaced by a discount store."

Chapter Six

"MY LAST picture is awful," Joan Blondell told me. "It's called *The Finks* and it's so bad they haven't released it yet. And maybe, I hope, they never will."

I got to Miss Blondell through the courtesy of her son, Norman Powell (Dick was his father); I got to Norman through his press agent, Frank McFadden, and I got to Frank through Herb Golden, who finally came back from Europe. Herb called Frank; Frank called Norman, and Norman, who was then producing TV features on what was left of the M-G-M lot, called his mother.

"Anytime, Norm," she said. "Ask him if he'd like to come for coffee early tomorrow morning at the house. I won't be working then."

So here I was, like they used to say in the fan magazines, having an intimate cup of coffee with a Hollywood star. I'm afraid this won't be much of a compliment to Miss Blondell, but I must say I felt more comfortable with her than I did with anyone else I ever interviewed. Miss Blondell, going on sixty-four, has gotten a bit heavy in the midriff; at least she's heavier than she was when I saw her in *Gold Diggers of 1933*. But I'll have to add she's still an attractive woman, and despite the fact that a fair portion of our conversation was devoted to a discussion of grandchildren (hers and mine), and in between she struck several blows for old nostalgia, Joan is *not* the grandma type.

The coffee was good and strong; my hostess served it herself after first opening the front door to reach for a bottle of table cream the milkman left outside.

"I have a day worker, once a week," she said, "and that's it as far as the hired help is concerned. The rest we [her recently divorced daughter and the latter's two children are living with her] do ourselves. But we were talking about the movies, weren't we, and I told you about *The Finks*."

I nodded and sat back to listen.

"We did *The Finks* in the grand old style on the Warner lot. It's supposed to be an attempt the studio made to keep up with the hip generation. They dragged out all the old props, those gorgeous chandeliers, furniture, and all they had stored somewhere. But it didn't help a bit.

"I'd read the script, the original I mean, and it wasn't too bad. But by the time they wound up they'd put in a hell of a lot of sex and nudity and I'm sorry to say it missed the point. I thought maybe the film would give me a chance to be 'with it,' but it didn't.

"This was the first time I'd been on the Warner lot in over twenty years when I wound up a series I did with Glenda Farrell. It was all horribly depressing to see it again, vacant and sad. The only person who recognized me was the cop at the gate who gave me a hug and a 'Hello, Miss Blondell. It's great to see you back again.' "

Joan shook her head.

"I walked over to see what, if anything, was left of the famous Green Room where Dick, Bogie, Bette Davis, Olivia, John Garfield, Eddie Robinson, and all the others—ghosts now—had such good times together. We worked hard all right—you can bet we did—but we loved it; we were stars and the studios took damned good care of us.

"The room was there, just—nothing in it but a lot of lovely memories. Not so long after that I went out to do a TV show on the M-G-M lot and it was even worse. Would you like to see what I wrote about that when I came back?"

I nodded; my hostess got up from the dining room table where we were sitting, and came back a few minutes later, a sheet of typed paper in her hand. She poured fresh coffee, then read what she'd written.

"Once in a while I get a strange, lonely feeling."

She paused and looked at me.

"Understand? This was written just after I returned to the house after I'd been on the M-G-M lot where I'd worked for a good many years and did a hell of a lot of pictures. We really had the good life; all of us were stars and were treated like royalty. M-G-M and the rest of the majors were teeming with people. There was action and the smell of success. But these last few years the lots were almost empty, every one of them. Well, so I wrote down how I felt."

She smiled and read some more.

"I get that strange, lonely feeling when we walk along the deserted Andy Hardy Street where Judy Garland and Mickey Rooney spent their childhood. At Metro, too, we come to the tree where the beautiful Garbo stood waiting for her car that long-ago day. When we pass Stage Eleven, Clark Gable's voice comes back to me: 'Don't marry that guy, Joanie, he's too jealous, too violent—marry me, Joanie.'

"Sometimes we walk in Warner's Sherwood Forest where Errol Flynn gleefully told tales of his youth during a picture we were making. I see a dilapidated carriage that proudly supported George Arliss and Bette Davis. At Fox, Shirley Temple and Bill Robinson dance before my eyes. . . ."

She shrugged her shoulders.

"Well, that's the way it is now on the lots—all empty. But M-G-M used to be the greatest, the epitome of everything. Protection for the stars was the ultimate and everything on and off the lot was glamorized, thanks to Howard Strickling. Warners was good, too, not quite as good, but the idea was the same. I did twenty-seven pictures in thirty-two months when I was with Warners and I did seven of these while I was carrying Norman. Sure I worked hard, damned hard; we all did, but the glamor was there and there was enough of it for everybody to share.

"I hate to keep harping on the past—I'm still working and doing all right. But it's so different today working with the Indys. They extract all they can out of you and then bang!— they let you go and couldn't care less what happens to you after they've finished with you. What a contrast to the way it used to be! I'll give you an example of what I mean."

She leaned back in her chair.

"It was while I was pregnant with Norman. I hate birds; it's almost psychological and I can't explain why, but when they get close to me I panic. I was doing a picture for Warners and I wanted to finish it before I went to the hospital. I knew it would cost them plenty otherwise; we all developed this kind of loyalty.

"At any rate, I was walking up the stairs on the lot when a bird flew in. I almost fell down the steps but I got a grip on the rail and hung on. In about half-a-minute there was a nurse and a doctor with me. They rushed me to the first-aid room and stayed there checking. Fortunately I was O.K., but they wouldn't let me move till they were sure.

"Not long ago I was doing a picture with Elvis Presley. It was for M-G-M, or what's left of it. We were out on the lot somewhere in Arizona and I stepped into a hole. It was covered lightly with sand so I didn't see it. Underneath there were hot ashes; the wranglers had had a cookout there; I burned myself badly and screamed with pain. They got a doctor but all he did was take a quick look and say, 'O.K., it's not burned much, only first-degree. Back to work for you.'

"But when I felt sick and sore after we finished the picture, I went to my own doctor in L.A. He told me I did not have first-, but *third*-degree burns. I never fully recovered and I always thought I couldn't sue. Nobody called to see how I felt; nobody today in TV or the movies really gives a damn."

I refused another cup of coffee; Miss Blondell poured one for herself and went on.

"I've been in show biz a long, long time, ever since I was three years old. I'm from a family of vaudevillians; my mother and father were troupers and they and I played all over the world. So I'm used to every kind of treatment, every kind of handling and, well, even every kind of dressing room. You name it and I've had it. Let me tell you about the dressing room I had on the Warners lot, then I'll get off this kick.

"My place there had a bedroom, a kitchen, and a bath, *and* a wonderful garden where I could relax after a hard day. I had my own maid and my own-practically-anything-else I wanted. I even had a solid gold mirror. While I was doing *The Finks* I couldn't resist the impulse to look at it and now I'm sorry I did. The mirror's gone; there's not a sign of the garden, I think it's part of a parking lot, and some producer—I don't know his name—has the rest of the suite for his office.

"You should have seen what they gave me when we made *The Finks!* I hate to think about it. And the matron was cold as ice—efficient, I'll give her that, but all business."

She smiled gently.

"Don't misunderstand me, I'm not complaining; that's just the way it is. I've had plenty of heartaches—three husbands and lots of other problems. Of course it's not the same now and I realize that; I'm happy to be working at all. And as long as they want me I'll keep working until they carry me off to Forest Lawn. But I got to remember. I've been a star! And that goes an awful long way for all of us."

Chapter Seven

EXCEPT IN Hollywood I don't imagine many people ever heard of Frank P. Rosenberg, but Herb Golden says he's one of the most knowledgeable producers in the Industry and, besides, his office on the near-deserted Warners lot used to be Joan Blondell's dressing room.

"Joan didn't leave anything personal around here when she took off," Frank said, "not even one of Norman's diapers."

Rosenberg is a New Yorker by birth but he's been around Hollywood for nearly forty-five years and, as an Indy, he has worked on most of the major lots. I suppose his best-known film was *Madigan*, starring Richard Widmark. He's also produced dozens of hour-length TV shows, but when I saw him, Frank, like so many of his colleagues who've remained in this abandoned city, was "reading."

He's a big, friendly guy, and since it was almost noon he asked me to join him for lunch which we ate on the lot in a small dining room. There couldn't have been more than fifteen or twenty tables and most of them were unoccupied.

"In the old days when Jack Warner ran the show, this used to be restricted to top executives; agents and other 'outsiders' were frowned upon and the chef prepared only gourmet foods. They called it the Green Room."

He smiled.

"Try the tuna on toast, not too bad."

On the way back to his office Frank asked me if I knew what was the greatest moment in recent motion picture history. I pleaded ignorance.

"It came in *Bullitt* when Steve McQueen says, 'Bullshit!' This really was the moment of truth and summed up everything the young generation feels about all the crap they've been handed. Your friend, Harry Kleiner, wrote that script and he knew what he was talking about."

Frank sighed.

"And out here nobody seemed to listen. I'll tell you what I mean. Take *The Arrangement* for example, starring Kirk Douglas and Faye Dunaway. Elia Kazan wrote the book and produced and directed the film which Warners released. I don't know how much it cost but I know it was a big-budget picture. This was one that was supposed to speak the truth, but instead of learning something from *Bullitt* they made the picture in Hollywood's old-fashioned style and it bombed. It was sexy enough and honest, I suppose, but this wasn't enough. The kids rejected it and so did everybody else. The way it looked to them was that it was just some more 'bullshit,' and the pile was high enough already.

"The masters of the Industry, Harry Cohn of Columbia, for example, are dead or too old to give a damn and there's no one around to take their place. I think *they'd* have gotten the message. But what we're getting out here now to run the studios are men who don't know a damned thing about making pictures.

"Take Charlie Bluhdorn. He sold coffee and groceries and came out here without any movie background and look what he's done to Paramount." [Oh, yeah. *Love Story* and *The Godfather*.]

Frank shook his head.

"To *say* you're a movie maker and keep repeating it time and time again just isn't enough. It reminds me of the story about the little Jewish boy who made a fortune in business, got married, had his own home and family but faithfully, every Friday night, visited his mother who still lived in the Bronx. One evening he arrived wearing a yachting cap which the old lady regarded curiously for a bit before speaking. Finally she turned to her son.

"*Nu*, Yonkele? Why the *capele?*"

A little annoyed, he answered, "I just bought a yacht and I'm the captain."

His mother smiled sadly.

"To me, Yonkele, you're a captain; to you, you're a captain, but to a *Captain*, you're nothing but a little Jewish boy."

We were back in Frank's office after walking along abandoned streets on the lot. He moved a few books aside; we leaned back on easy chairs and put our feet on the desk.

"Regard that chair as sacred," he smiled. "It's the only thing left from Miss Blondell, so lay your ass on it gently."

I did.

"What's happened to most of the new studio heads is that they're mesmerized by the talent and can't say no. Most of them are at least young-middle-aged, and all their lives, from the time Mom gave them a quarter to go to the Saturday matinees, they've been dreaming of meeting the stars. Now they have their chance and they're scared to death to do or say anything to offend these beautiful women and handsome men they always envied. They've never accepted the fact that the kids regard these same stars as has-beens and avoid them like the plague.

"Listen to this. I was doing *One-Eyed Jacks*. Brando was the star and we were out on location at Monterrey. Naturally I had my shooting schedule worked out, but before we'd been there two days we were already two weeks behind because our star was acting like a prima donna. We were *bound* to go over our budget.

"Brando kept insisting on doing expensive scenes which didn't belong in the picture and which weren't even in the script in the first place. Well, there was one particular scene I recall. He wanted a fiesta; I didn't and told him so. But he

64

went over me; complained to the studio head and, because he *had* been a star, Marlon got his way. That particular scene cost over half a million dollars."

Frank paused to light his pipe and then went on.

"*One-Eyed Jacks* bombed. Nobody, least of all the younger generation, wants to see Brando anymore. Maybe he'll stage a comeback—you never know for sure—maybe they *all* will, but I doubt it. [But Brando did—in *The Godfather*.] The kids have had it with those old faces; they want new people and new faces and they want somebody out here with the vision to close the generation gap. They won't stand for the junk their parents stood for.

"Sure they like Peter Fonda and Jon Voight. But let either make a film the younger generation doesn't care for, something phony they can't believe in, and they'll not shell out a nickel to see them.

"Everybody knows by now—except maybe the men they're sending out here from New York—that what made the old-time stars, the ones on your list, was block booking—forcing theaters to accept a given allotment of pictures made by these same stars every year. Harry Cohn, for example, used to average five pictures a month. He called them 'Super A's,' 'A's,' 'Nervous A's,' and 'B's.'

"Cohn had a great deal of the zealot in him and he was ashamed of the pictures he produced which weren't good. And this was a quality of all the big men of Cohn's time. They took tremendous pride in their pictures and wanted their trademark to stand for something. Of course they were extravagant and reckless gamblers, but they did get something good out of the films.

"At any rate, under block booking, theaters were forced to accept a given annual allotment of films. People used to go to the movies automatically; it was the thing to do; they really didn't give a damn what was playing."

He chuckled.

"I don't know if this'll strike you funny and maybe it really isn't funny at all, but I think it illustrates what I mean about the 'loyal' public we used to have. At any rate, a good many years ago when I was doing p.r. for Columbia I was in New York and had to go up to Loew's Eighty-third Street Theater. I can't remember any more what the picture was, but I recall there was a good-sized crowd standing outside waiting for the box office to open.

"First in line was an elderly woman. As I passed her to enter the theater, she tugged my sleeve.

" 'Why are so many people here today? Do you know what's playing, mister?' "

I told Frank about an old Philadelphia friend, Arthur Myers, who was the most avid movie fan I knew. He and his wife went to the movies at least five nights a week and Arthur used to sneak into a matinee every couple of days. Late one afternoon I saw him emerge into the sunlight from a Market Street theater. I asked him how he liked the picture. He shrugged his shoulders.

"I didn't mind."

Frank nodded.

"That's what I'm getting at," he said. "No more 'loyal' fans; they're all home watching their favorites on TV. The bankers, the finance companies, and the conglomerates who've been putting their dough into the movie business are no longer interested in who the star is. They want to know what the picture's all about so they can assay its chances for success and a return on their money.

"And the ridiculous thing is that these masters of finance turned out to be just as poor guessers as anyone else. Hollywood is in such a state of flux, nobody can predict anything. They got inspired with *The Sound of Music*, which as you know was an enormous box-office success.

"Julie Andrews leaped to fame and everybody thought the star system made a comeback. But Julie's next few pictures were ruinously expensive bombs. Paramount, envious of the gold in *Sound*, tried it out with *Paint Your Wagon*, a *very* big-budget picture. I understand *Paint* was close to twenty million dollars. Then they did *The Molly Maguires*, a drama, which cost nearly fifteen. They were both disasters. Now we're all back trying to figure out the next move."

He sighed deeply and turned his palms open.

"Let me sum up what I believe. First of all I think Hollywood, the Hollywood you and I knew with all the glitter, is dead. I know the *star* system is dead, and many, not all of course, of the people you're going to see remain glamorous only in your mind and in the minds of members of our generation.

"So what's left for Hollywood? Well, for one thing, it still holds the greatest collection of technicians in the world, even though most of them are out of work today—directors, cinematographers, producers, electricians, grips, and actors. So, if pay-TV ever comes into being, I think this will be the center for it. At any rate, that's what I hope."

Frank stood up and I joined him at the window overlooking what used to be Miss Blondell's private garden. Pulling out of it was an ice-cream truck, the only action visible in any direction.

"If you ever see Joanie again [I did]," Rosenberg said, "tell her she's better off never to come back here. Next time even the Good Humor truck might have deserted us."

Chapter Eight

WHEN I returned to my apartment there was a message to call Bill Kirk who runs what is technically known as the Motion Picture and Television Country House and Hospital, although everybody in the Industry calls it simply "The Country House."

Bill said I'd been "cleared" by Margaret Herrick, and that if I had no other plans for the next day he'd be glad to give me a guided tour of the institution and, if they were available, introduced me to some of the personalities living there.

Bill, a pleasant man in his early sixties, never was in the Industry. His background is social welfare and he's been at The Country House for the past ten years. Together we drove out to the institution (a misnomer, I suppose) in suburban L.A. The Country House, located on spacious grounds, is beautifully maintained and is a far cry from what we used to think of as the "Old Folks Home." It's supported mainly by Industry payroll deductions ranging from one-half to four percent.

I've visited many nursing homes and am aware that a large percentage of these are operated by venal promoters who couldn't care less what happens to "guests" as long as their bills are paid. The hired help in these places usually is ill-trained, underpaid, and, with rare exceptions, no more interested in patients' welfare than their greedy employers.

If they're well enough physically and mentally, guests at The Country House live in beautiful private cottages and, if they need constant nursing, there's the Pavilion, a seventy-nine-bed, long-term-care center, staffed in the main with R.N.'s who actually go about their work smiling. They have convalescent aid for those who've been seriously ill but are recovering and nobody ever gets kicked out of The Country House. No matter how badly his condition deteriorates, there's always a place for a person somewhere on the grounds.

Guests include actors, directors, cameramen, writers, film editors, electricians, laborers, secretaries, in fact all branches of the profession, reaching up to the stars and down to the grips.

For entertainment of the physically fit, there are golf club affiliations nearby, and on the grounds, bowling and croquet. There's a well-stocked library and a theater where guests either put on their own shows or watch top stars from the profession perform. Ironically, in every room there's the figure of the "enemy," a TV set (color at that), cause of a good many guests' involuntary retirement.

"One of the things we don't have here," Bill said, "are funerals. Not that guests don't die—we can't promise immortality—and you have to consider that the average age is fairly high. But services are held off the grounds and you know, if you've ever been in welfare work, this is important. Something else we don't have here is discrimination—racial, ethnic, or religious. We *do* have a chapel which is interdenominational."

For members of the Industry who didn't hang on to their dough, The Country House is a good place to wind up interesting, even glamorous, careers. Beyond noting the fact that there is a forty-million-dollar, fifteen-year expansion program, I'll spare other details except for mention of a completely modern forty-bed hospital, with only private rooms.

It was in one of these rooms that I spent a few bittersweet

hours with Miss Betty Blythe whom I had not seen for slightly more than half a century. The star of *The Queen of Sheba*, according to the pretty nurse who was in attendance, was "resting comfortably" and would be happy to receive visitors when she awoke from her mid-afternoon nap. Miss Blythe had been a hospital patient for several weeks, with an illness not disclosed to me although I have reason to suspect it was hardening of the arteries, but she was expected to return to her cottage shortly. It may very well be that she did. At any rate, I hoped so.

"Don't push too hard," the nurse cautioned me. "She does get a bit forgetful at times and this seems to trouble her. And she tires easily, so if you notice that she's drifting off to sleep again I'd appreciate it if you'd walk out of the room quietly."

So I sat in a chair near her bed waiting for the white-haired old lady to awaken. Meanwhile I had a chance to read a clipping which Ray Crossett dug up somewhere and handed to me that morning. It was from an unnamed fan magazine interview—"Miracles of Beauty," written by Eleanor Hold James and printed, according to Ray, about 1918 or 1919, a few years before *The Queen of Sheba* was released.

"There must have been hundreds of similar interviews in dozens of different fan magazines," Ray said, "and all of them, I'm sure, equally nauseating. If you want to take the trouble to check newspapers of the day I'll bet you'd find thousands and thousands of stories about Betty. You must remember she was one of the most popular stars of the time; everywhere she went she was treated like royalty. I remember her myself when she made a personal appearance at the Criterion. Crowds lined the streets in front of the theater and it took a cordon of cops to protect her from loyal fans."

The subtitle of the piece Crossett gave me was "Being the Northern Lights and Betty Blythe, Who Declares That Today Is the Day of Miracles."

It was a false night. Nature was staging one of her miracle pictures. Against the heavens were filmed the most awe-inspiring masterpiece I have ever seen. It was the night of the Northern Lights. Fingers of brilliant color stretched forth in fan shape against the deep violet sky. They were crimson and gold and bold of hue. Every now and then they trembled with the flush of color, like blood pulsing through delicate veins.

Miss Blythe, with other members of the Goldwyn Company, happened to be filming scenes of the coast of Washington for Rex Beach's picture *The Silver Horde* when I was in Seattle, and they invited me to visit their camp on a wood island. . . . This was my first meeting with Miss Blythe, whose beauty has only partially been reproduced by magazines. Heretofore she has been in the eastern studio of Vitagraph where she appeared in *Beating the Odds* and other plays, with Harry T. Morey.

As I stood on the veranda, spellbound by the beauty of the night, a figure in ethereal draperies of chiffon suddenly came forward out of the picture. Against that background of rose and blue and golden shadows, she seemed a goddess descended from Olympian heights. She is unusually tall and slender, with a cloud of dusky hair wound around a small head.

Silhouetted against the lights, she presented a study in lines and movement—gracile, lithe, regal. Her long throat and exquisitely molded shoulders and arms shone pearl in the radiance. The outline of a gracefully etched figure could be discerned through the draperies flowing behind her. . . .

Miss Blythe stirred; I glanced over at the bed. Unconsciously she brushed aside a strand of snow-white hair which fell over her pale face and she continued to sleep. I read on.

"Isn't this night marvelous." Her voice came floating forward. It was a musical voice, and, as I learned later, it was carefully trained for opera. Miss Blythe devoted two years to the study of music in the Conservatoire of Paris with the intention of pursuing an operatic career. But she was handicapped by beauty! The pictures demanded her, or rather, they offered her greater rewards than the stage. . . .

There wasn't any question about the fiscal advantages of Miss Blythe's decision. During the decade which ended in 1928, her salary reportedly ranged between three and four thousand dollars a week, which in those days of comparatively gentle tax bites was an awful lot of money. Unfortunately, Miss Blythe didn't keep her dough; bad investments, foolish extravagances (two Packards and a golden Pierce Arrow at the same time), plus an ailing husband took their toll of the former *Queen of Sheba*'s bank account at about the same time the public tired of vamps. Clara Bow, the pretty, unsubtle "it" girl entered the scene and forthwith Miss Blythe and the rest of the slinky sex sirens, including Theda Bara, whom Miss Blythe replaced, crept back into the shadows of oblivion.

Miss Blythe emerged a few times during the next four decades to play character roles. She was the matron in Majestic's *The Perfect Clue*, starring David Manners. The play opened at the Criterion in New York.

The New York *Times* reported:

> Of interest perhaps to the older generation of film-goers is the line on the cast sheet reading: "Ursula Cheesebrough . . . Betty Blythe." Yes, it is the same Miss Blythe who was The Queen of Sheba for Fox in 1921.

The year was only 1935 and Miss Blythe then could not have been more than forty, yet she'd already been relegated to the ancients. I looked at the gently snoring figure in front of me and wondered into which category that *Times* critic would place anyone who actually saw the actress perform in 1921.

Miss Blythe tried again a few years later in a Columbia production called *Before Midnight*, starring Ralph Bellamy and June Collyer. Of this film, Mordaunt Hall, the New York *Times* critic, reported:

> . . . It is just a puerile puzzle in which a zealous attempt is made to deceive the audience. Miss Betty Blythe, the vet-

eran queen of several silent pictures, portrays Mavis Fry, who, it might be said, had a very good reason for poisoning at least two men. Miss Blythe's performance is not especially impressive.

I'd been in the hospital room for almost an hour by then and the star was still sound asleep. Even though I had plenty of time, I wondered whether it might be a good idea for me to leave. I was trying to make up my mind when the floor nurse returned.

"Why don't you stick around a bit longer," she suggested. "Miss Blythe doesn't get much company and I think it would be helpful for her to talk to someone for a little while. Come on, I'll wake her; she sleeps a lot and I think this'll do more for her."

Very gently the nurse walked over to the bed and whispered, "You've got a visitor, Miss Blythe," and the patient, a lovely smile on her face, sat up and greeted me.

"You're from the press?" she asked in a husky voice, and I nodded even though this wasn't exactly the truth. "If there's a photographer with you, ask him if he'll please wait until I get ready."

I assured Miss Blythe I was alone; she seemed a bit disappointed. Then she reached over to a night table beside the bed and from an already opened pack removed a crumpled cigarette which I lit. She inhaled deeply and with obvious pleasure; I sat back in the chair ready to explain my mission. No explanation was necessary; Miss Blythe simply assumed I was there for the kind of interview she must have given a thousand times in the past. Without any prompting from me she led the way.

"I suppose," she said, "you want to know how I got into the movies." I nodded and she told me she'd gone to Vitagraph's Sheepshead Bay studios with a girl friend who'd been summoned to take a screen test.

"But one of the directors saw me sitting there and insisted that I take this test. I told him I wasn't interested but he refused 'no' for an answer. Well, from the moment they saw the results I was in and that's how it's gone ever since."

She paused to take several more puffs, then went on.

"Of course you saw me in *The Queen of Sheba*, didn't you?"

I answered, "Of course," then told Miss Blythe the circumstances under which I'd seen the film and confessed my great and instant love for its star. I think Miss Blythe was pleased; she smiled graciously.

"Did I ever tell you how I got the part?" she asked. I answered no and the former Queen went on.

"This was going to be the big picture of the year and maybe even the century and the studio handed out all manner of publicity about how they intended to choose the star. Every actress in the world was trying to be the Queen and didn't hesitate to use whatever she had to get it, if you know what I mean.

"But all *I* did was recite a few verses from the Bible. This is the way it was. The director was named J. Gordon Edwards and it was his duty to recommend who would be the star. He'd already interviewed dozens of actresses before he reached me. He had an opened copy of the Bible and asked me to read.

"I looked at Mr. Edwards, closed the book, and without any notes proceeded to quote from 'The Song of Solomon.' I remember it to this day. Would you like to hear me?"

I nodded. She crushed her cigarette in an ashtray so full of butts there was scarcely room for another, ran a comb through her thick, white hair, and sat erect. She looked at me, frowned slightly, and went on in a voice as husky as I remembered Tallulah's was.

The Song of Songs, which is Solomon's.

Let him kiss me with the kisses of his mouth; for thy love is better than wine.

Because of the savour of thy good ointments thy name is as ointment poured forth, therefore do the virgins love thee . . .

74

A bundle of myrrh is my well beloved unto me; he shall lie all night betwixt my breasts. . . .

Make haste, my beloved, and be thou like a roe or to a young hart upon the mountains of spices. . . .

Admittedly my knowledge of the Bible is limited, but I'm inclined to believe Miss Blythe's rendition of "The Song of Solomon" was perfect. When she finished I applauded briskly and the actress relaxed, a look of triumph on her pale face. It had taken at least a half-hour for Miss Blythe to finish all eight chapters (I herein confess I didn't know at the time just how many chapters there were). Then she asked me to light another cigarette for her, but by the time I'd struck a match Miss Blythe had fallen asleep again. I thought this was as good a time as any to leave.

I'm glad I saw Miss Blythe. She died a short time after my interview with her.

Chapter Nine

UNLESS YOU'RE one of the several hundred guests at The Country House, it's not likely you will ever have heard of Theodore "Doc" Joos. Doc never made it big; his name never appeared on theater marquees and at no time was he a featured player. In fact, Doc hasn't been listed in the Motion Picture Almanac for the last half-dozen issues of that publication. A very modest man, I think he'll be quite surprised to find himself included in this compendium of Hollywood's great.

But Doc had been making movies out in Hollywood even before it was called Hollywood and by 1914, when he played an "extra" in *The Birth of a Nation*, he was considered an old-timer. He and I had lunch together in The Country House dining room. Then we walked hurriedly to the far end of the grounds where the actor and his wife live in an attractive cottage. Doc apologized for setting such a rapid pace.

"I haven't seen Betty for a couple hours," he explained, "and I'm a little worried. She wasn't feeling too well this morning. We all get upset that way; you know, you never can tell; none of us are young."

Doc's concern became greater when we neared his house

and saw a nurse emerging. He actually sprinted the last few dozen steps, forgetting to use the cane he'd been leaning on. But the nurse, pretty, young, and blonde ("We try to pick them all that way," Kirk told me later. "It's great for morale"), said everything was O.K., she'd only been making a routine check, and that Betty, Doc's wife, was over at the rec hall helping assemble equipment for an oncoming stage production. So Doc unfolded a couple of beach chairs and he and I stretched out in them under a warm California sun.

Now that I looked at my host more closely, I thought his tanned, rugged face, topped with close-cropped white hair, seemed familiar. The Doc smiled.

"No wonder. I've been in a thousand westerns from Tom Mix to James Arness. You can't see my name listed in the cast of characters but I'm there just the same; getting shot off my horse or taking a poke at some cowhand, or bending an elbow at the Lone Eagle Bar."

The Doc was born in Sierra City, California, on January 16, 1883.

"It's only a small town up near Tahoe and I couldn't wait to get out of it. Ever since I was a little kid I wanted to get into show biz. I don't know why; nobody in my family ever was. But my mother was musically inclined, we had a small pump organ in the house, and my older brother and I took lessons even though we didn't want to. Believe it or not, that's how I got my 'big' chance.

"I quit school in the eighth grade to work in a grocery store. I was the delivery boy and I had to take care of the horses and wagon my boss owned. Besides, we had our own mare when my father was alive so I knew how to ride and handle animals.

"Every season at least one stock company used to play in Sierra City and of course I didn't miss a performance. I must have been around twelve or thirteen when the manager of one of those repertory groups came 'round to our house and asked my mother if she'd rent them her hand organ. Seems that a stagehand was drunk the day before and dropped the company's organ from the wagon they traveled on and it got smashed to smithereens. Somebody in town told the guy we had an organ in our house and that's why he was there."

Doc paused to relight his pipe, then went on.

"Well, my mother said it would be O.K. but there was one condition the manager had to meet. My mother knew I was crazy about the theater so she said she wouldn't charge anything for renting the organ providing they'd pay her son, which was me, to play it. The manager must have been pretty desperate, so he said if that was the only way he could get the organ, he was prepared to accept the terms. Of course I had to be able to play.

"So he handed me some sheet music and told me to go ahead. I always was good at sight reading and I must have done all right because the manager clapped real loud when I finished and said, 'O.K., kid, you're hired.' "

Theodore "Doc" Joos sighed and shook his head.

"That was the best week I ever had in my life. Man, I really lived it up. This was a long, long time ago, and I wish I remembered what our entire repertoire was but I recall only two plays, *East Lynne* and *Two Orphans*. We had eight plays altogether and a company of six, including me.

"Sierra City was too small to have its own theater so the company performed in the center of the town from a wagon with the back end as the stage and the organ inside. It wasn't much of a company but when the lights went on at night, man, it turned into magic.

"The manager was a nice guy; he paid me what he promised when my week was over. I think my mother was surprised; she expected to have some trouble on that score. He asked me what other talents I had and, believe me, I told him. I said I was an actor; actually that wasn't all a lie; I used to be in our church cantata every year. But what really sold him was the fact that I knew how to handle horses, and the actor they had doing that was a lush."

Doc smiled.

"You'd think a kid my age would have fallen in love with

the leading lady or at least the ingenue, but not me. I fell in love with the magnificent matched team of dapple grays they had. The manager asked me how I'd like to join his company and travel with them and I don't have to tell you what my answer was to that. He first had to get my mother's permission and in the beginning she refused flat. But I kept nagging and nagging. She knew I'd run away if she said no, so she finally said yes and off I went. I was in show biz.

"That's how it all began almost seventy-five years ago. I never got top billing or anything like that, but if I had to do it all over again I wouldn't ask for any other way to spend my life."

Doc sighed.

"Well, let me tell you how I got into the movies. I'll start with that repertory company that traveled by wagon. First of all, the wagon was a Studebaker. They really made them good in those days and this one must have been built about 1885, so it had done a lot of traveling 'round before I got behind that pair of grays.

"We played mining camps and tank towns all through British Columbia, Alberta, Saskatchewan, and even up as far as the Yukon. Then we'd swing south to the Great Northwest into Montana, Wyoming, Washington, and Oregon. When we came to some of those places it was an *event*. Everybody— Mom, Pop, the kids—turned out to see us. I can picture them now going crazy with joy, watching every action; never taking their eyes away from us for a second; standing out there in the cold but not minding it a bit. And it was bitter cold most of the time; you can believe me."

Doc shook his head.

"We'd be the only excitement they'd have for another whole year and they knew it. But, even so, there wasn't much dough to share. On a *good* night, a *really* good night, we might take in as much as thirty bucks. I was low man on the totem pole so there wasn't much left for me.

"But the experience was wonderful. I had twelve years of repertory and by the time it was over and I was ready for

Hollywood, I was an actor, a stage director, lighting expert, and organist. You name it and I could do it. And besides, some drunk we had traveling with us for a season taught me to play the clarinet and when he took off for parts unknown he left me that licorice stick.

"I forgot to tell you that first outfit I was with was called The Robert Buchanan Repertory Company. We stuck together for around four years before we broke up. Mostly we played one-night stands although a few times each season we'd play a whole week in the same town. That'd be cities like Dawson up in the Yukon or Great Falls, Montana. If we played for a week we changed bills Monday and Thursday. We bought our plays from Nat Goodwin who pirated them."

My host excused himself, went into his cottage, and returned a few minutes later with a large scrapbook and a couple of smaller ones under his arm.

"My diaries," Doc explained handing me one. The initial entry was July 17, 1902, and the place appeared to be Sonora, California. While the handwriting, like everything else about my host, was neat and clean, the ink had faded and what the Doc had written was difficult to decipher. This entry, as were all the others, was brief.

Played the Grand [?]. Stayed at the Mansion House, first class. Saw Goldie.

I looked up at Doc.
"Who was Goldie, and did you make out?"
The Doc's eyes twinkled.
"A local and I wouldn't tell you even if I did."
I protested.
"But that was more than seventy years ago. You don't think Goldie would care anymore, do you?"
My host grinned.
"Who knows? Can't take any chances. Might be going back there again some time."
I followed Doc's pre-Hollywood career, the girls he met, the

towns, the mining camps, the theaters, the roles he played, and the hotels he stayed in, all long since vanished. Up and down the West Coast Doc went from California to the Yukon and as far east as South Dakota where, according to an entry made in 1904, he went broke. I asked my host if he remembered that incident. He nodded.

"I sure do. The Buchanan Repertory folded up in Calgary, Alberta, long before that and I joined up with the White Minstrel Show who booked out of Minneapolis. I doubled as end man and played the clarinet in the orchestra. I was damned good by then. The company was doing all right until we got to Thunder Butte, South Dakota. On Saturday night one of the show people absconded with the week's receipts and, like the rest of the show, I was dead broke and hungry.

"I had two clarinets and I hocked them both for twenty bucks and never reclaimed them and for all I know they might still be in that Shylock's place up in Fargo. That saw-buck didn't last very long and I got hungry again. I left show biz to take a job as attendant in an insane asylum at Des Moines. Then I heard about a fiddler who was looking for an advance man and press agent."

Doc rubbed his chin.

"I never can remember the guy's name and you won't find it in my diary or scrapbooks so there's no use looking. At any rate, this fiddler billed himself as Ole Bull's successor but he sure wasn't! I stuck that out for two seasons. Then I got tied up with another road company, still traveling on wagons. And that's where I got the break that led me to Hollywood."

My host looked at me.

"You heard of Wilfred Lucas, didn't you?"

I was ashamed to admit I hadn't so I said, "Sure."

The Doc obviously wasn't convinced and thumbed through one of his scrapbooks until he came to the page he was looking for. It contained a faded picture of a theatrically hand-some gentleman who looked to be in his mid-forties. Beneath this was a clipping from the *Motion Picture News* of October 21, 1916. Lucas, according to this long-since defunct publication, was one of Hollywood's earliest and brightest stars. He arrived there, or rather in nearby Santa Monica, in 1911 to play opposite Linda Arvidson, D. W. Griffith's wife, in a two-reel version of *Enoch Arden*. Later he starred in a number of films with Blanche Sweet, Donald Crisp, and Mary Pickford. Biograph paid Lucas one hundred fifty dollars a week, the highest salary the company had ever given anyone. Among his other credits was a starring role in *The Trey of Hearts*, this one mentioned by Doc.

"Wilfred stayed with our company," Joos continued, "for some three or four years and we got to be close friends. He went to Hollywood around 1909 or so—that's just about the time they started to make pictures there—and he got in touch with me. Said he needed an assistant director who knew his way around and thought of me right away.

"Hollywood wasn't much those days, just lots of wide-open spaces. But the weather was good, sunshine almost every day in the year, and that's why the movie makers from New York came out here. We were making two-reelers then and serials. I can't recall anymore what most of them were except for one, *The Trey of Hearts*."

Doc paused to fill his pipe which he lit, sat back contentedly, and went on.

"I did everything—direct, act, work in the production department. I even was assistant to the first-aid man. That's how I got my nickname, 'Doc.' "

He smiled.

"Remember Tex Guinan?"

This time I could answer yes truthfully.

"Well, Tex was the star of a two-reeler we were doing. She was supposed to be a great horsewoman and that's one of the reasons Wilfred hired her. Maybe she knew how to ride once, but by the time she came to Wilfred she was so damned fat she couldn't mount her horse. So Wilfred told me to put her on the animal every day before the shooting started. Then, when it was over, I had to get her down again.

"About 1916 or 1917, William Randolph Hearst, the publisher, started his own company, Cosmopolitan Productions, and I went to work for them doing everything. I had two main jobs there besides acting. I was assistant supervisor of the studio hospital and assistant director. We had a pretty good cast of stars. There was Irene Castle, Noah Beery, and Milton Sills, and I don't remember how many others.

"When Cosmopolitan folded I went out to Universal and stayed with them for the next twenty-five years. I guess these were the best times of all."

A pleased smile swept over my host's face.

"I knew the business from top to bottom, I can tell you. Maybe I never had my name up in lights and maybe I didn't make very many screen credits, but whenever any question came up, when nobody else could answer, they used to say, 'Ask the Doc. He'll know the answer.'

"I guess it's over now, but I had some good moments and I got lots of memories to take with me. I was even on the Universal lot when they made their first sound picture with equipment I helped borrow from Fox Movietone News. I had another five good years with Hopalong Cassidy and once in a while, on the Late, Late Show, I can watch myself get shot off my horse or bend an elbow at the Western Bar, or help put out a burning arrow on the wagon train."

Doc glanced at his watch and told me he had to leave for a rehearsal.

"I'm assistant stage manager for a show we're putting on next week. Gene Raymond and Cesar Romero are in it and it's got to be done right. So that's why they called the Doc."

We shook hands.

"I got one favor to ask you, young fellow," he said. "Please don't say I'm spry. I don't like that word."

I kept my promise even though I can't think of a better adjective to describe this little ninety-year-old gentleman. He walked me over to a cottage at the other end of the grounds, then called out, by way of introduction, "Chester! Chester! Here's a young fellow wants to interview you."

Doc turned to me and whispered.

"You might have to talk a bit loud. Chester's hearing just ain't what it used to be."

Then, swinging his cane jauntily, he darted off toward the L. B. Mayer Theater where I'm sure the director, stage manager, and others were anxiously awaiting the arrival of Theodore "Doc" Joos to assist in the production.

Chapter Ten

WITHOUT THE famous black "soup-strainer" mustache, his trademark for a good many decades, I know I wouldn't have recognized Chester Conklin. Mr. Conklin had been around Hollywood for as long as Doc and had lived alone since the death of his wife a few years earlier. (As they say in Hollywood, Mr. Conklin "passed away" recently, and I hope I haven't put a hex on guests of The Country House.)

I'd heard that Conklin, who earned as much as four thousand dollars a week over a period of many years, lost most of his fortune in the Wall Street crash of 1929. However, Bill Kirk told me the old comedian was by no means broke and could afford to live almost anywhere he chose but came to The Country House because he felt at home only with movie people. Despite this fact, Conklin kept to himself most of the time, venturing out to visit friends upon rare occasions. He spent many hours listening to classical and semi-classical music on a huge stereo which occupied a large portion of the living room. Almost all the space left over, except for a couple of easy chairs, several pipe racks, and assorted tables, was taken up with stacks upon stacks of record albums. He was playing one of his favorites, a Bach chorale sung by the Mormon Tabernacle Choir, when I interrupted him.

He motioned for me to sit down opposite him and together we listened until the record came to an end. Then my host smiled very sweetly and asked me what I wanted to see him about.

"I wish I had my scrapbooks," he said with regret, "but they were burned a while ago. Some of the clippings went back nearly sixty years, the time when I came out to Hollywood. You could have gone through them and have a pretty good idea of what this town was like then and how it's changed. I wouldn't say for the better and I wouldn't say for the worse. I don't know, I'm out of touch, I'm afraid.

"I guess you know my first director was Mack Sennett and the first pictures I made were with the Keystone Comedy Cops."

I nodded. I couldn't have been more than six or seven years old when I saw these two-reelers at Mahanoy City's old Palace Theater just around the corner from our home on Mahanoy Avenue. The films were usually sandwiched between four acts of vaudeville. I sat back looking at this dignified little old man, puffing away on his pipe, and thought of those endless hours of delight he gave me and my companions during those wonderful Saturday matinees so long ago.

For us, or for me at any rate, Chester Conklin was *the* Keystone Cop, a constant victim of pratfalls, a frustrated officer of the law who spent his time wiping custard pie from his face and from his ill-fitting uniform, and never catching his man. Maybe in this era of sophistication all this doesn't sound funny, but I thought it was then as did quite a few million others.

The comedian faded into oblivion nearly forty years ago so that a true Conklin fan would have to be at least in his early fifties. I'm sorry to say I qualify with a considerable number of years to spare. For those who require a briefing, I should point out that Chester Conklin ranked with the great funny men

86

and women of his day—Chaplin, Ford Sterling, Slim Summerville, Roscoe "Fatty" Arbuckle, Mabel Normand, Buster Keaton, Ben Turpin, Louise Fazenda, and Mack Swain. Of these, only Chaplin survives.

"I worked with Charlie back in the old days," Conklin recalled. "Mack [Sennett] hired him to play the part of a drunk. I think he paid him one hundred fifty dollars a week and Mack was sure it was too much. All Charlie did in the beginning was to portray drunks; he went from one set to another doing it. Then, finally, of course, Charlie got other ideas, perfected his little tramp role, and before long he was stealing every scene from us. And with good reason, I guess; the man's a genius.

"I believe it must have been around 1914 or maybe a year later when I met Charlie and first started to work with him. The picture was called *The Auto Race* or something like that. It was a Keystone comedy, naturally. I don't recall who else was in it but I imagine it was the usual cast."

I was aware that after a lapse of more than two decades, Conklin and Chaplin worked together in the latter's 1936 film, *Modern Times*, and again in 1940 doing *The Great Dictator*, another Chaplin classic. I brought this up but for some reason or other my host shied away from any discussion of these pictures and the parts he played in them. Instead he spoke of his pre-Hollywood days.

"I came from a small town in Iowa. It's called Oskaloosa and whenever I mentioned the place it always got a laugh. Maybe that's why I became a comic. I was only a kid when I left home for the stage and later to join the Al G. Barnes Wild Animal Show as a clown. It was a good life and I stayed with it until I went to Hollywood. Like everybody else who wanted to be in the movies, this was the place; this was where the action was even that long ago.

"We had the one ingredient necessary to make pictures—the sun. In those days there were no artificial lights worth thinking about, so we shot everybody out of doors. They were

coming out here from the East; every day there'd be more and
more of 'em—studios, actors, and everyone else attached to
the Industry."

He shrugged his shoulders.

"I understand there's not too much going on in Hollywood
these days. But it'll all come back sometime; I'm sure of that,
or I hope so at any rate."

I don't know and didn't ask what brand of tobacco my host
was smoking, but it reminded me of Miners' Extra, a noxious,
long-cut weed my father used to pack into his corncob and
almost asphyxiate our family. I must have winced involun-
tarily when a thick cloud of heavy black smoke from Conklin's pipe suddenly surrounded me. He noted my discomfiture
which took the form of a hacking cough and, without saying a
word, rested the pipe on an ashtray. He didn't pick it up again
while I was present.

"Did you know I was the first of the Conklins to go in show
business?"

I shook my head.

"It's true. My father was a salesman. He and my mother
were good church-going people but they didn't object, well,
not much, when I told them I wanted to be an actor. I wasn't
very tall—around five-foot-five—so I wouldn't likely be playing heavies. I started out with an Omaha stock company, then
got a vaudeville act together and traveled all through the
Midwest. That was before I became a circus clown.

"Well, when I came out around 1913, I was twenty-five
years old and this town was getting to be quite a place. I went
with Triangle in 1915. We had a good outfit, Mae Marsh,
Bessie Barriscale, Norma and Constance Bennett, Wilfred
Lucas, H. B. Walthal, and I don't know how many others.

"I guess I must have been on most of the major lots—Ince,
Pathé, Vitaphone, Christine, First National, FBO, and Paramount. They're all gone now except Paramount and I hear
they're not doing too well nowadays. But I made some good
ones with them. Remember *Two Flaming Youths?*"

I nodded.

"My co-star in that one was W. C. Fields, a really great performer. Then I did *Tillie's Punctured Romance* with Marie Dressler. I worked with Buddy Rogers in *Varsity* and with George Bancroft in *Tell It to Sweeney*. George was another fine actor. But all this was a long while back. I haven't been doing too much lately."

He paused.

"Last film I was in was *A Big Hand for the Little Lady* out on the Warner lot. Young fellow named Fielder Cook directed; stars were Hank Fonda and Joanne Woodward. Did you see it?"

I said yes; this was the truth and I did have a fleeting kind of subliminal recollection of Conklin somewhere in the film.

"Central Casting called me, asked how I'd like to go back to work. They apologized, told me it was only a bit part without lines, but I said sure anyway. Got a program some place."

He stood up; walked over to his desk, pulled a single sheet of paper from an opened drawer, and handed it to me.

"Far down the line," he said, "it's there all right."

It was.

Man in Saloon——Chester Conklin

Chapter Eleven

I WAS having dinner one evening with Professor Arthur Knight and his wife, Maryanne, when the subject of dirty films—"Nudies" as they're known in the trade—came up in our conversation.

"It's getting to be a pretty big branch of the Industry," the Professor said. "Don't neglect it."

So with this admonition in mind I hastened to arrange an appointment with Mr. (also known as Doctor) David F. Friedman, the Number Two and possibly the Number One producer of American "sexploitation" films. You may recall that Dr. Friedman was the guiding genius of *Trader Hornee*, a feature film Professor Knight's students and I were privileged to see screened at the University of Southern California's motion picture workshop. My contact with Friedman resulted in a productive fringe benefit, the opportunity to interview Miss Chris Mathis, youthful performer in such film classics as *Weekend Lovers, Thar She Blows, The Ramrodder,* and *Starlet.*

After the initial shock of watching a nude couple wore off, I can truthfully say I didn't mind *Trader Hornee* and I am almost tempted to present my own critique of the film. But with so many reviews written by professionals and available to me through Dr. Friedman's good offices, I intend to bypass this opportunity and instead offer excerpts from the columns of Mr. Don Morrison of the Minneapolis *Star* and Mr. John Dwyer of the Buffalo *Evening News*.

Mr. Morrison wrote:

Somehow, in all the close scrutiny given to emerging nations of Africa and the reams of copy written about the peoples of that continent, very little has been said about the Meshpoka Tribe.

One school of thought contends that the less said about the Meshpoka, the better. Another school, which happens to be on strike at the moment, is not available for comment. Still a third school claims there is no such tribe.

We are indebted to Dr. David F. Friedman, anthropologist, historian, world traveler, scholar, raconteur, wit, licensed zipper repairman, and bon vivant, for what little we know of this fascinating lost culture. (It should be pointed out that Dr. Friedman's title is an honorary one. He used to give sex lectures at drive-in theaters, to be sure, but he flunked out of medical school because he tended to faint at the sight of a Band-Aid. Failing in a childhood ambition to become a dermatologist, he chose the next nearest thing and now is eking out an opulent living as a leading producer of skin flicks, known in the trade as nudie movies.)

His *Trader Hornee*, now playing at the Astor Art Theater, fills us in satisfyingly on the Meshpokas. Dr. Friedman accompanied the film to Minneapolis to save freight charges. However, he cannot give a satisfactory philological explanation for the similarity of Meshpoka and *meshpochen*, a Yiddish word meaning family or clan. "Go ask," he says.

In all events his gripping documentary belongs in anyone's syllabus.

Mr. Morrison's next few paragraphs are devoted to a résumé of the plot, which involves one Hamilton Hornee, an Indianapolis private eye, hired by a local bank "to find a missing heiress, lost sixteen years earlier at the age of five when her multi-buck parents were killed on a safari."

I have no intention of whetting the appetites of literary voyeurs by detailing any of the several heterosexual and homosexual scenes to be found in *Trader Hornee*. Nor do I wish to be a spoilsport and reveal the plot to those who have not yet seen the film. So I will state only that Detective Hornee, his secretary Jane, a female reporter named Tender Lee, plus other members of the search party reach Meshpoka territory, there to be captured by the natives. Preparatory to being boiled in a huge iron vat for the chief's dinner, Miss Lee, in desperation, shrieks, "Stop! I'm a friend of Sammy Davis, Jr."

I may have gone too far already but I cannot resist describing one more scene in which a Meshpokan is administering a savage beating to Jane. "I like it! I like it!" cries Detective Hornee's secretary, a masochist.

I gather that Mr. Morrison had as much fun interviewing the producer as I did. The Minneapolis *Star*'s columnist concluded:

> I commiserated with Dr. Friedman on the hardships the company must have suffered in capturing this priceless record. His eyes squinted wearily into the distance of unseen horizon: "There were times when we were as much as ten minutes away from the Beverly Hills Hotel," he said.

And from Buffalo comes John Dwyer's comment, one which must have sent Dr. Friedman into paroxysms of joy.

> *Trader Hornee* is the funniest film ever made.
>
> It has dialogue from Harry's 24-Hour Kosher Delicatessen, girls from Surfside Beach, color shots of Africa, and a painted tribe from Lenox Avenue, assorted characters from *Tarzan, The Bengal Lancers, The Maltese Falcon, How to Be a Jewish Mother, Uhuru,* and *Candy.*

The great thing about Dave Friedman is that, while accumulating several million dollars, an attractive wife, a mountaintop mansion, and a Rolls Royce, he takes nothing seriously and that applies particularly to the films he continues to make with astonishing financial, if not artistic, success.

"I make dirty pictures and I sell 'em," he says. "It's no secret. I even told that to the President's Commission on Obscenity and Pornography when I testified in Washington a couple months ago."

As proof of this, Dave showed me a letter he received from the Commission's chairman a few weeks later.

> On behalf of the Commission . . . I wish to extend a sincere "thank you" for your efforts. . . . Everyone in attendance learned a good deal from your candid discussion of some of the problems involved with the exploitation motion pictures. The meeting was quite a success. Obviously the reason . . . was your frank and open discussions of the subject and the candid expression of your opinions.

Dave (he prefers this familiar appellation to the more formal "Doctor") is a tall, slender, pleasant-looking gentleman, fast approaching the half-century mark. Except for jet-black sideburns which sweep down almost to his neck, he could be mistaken for a banker which, in a sense, I suppose he is, because among other varied chores he handles the fiscal affairs of his company, Entertainment Ventures Incorporated. He has been in some area of the entertainment world since childhood.

"My father owned an amusement park in Birmingham, Alabama, a half-interest in the O. J. Hess Carnival which quartered there and a share in a theater, also in Birmingham. In addition, he happened to be editor of the Birmingham *News*, but I never did find out which end of these activities was avocation or vocation. There never was any question about *my* interests—it's always been show biz.

"What a wonderful way for a boy to grow up, the envy of

93

every kid in Birmingham. Never a dull moment for me or wondering where I'd spend my time away from school and whether I'd have a summer job. I had my choice of three fascinating arenas. Before I was ten years old I had more than a rough idea of problems involved when you furnish entertainment to the public.

"My mother also was in show biz—well, kind of, anyway. She was organist for the biggest Methodist church in Birmingham. One day when my father's theater organist didn't show, he sent out for a substitute and my mother arrived on the scene. That's how they met. The marriage lasted until I was around twelve, then broke up; my mother remarried, this time to a chemist and we moved to Buffalo, New York.

"I was graduated from high school there, but during those four years I spent all my spare time working for Buffalo film exchanges, learning that important business end of the Industry. Believe me, what I gathered about distribution there really stood me in good forever after."

At his stepfather's insistence, Dave went to Cornell University where he received his E.E. degree.

"I hadn't the slightest interest in engineering, but in those days you didn't argue with your parents, you did what they told you to do. Meanwhile, though, I spent a good many hours working with the Cornell Dramatic Club, which consisted solely of amateurs, and a good many more hours as a member of Local #377 of the Ithaca Motion Picture Operators Union, which consisted solely of professionals. I still hold my card there.

"Then came a stint in the Army Signal Corps where I made training films and set up a theater in Astoria, Long Island, to show them in."

He sighed.

"No girls in any of these and if they don't have girls I don't want any parts of them. I forgot to tell you I wasn't more than sixteen years old when I was the talker for a carnival kootch show—not my father's, although he might have let me

do it at that. He was pretty broadminded, and no pun intended. I *really* enjoyed doing that."

Dave's voice took on the raspy tones of a carnival talker and
a sudden glint came into his eyes.

"We're gonna show you," Dave barked, "what yuh can't
see at home."

Showing them what they can't see at home is what David
F. Friedman is currently doing at the rate of one full-length
skin flick every seven or eight weeks. Hollywood's major
studios, most of which are in grave financial trouble, might
learn how to lower their enormous production costs by studying EVI's methods. While almost all the big movie companies, as everyone knows, have been losing vast sums of
money annually, EVI's been making it. During the 1969–70
season, for example, one division of Dave's company netted
$170,000 out of less than a million gross.

"We don't waste time or money anywhere. We *keep* our
production schedules. And when we budget fifty thousand
dollars for a film, we're spending more than we usually do.
Most of our pictures cost much, much less; you'd be surprised."

He chuckled.

"No Academy Awards for us, that's for sure. You might like
to see a letter I received recently from an anonymous gentleman who claims to be a part of that Establishment. I'll read it
to you:

Feature Documentary Committee
Academy of Motion Pictures
Los Angeles

Gentlemen:

I am a member of the Feature Committee. My wife and I
happen to own two parakeets, male and female, of which we
have been so fond that we would often take them with us to
concerts and theaters, carrying them unobtrusively in a venti-

95

lated purse or pocket. They have never given us any trouble, and rewarded us for our care by sweet song and innocent chatter.

Unfortunately we took the parakeets with us on the night the Committee screened *Sex and the Animals*. Since then the behavior of the birds has been alarming. From clean-living, discreet parakeets whose modest character would have given joy to Saint Francis of Assisi, they have become leering and sensual fowl, constantly displaying their wattles and uttering hoarse peeps that can only be described as ornothological obscenities. Perhaps worst of all is the change in the attitude of the male parakeet. I thought the low point of his new aggressiveness had been reached when he approached my wife in a suggestive manner, but unhappily he went even further. He approached *me*.

Of course I do not hold the Documentary Committee responsible for the films it judges, but I respectfully suggest that in the future, a subcommittee conduct preliminary screenings, so as to warn members of any picture that should be classified "X" for household pets.

I apologize for writing anonymously, but I have withheld names to protect the innocent.

> Yours cordially,
> (signed)
> A Member

Dave sighed.

"Even though the Industry doesn't recognize us and you won't find my name in the *International Motion Picture Almanac*, we—four or five of my competitors and I—are the only people out here besides Disney making money; at least three of us have become millionaires. And we're giving the customers what they're willing to spend money for. Let me tell you something about the sexploitation market so you'll realize I'm not talking about pennies.

"Right now there are approximately four hundred hard-core sexploitation theaters in the United States showing nudies regularly week in and week out and their number is growing while at the same time the 'regular' houses are fading out of existence.

"I'm going to exclude New York City, where most of the adult houses are in the Forty-second Street area and which are dark, dingy, and dirty with terribly bad equipment. The fact is that the great majority of skin-flick theaters are nicely appointed and immaculately clean. I happen to believe the adult theaters on the West Coast are the best as far as projection, seats, and sound are concerned. But they've got some beautiful places in Augusta, Georgia; Cleveland, Ohio; and elsewhere."

He paused.

"I'll tell you something else. We're looking for additional markets and we're getting them from lots of regular theaters which don't normally play nudies. Theater owners throughout the country who play Paramount, Fox, M-G-M, and all the other majors day after day to damned slim audiences welcome us. Lots of times we're the ones who pay the rent and if the guy is in hock, our nudies pay off his notes.

"Take my picture *Starlet*, for example, which has played in approximately three hundred fifty hard-core houses and is now starting to play the 'legitimate' movie houses. I expect at least five hundred play-dates from this non-sexploitation market. I know they have to whittle down about three or four minutes from the strongest sex scenes. I'm now signing *Trader Hornee* for general-release houses.

"I'll talk about profits for the moment. The average skin flick, *in color*, runs eighty minutes and costs about twenty-five thousand dollars, up to and including the answer print. I'm speaking of pictures like *Daisy Chain*, *The Head Mistress*, *Space Thing*, and so on."

(I might point out, although I'm not sure it's necessary, that a great many skin-flick titles have double-entendre, as for example, *The Head Mistress*, *The Ramrodder*, and *Down to the Sea*, and, of course, *Thar She Blows*.)

Dave went on.

"To the production cost you have to add another ten thousand dollars which takes care of prints and advertising. So you've got thirty-five thousand dollars going in. Any of these will return one hundred thousand dollars to the distributor at the end of one year. Some of 'em, like A *Brand of Shame*, can bring in as much as one hundred sixty thousand. *Thar She Blows*, at this writing, has brought in two hundred thousand dollars. If you release seven pictures a year, and that's about average, you're talking about a quarter of a million dollars net profit."

Dave shook his head.

"I wouldn't want anybody to get the idea all he has to do is to come out here to Hollywood, turn out four or five nudies a year, and make a fortune for himself. *Distribution* is the main problem, although fortunately not for me. There are approximately one hundred twenty-five sexploitation pictures made annually. And there is one indisputable fact—there are only fifty-two weeks in the year. So this means seventy-three of these one hundred twenty-five skin flicks aren't going to be shown anywhere."

Dave's mathematics confused me but I had to assume he knew what he was talking about and, without asking for an explanation, I let him continue.

"If you're thinking of going into the Industry you *must* be on top of the costs all the time and save wherever you can. I know the business from beginning to end. I write the scripts, I cast, I direct, I produce, I edit, and when the films are ready for distribution I know how they should be handled."

He grinned.

"Besides all this, I do a little acting. Naturally, I'm a frustrated ham. As a matter of fact, you'll rarely see an EVI picture without me in it somewhere. Remember the bar-room bum in *Trader Hornee?*"

I confessed I did not.

"Well," Dave said, "that was me. A magnificent portrayal which lasted for some twenty seconds. Now I'll give you a few more reasons why we make dough instead of losing it like the majors are doing. We don't go in for fancy fronts, expensive real estate and plush offices. Who needs 'em?"

The question was rhetorical. A cursory glance at EVI's minuscule lot and modest headquarters located in a rundown section of East Los Angeles should be enough to convince the worst skeptic that Dave Friedman speaks the truth. Even a neophyte such as I had to observe that EVI's non-filming costs were minimal. The building the company occupies is a simple one-story structure, small enough to be tucked behind Ann-Margret's suite on the Paramount lot. Dave's office—it would be a misnomer to call it "private" since he shares it with any fellow worker who happens to be around at the time—is modest and functional.

Dave introduced me to his secretary (everybody else's as well; she's a sort of one-girl stenographic pool) who looked vaguely familiar. Naturally, I didn't listen to her name and kept staring, trying to figure out where we'd met. She noted my confusion, stared right back, then, in a moment or two, burst out laughing.

"Don't be upset," she said, pulling an old burlesque gag. "Just that you don't recognize me with my clothes on."

Then, of course, I realized that the pretty young lady behind the typewriter transcribing notes was the aforementioned Chris Mathis, the lead in many an EVI feature. I'd seen her in *Starlet*, which Dave ran off for me the night before in the projection room of his home. I evinced an interest in how Miss Mathis regarded her dual career in which she appears to leap unconcernedly between the glamor of stardom and the routine of a stenographer. She looked first at me, then at her boss.

"With Dave around," she said, "nothing's ever dull."

With the exception of Miss Mathis, her employer, and a black technician working in a room in back of the office, there seemed to be a dearth of EVI personnel. I'd expected to see at least a *few* writers, actors, grips, producers, directors, cinematographers, publicity men, the usual assortment of studio personnel. Even at those nearly deserted M-G-M, Twentieth

Century-Fox, and Warners studios I'd visited earlier, lots on which a few films were being made annually, I'd seen at least scores of male and female employees.

"Where's everybody?" I asked Dave.

His answer, too, emerged from ancient burlesque.

"Ain't nobody 'round here but us chickens."

He smiled, even if I didn't.

"I'd be kidding you if I said this was a one-man business and that Chris, Charlie [the technician], and I were EVI's only full-time employees. There's Jerry Persell, our general sales manager, but you won't see him hanging around the studio; he's out on the road selling. The company treasurer is Dan Sonney and you won't find *him* on the lot either; he's out somewhere getting production costs for our next film.

"Let me tell you, both Jerry and Dan have had even more experience in the Industry than I've had. They *really* know their way around, every single angle, every pitfall. I shudder when I think of the helpless misfits they're bringing out here to Hollywood from New York to run the majors."

He shook his head dolefully.

"These are guys whose previous experience consisted of operating parking lots, running window-cleaning outfits, or running janitor-service organizations. But they haven't the slightest idea what the movie business is all about. They're happy to spend money—mostly stockholders'—because they still are under the illusion that Hollywood's glamorous like it once was. And they're convinced being identified as Industry tycoons will get them recognition and a better table at Sardi's when they go back east.

"These guys say to themselves, 'Oh, Boy! The beautiful stars I'll be casting,' and they're filled with dreams of the old casting couch. What stars? I ask. The only ones these aging Lotharios remember are as ancient as the guys themselves. That's the truth of the matter."

According to Dave the skin-flick branch of the Industry has no star system. I asked him why; he thought for a moment before answering.

"My own belief is that customers prefer a new face or a new body every week, so I'm constantly on the lookout for beautiful young girls willing to take off their clothes and emote. I've used Chris, here, in several features, but I don't want our patrons to get tired of her body. You understand my opinion of not having nudie stars isn't shared by some of my competitors.

"Don Davis, for example, uses one particular woman in almost every picture he does. She's a really nice gal, worked for us in two or three pictures. But she's a woman thirty-five or thirty-six years of age. The silicone job is beginning to dissipate, she has false teeth, and she doesn't turn *me* on. However, a lot of fat, elderly exhibitors around the country get tremendously turned on by her. In addition, I'd say she's a good thirty pounds overweight, at least by my own personal preference in women."

I glanced at Chris and I understood exactly what Dave meant. Dave's eyes took on a dreamy look and he sighed deeply.

"If there ever was a girl I could have starred it was Stacy Walker, the actress who made *The Daughter of Fanny Hill* and *Smell of Honey* for me. She *really* exuded sex; it was sheer animal magnetism; no woman could compare with her. She was sexploitation's Marilyn Monroe. I made those two pictures almost four years ago but we still get fan letters addressed to 'Stacy Walker, Daughter of Fanny Hill.'

"Once I showed her pictures to an important major studio and a couple of producers flipped when they saw this girl. But she never showed up for appointments to meet these fellows who had parts for her in big pictures. Suddenly she disappeared from the scene and nobody knows where she went. Boy! She could have been a real star. I know I would have used her again and again."

He turned to Miss Mathis.

"Am I right, Chris?"

The latter nodded and Dave continued.

"There is another girl who's made around twenty-five

101

nudies, worked for everybody in the business. She's pretty, she's an excellent actress, and she can carry a heavy dramatic scene. She's dark and she's cute, but she doesn't turn me on. Most of the girls in skin flicks are what we call 'ding-a-lings.' They're here today and gone tomorrow. At the end of the picture you're glad to give them their checks and say good-bye forever—you hope.

"But, I always used one girl steady as a lesbian. In fact, she became known as our house dyke."

At this point I may have looked a trifle confused; Dave noted my raised eyebrows and elaborated.

"You *have* to have a lesbian in every sexploitation film. The customers expect one and look forward to the inevitable homosexual scene, just like they know they're going to get a bloody scene and at least one orgy. I wouldn't want to disappoint all those nice people."

He grinned.

"Let me tell you about our customers—God bless 'em! I said before the patronage is very regular. You can almost call the roll on opening days in the skin flicks. Same fellows come back week after week, year after year. Tell you something else; we're about the only branch of the Industry that has matinees regularly and where they're as profitable as evening shows.

"During the day you get basically three types of patrons, and with very rare exceptions they are males. First you get the real voyeurs, the black-jacketed 'panter' who sits by himself, puts a newspaper or overcoat over his trousers, and groans.

"Then you get the attaché trade; the guy wearing a suit, shirt, and tie, and carrying a briefcase. He's generally a salesman or an executive waiting for an appointment or he's goofing off in the middle of the day. The third category in daytime audiences is the postman type. It's his day off, probably the middle of the week. Out of sheer force of habit he comes downtown and goes to the nudies."

I asked Dave how it paid theaters to run daily matinees. He shook his head at my ignorance.

"If the skin-flick house has a daily gross of one thousand

dollars, for example, I'd say six hundred of that comes in before five P.M., not that we don't have customers for the evening performances. You may be surprised to hear there are plenty of couples—I mean boy-and-girl couples. Some of the guys are there taking the girls to a nudie to ready her up. And women laugh loudest; college kids are great enthusiasts. It's the 'in' thing for them."

He grinned.

"Actually, some of the cracks college kids make are funnier than my scripts. But I can't use 'em; too risqué even for skin flicks. So forget about sexploitation films corrupting the morals of America's youth. If the average high school boy wants to see a naked female, all he has to do is ask his girl friend to take off her clothes. And when Pop finally sits down with his adolescent for a talk on sex, the kid's likely to say, 'O.K., Pop, what do you want to know?'

"Seriously, though, unlike 'regular' X-rated feature films which rely on the eighteens to twenty-eights for admissions, nudies, except in college communities, don't. Kids today look upon sex as a participant sport, not a spectator activity. When they do come to our skin flicks they come to laugh; for them it's camp. These kids will get old, too, and when that happens they'll do less performing and more looking. Our dough comes from people at least thirty and a great percentage a hell of a lot older."

The attitude of most sexploitation film companies, those skin-flick majors which annually produce at least five full-length features and are in a position to market them, is extremely bullish. Like Friedman, these entrepreneurs of dirty movies are convinced the future of the entire Industry, in fact the future of Hollywood itself, lies with them. This optimism was encouraged by a story which appeared recently on page one of the New York *Times*.

Pornography has become big business in America. In a nation founded by Puritans, there has developed a huge and often shadowy industry devoted to the exploitation of sex.

Using the techniques of modern business, from mass production to mass distribution, the pornography industry makes a variety of books, magazines, movies. . . . Its customers are millions of Americans every week.

There appear to be two main reasons for this explosion of erotica. The Supreme Court has, over the last decade, deemed most pornography legal. Only so-called "hard-core" pornography, or "obscenity," is considered illegal, although local interpretations vary.

The annual volume of the pornography business is difficult to estimate. Some observers have said $2 billion; most experts put the figure at closer to $500 million. But what is not disputable is the industry's tremendous recent growth.

Five years ago about ninety theaters around the country showed "sexploitation" movies or "skin flicks." Now there are more than 600 and the number is growing weekly. Some have abandoned seedy downtown areas for the suburbs; many are clean and respectable looking, with admission prices as high as $5.

Another New York newspaper holds a divergent opinion. Said Mr. Jack Robbins of the New York *Post*:

The dirty-movie business is being ruined by dirty movies. For several years young film makers have learned their trade and made a few dollars, sometimes a lot of dollars, making 35-millimeter feature-length films that included a lot of sex but also had a story line and sometimes some vestige of film art. . . .

In the last year the market has been virtually taken over by 16-millimeter films, often without sound, that include—genuine, not suggested—a lot of sex, no story, and no art. . . .

"It's degrading, it's illegal, and there's no money in it," says Leonard Kirtman who made about 70 skin flicks over the last four years and says he will probably make no more. . . .

"They're going to flood the market and ruin it. Nobody will

make any money. A lot of skin houses in California are closing. People are bored with it."

But Friedman shook off this pessimistic point of view and reiterated his claim that without effective theater distribution and know-how, the inexperienced amateur was bound to fail and presented no more danger to EVI and its competitors than, for example, "a few flies around a race horse."

Chapter Twelve

THERE ARE some very important Hollywood personages I interviewed and haven't mentioned yet except in passing—Lana, Zsa Zsa, the Duke, Joan, and Barbara, for examples. But I simply can't seem to tear myself away from David F. Friedman. It may be that I'm reluctant to dispose of him because I'm convinced it will be he rather than Miss West who is destined to save Hollywood. On the other hand I will not deny it may be that the Doctor's frank approach to and historic interest in a hitherto forbidden subject intrigue me.

"As far back as 1958," Dave said, "I introduced sex to New England."

A brash statement indeed.

"That particular exploitation film was called *Because of Eve*," Dave explained. "It's the story of Bob and Sally and we held back nothing, including all areas of male and female equipment. This is what we in the trade call the 'pickles-and-beaver' bit, if you know what I mean. I showed 'em how to do it right in Maine, Vermont, New Hampshire, and so on. I was the pre-film 'lecturer.' Wanna hear my pitch?"

I nodded. Chris brought us a couple of cold beers from the office refrigerator and poured them expertly. I sat back to listen.

"I should preface this episode in the life of David F. Friedman," he said, "by telling you back in those days we showed our films mostly in drive-ins. And I also ought to add that the lecturer's name traditionally had to be short, of Anglo-Saxon derivation, and end with the letter 's.' This made them euphonius, confidence-inspiring, and brief enough to get on a theater marquee. It would be quite inappropriate to be Herman Cohen or David Friedman, Patrick Casey or Abner Runkelmeyer. The Professor's name either was Elliot Forbes, Curtis Hayes, or Alexander Leeds.

"I loved every minute of the lecture platform. For me it was a happy combination of carnival and movies. There were four of these original sexploitation films, only then we called them 'Sex Hygiene' pictures—*Mom and Dad, Bob and Sally, Street Corner,* and *Because of Eve.* That year of '58, I was Curtis Hayes and, as I said, the picture was *Because of Eve.*

"Like the rest of them it had a rigid format—the story of a young girl whose parents denied her the kind of sex knowledge she should have had. Naturally, on her first date with a boy she gets pregnant and can't tell her parents. So she always winds up telling her schoolteacher or an old family friend. Then what do you suppose she does?"

I had no answer.

"Naturally she goes to her friendly neighborhood abortionist; the parents find out. It was one hell of a scene. Then, at the crucial moment the movie would come to a screeching halt, and the title would flash on the screen: 'We pause in our presentation to introduce, in person, the eminent hygiene commentator, Mr. Curtis Hayes,' or Mr. Elliot Forbes, and so on.

"There were four units on the road; my territory was New England, and I was Roger T. Miles. My lecture went something like this."

Dave took a deep swallow of beer; cleared his throat, and began.

"Good evening, ladies and gentlemen. This is Roger T. Miles speaking to you from the projection room in the beautiful Starlight Drive-In Theater in Bellows Falls, Vermont. I'm very happy to see so many of you here tonight and I'm sure you will agree with me and so many others after you've seen all of the story of *Bob and Sally*. I know this will greatly benefit not only the people of this charming community but every community in our great nation if they were privileged to see all of it.

"Now I'd like to warn you at this time that in the final reels of *Bob and Sally* which you are going to see shortly, you are going to observe on our screen the shockingly frank facts of life. Among other things, you are going to see the actual birth of two babies. First you are going to see a normal, natural birth and second, what is known as a Caesarean section.

"I'd like to warn you at this time that some of you may get sick, and it's usually the big, strong men who do. Well, gentlemen, if any of you feel sick, put your head down between your knees and raise your hand and one of our nurses in attendance will come to you and give you aid."

Dave paused to call for a refill for his guest and himself; Chris obliged and my host continued.

"So many of you fine parents here in Bellows Falls do not give your children proper sex education. And *that* is the reason for this presentation of *Bob and Sally*. Naturally, with one showing we cannot *possibly* cover the many and varied problems in the field. So, it is for this reason that the sponsors of this film, The Women's Research Guild, have put together two books which I am going to describe to you now. Please bear with me."

Dave, who all the while seemed to be back in Bellows Falls at the beautiful Starlight Drive-In Theater, dropped his voice, grinned again, and turned to me.

"You know where I just was, don't you?"

I nodded.

"Well, I'm going back there now and give 'em the hard sell. Here she goes! Listen."

I did.

108

"Ladies and gentlemen, I have in my hand the 'Sexual Guide' *complete* with pictures and illustrations. It tells you *exactly* what to do on your wedding night. And, furthermore, it graphically tells what you should *not* do.

"Chapter Nine, for example, describes the six erotic zones in a woman's body and it tells you how they are to be fondled, caressed, and handled by the husband to bring his wife to the fulfillment of their passion. Each of these six zones is *fully* described and illustrated."

Dave's pitch was interrupted momentarily by the arrival of a pair of gentlemen who I learned later were owners of an Atlanta, Georgia, "adult" theater and old customers of EVI.

"Go on, Professor," one of them, a pleasant-looking man in his early thirties, called out. "I'm itchin' to buy your ole 'Sex Guide.' "

There were introductions all around. The Southern gentlemen's preference was for bourbon and branch water and Chris obliged.

"Well," Dave said, "it went on like that for a couple more minutes. About this time there's always a couple of idiots in their cars wanting to get on with the picture and they keep honking their horns. So you stop and say . . ."

The other Southerner, this one a tall, white-haired, sunburned Atlantan who looked about sixty-five, raised his hand.

"Let me give the squelcher, Dave," and Dave yielded the floor.

The distinguished gentleman's soft voice turned raspy.

"By the way, ladies and gentlemen, there is one chapter I would like to mention now. It is Chapter Fourteen and the subject is masturbation. It should be read by the parents of every boy in the audience, *especially* by those who are blowing their horns."

The speaker turned to Dave.

"Did I do it right?" he asked, and his host's answer was several seconds of vigorous hand-clapping.

"Couldn't have done it as well myself."

And with this generous response Friedman went on, if not with the pitch, at least with a further elaboration of the sales talk.

"There were some frames on V.D. in the film although we didn't always show them; they were pretty strong. But in the book for men they were included and some of those illustrations showing the deterioration of the male sexual organs . . . well, they weren't funny. The final chapter of the book for women we called 'Vatican Roulette.' It went something like this:

"And now, ladies, I want to talk about the control of conception. Understand me, I am not advocating birth control. We of this organization do *not* advocate birth control. However, nature does operate in patterns and every young woman, upon reaching puberty or womanhood, enters into her own menstrual period each month . . . the fertile period, and so on and so on.

"And I believe with all my heart that the set of books belongs on the bedside of every man and woman in America. They are made available to you at a fraction of their cost of printing, mailing, and distribution. We sell them not for ten dollars a set, which would be a very fair price, not for five dollars, not even for three, but only two dollars a set. *They cannot be obtained anywhere else!*

"Young men are now on the grounds. If you want to buy this invaluable set of profusely illustrated books, turn on your headlights. And if you would like to talk to me personally, I will be in the concession stand and be more than happy to speak with you. Now I want to wish all of you wonderful Bellows Falls folks a very happy life. God bless you!"

Sexploitation, or simply exploitation films, as they used to be called, have a long if not a particularly honorable history. Dave, who made a study of the subject, claims the idea began in the fertile mind of Manny Brown, whose first film, *The Evils of White Slavery*, was presented to an eager American public the year before World War I began.

"Manny, a tall, gaunt, distinguished-looking guy, was the

lecturer and naturally he was billed as 'Professor Emanuel Brown.' The film which he produced himself was supposed to be an exposé of white slavery in cities of the United States. I never saw it; no prints were left when I went to work for Manny, but he told me it was wild and woolly and didn't miss much that would titillate his audiences. And I wouldn't doubt that gentlemen present could hardly wait till the movie was over to rush to their local prostitute.

"I guess Manny played every tank town in the country over the years. He told me how he wound up the lecture. It's been a hell of a long time since then but I think I can still remember how it went."

Dave stood up and opened his arms in supplication.

"And now, dear friends, I hope that when you and the rest of the people in our great nation see what horrors lie ahead for those who fail to heed my advice, instead of the harsh noise of hurdy gurdy bands in America's red-light districts there will be heard the inspiring sounds of 'Rock of Ages.'"

We all applauded, Dave took a bow, and sat down.

"Of course," he continued, "if the Professor showed his picture to a lower East Side audience in New York, the sounds to be raised were 'Eli! Eli!'"

Then Dave, joined by one of the Atlanta gentlemen, hummed a few bars of that venerable Hebraic hymn. After which Dave went on.

"Not too much sex *per se* in those early exploitation days. It was dope or the evils of crime, and, believe me, religion. For example, in *The Prince of Peace*, the life of Christ was exploited to the nth degree. That picture took in more cash than anybody ever dreamed was possible. Babb really raked in the dough with *Prince*; must have made himself a couple hundred thousand bucks. He was an old timer."

Dave sighed.

"Like we used to say in carnivals, 'He turned 'em to the right, he turned 'em to the left, he turned 'em on, he turned 'em off, he turned 'em every way but loose.' In my time I've exploited the marijuana theme with a couple of films, *She*

Should Have Said No and *The Devil's Weed,* and did O.K. with both of them.

"Today, with such all-around permissiveness, the theme naturally is sex. Right now EVI and the rest of the skin-flick producers are showing more than the majors dare, although in *Midnight Cowboy,* for example, there's a full intercourse theme, done very well, too. What the majors are going to show on the screen six months or a couple of years from now is anybody's guess."

He smiled confidently.

"But whatever it is, we'll be ahead of them. You can bet your ass on that."

The younger of the two Southern gentlemen, who'd been listening appreciatively to Doctor Friedman's discourse, interrupted to mention that he'd like to see a screening of EVI's latest production, *The Ramrodder.* Dave was more than happy to oblige a customer and asked me to join him and the Atlantans in a rear projection room. But I thought this would be a good chance to interview Chris, so I thanked him politely and remained to talk with the star of *Starlet* and other feature films.

I don't know how old Miss Mathis is; I didn't ask and she didn't volunteer to tell me, but my guess is that she hovers somewhere between twenty-five and twenty-seven. In the brief period of elapsed time from her birth in Baltimore, Maryland, to the present, her work has been varied.

"Believe it or not," she said, "I started out wanting to be a lady cop. I was living with my parents, eight brothers, and six sisters. I'm the oldest. I heard there was an opening on the Baltimore Police Force and I applied. But I got there too late, the position was already filled. So, naturally, I became a bunny in the Baltimore Playboy Club."

This last statement sounded like a nonsequitur but I didn't want to probe the possible connection, so I let Miss Mathis continue without interruption.

"I stayed there for three years and then I transferred to

Hefner's Club in Jamaica, British West Indies. I didn't like it. I returned to Baltimore and went to work as a file clerk at Fort Holabird, but I didn't like that *at all*. I quit and went down to Miami to do modeling—that's what I always wanted to be, a model, not an actress. In case you're interested, I'm five-feet, five-inches and 35–23–34; I'm a natural brunette. But I didn't make it in Miami and I was so broke the only dough I had was a dime to call my father and ask for plane fare home.

"I got tired of Baltimore, came out to Hollywood in 1968, and got into the movies almost as soon as I got here. My first picture was *Alimony Lovers* but it was only a bit part, a walk-on, for Clover Films, one of Dave's competitors. Then I got to play the lead in Box Office International's film, *Weekend Lovers*."

I asked Chris what the difference was between a weekend lover and an alimony lover. She looked puzzled and shrugged her shoulders noncommittally.

"Then I did a picture for Filmco, *Temporary Lovers*, I think it was called. [This brought to mind still another unasked question.] Meantime I got married. I have a little girl born October 1969. Name's Vanessa, and I guess you might say after Vanessa Redgrave, an actress I admire very much. But to tell you the truth I didn't have that in mind when I went to the hospital for confinement; I expected a boy. We have so many in our family, the proportion's like three to one.

"I met David in 1969 and he said he could make a star out of me although actually he hired me to be his secretary. Later he made me the office manager, which is what I am when I'm not acting. The first picture I made for David was *Thar She Blows*, which he wrote, produced, directed and, of course, acted in. He likes to have his hands on everything.

"I had only a small part, too, really just a walk-on, but I learned a lot. David is very conscientious and thorough, you know. People who work for him soon find out he thinks of

113

every detail. Let me give you a copy of the shooting script for *She Blows*. Read it when you get a chance and you'll see what I mean."

Chris reached into a filing cabinet and handed me copy number thirteen which I glanced at hastily while the actress answered the telephone. Actually it wasn't necessary to go beyond page one for proof of Dr. Friedman's painstaking attention to details.

> Low Angle Shot—Sally.
> As she goes up the stairs, Camera sees the lush little bare behind under the micro-skirt.

Clipped to the back of copy number thirteen was a color-fully illustrated promotion folder of the film itself. In this were displayed those scenes which Dave had told me were the sine-qua-noniness of all skin flicks. Even for eyes as untrained as mine, it was no problem to pick out the masochistic bit, a sea-going rowdy using a dead fish to flog a naked woman who obviously was enjoying every lash and asking for more.

Superimposed over the copiously endowed body of Miss Shari Mann, the star, was a brief synopsis of the picture. I'd read no more than the opening sentence—"Filmed against the endless splendor of the sensuous sea, the David F. Fried-man–William Allan Castleman color production *Thar She Blows* relates the classic tale of a tortured soul, Bob Frigate, captain of a hundred-foot, ocean-going charter yacht"—when Miss Mathis concluded her telephone conversation and turned to me. I commented on her employer's thoroughness and imagination.

"I know," Chris agreed. "He's a genius. And modest, too. I bet he didn't even tell you he owns a chain of adult theaters, did he?"

I shook my head.

"Well, he does. They're all called 'The Pussycats,' eight in Los Angeles, two in San Diego, and a couple more in Sacramento."

I looked properly impressed.

"But we were talking about my career, weren't we? I told you my big chance came in *Starlet*. It was a tremendous role and called for talents I didn't even know I had. David said I performed magnificently. And the publicity he got for me was simply *tremendous*. Did you see the last issue of *Adam Film World*? You know what that is, don't you?"

I was afraid to say no to both questions, but conscience compelled me to speak the truth. Chris smiled tolerantly.

"That's all right. I understand. It's just one of the most important fan magazines for skin flicks. Here, I'll give you a copy. I have a couple left."

I thanked Chris and while she sat by, eyes modestly averted, I counted ten full pages of *Starlet* publicity, including a dozen or more photographs of Miss Mathis, showing the young lady in varied positions of pre-, actual and post-copulation. I observed Dave's fine hand in one caption which read:

> A couple, Doug and Carol (Miss Mathis), are lying nude in bed as the film opens, then somebody says harshly, "Commence to yence."

On this note I think I should conclude my explorations into the realm of skin flicks and let posterity decide whether David F. Friedman's and Hollywood's future are to be inevitably entwined.

Chapter Thirteen

"OUT IN Hollywood, when they put their arms around your shoulder, look you square in the eye, and say, 'Remember, kid, I'm with you all the way down the line,' that's the moment to be on guard. It's a signal they're getting ready to cut your throat or stab you in the back. And if it can be arranged without danger to their own person, they do both at the same time."

So states Mr. Dore Schary, New York City's recent commissioner of cultural affairs, a job which at thirty thousand dollars per annum paid him less than one-tenth of what he received for running Metro-Goldwyn-Mayer in the good old days. I'd had to came back east for a week to handle some personal affairs and Dore agreed to see me before I returned to Los Angeles. We finished dinner in his Manhattan apartment and were sitting around talking in his study which looks out on Central Park.

While my host claimed his opinion of Hollywood's perfidiousness would hold true in general, he admitted he was referring specifically to a pair of incidents in which he himself was involved.

"The first time was in 1948 when I took over the job of production chief at M-G-M. I succeeded Louis B. Mayer whom they let out. There was considerable bitterness on both sides, Louie's and management's. Louie'd been on the lot for a good many years and had reason to think he'd built up a strong personal following of men and women whose careers he'd made. He felt sure that when I came on the lot there'd be many resignations out of loyalty. As a matter of fact, so did I.

"I remember discussing this with Nicholas G. Schenk, then president of M-G-M. I said, 'Nick, I'm prepared to release everybody who wants to go, regardless of their contracts.'

"I'll never forget the way Nick looked at me. His face had an Oriental cast to it and his eyes could narrow into slits, as they did at that moment. He gave me what I can only describe, and tritely I know, as an inscrutable smile.

" 'It's all right with me, Dore,' he said. 'If anybody wants to quit, we'll pay him off.'

"But *everybody* stayed on, even Louie's private secretary and personal assistant. Not one person resigned to follow his erstwhile leader. Nick wasn't the least bit surprised. So I said to myself, 'Dore, remember when your time comes, you'll know what to expect,' and that's the way it was eight years after.

"Late in 1955 murmurs began to circulate out in Hollywood that I was going to get the axe and calls from my 'loyal' supporters began to come in. Stars, directors, producers, secretaries, and writers flocked to me all singing the same tune, 'Don't forget, kid, we're with you all the way down the line.' What happened to me was exactly what happened to Louie eight years before."

Dore paused.

"Well, that's not quite true. After they let me out, two people did come through. Spencer Tracy was one of them. I was in New York by then and he phoned me.

" 'I just read in the papers you got fired, Dore. What the hell for?'

"So I gave him some, if not all, of the background. When I'd finished he said, 'I love you, kid,————Hollywood. If you ever need me for anything you can count on me.' I knew he *meant* what he said and he didn't care *who* knew it. He was a great and wonderful man and we remained friends until his death, although I never had the occasion to ask him to do anything.

"The other real friend was Montgomery Clift. Monty'd hurt himself while he was making *Raintree County* for me. He was a fine actor and a nice guy and I was more than glad to protect him until he recovered from his accident. He reached me at home the day after Spencer called.

" 'I just want you to be sure, Dore, any time you want me for a picture I'm available.' "

Dore smiled with obvious satisfaction.

"He delivered. Two years later I called him. 'Monty,' I said, 'I'd like to talk to you about something.' He knew what I meant and he answered, 'When do we start?'

"The film was *Lonely Hearts*, based on a best seller, *Miss Lonely Hearts*, and I produced it independently on a small budget. In addition to Monty, it starred Robert Ryan, another fine actor and a gentleman, and Jackie Coogan. Unfortunately, we didn't do as well as we might have."

Critics in general dismissed the film as just another Schary "message" picture. The New York *Times* said:

> It [*Lonely Hearts*] is an endeavor to say something profound about the danger of quick moral judgments and the virtue of loving thy fellowman. . . .

Lonely Hearts was neither the first nor the last product of Schary's awareness of social injustice and his ardent desire to make movie audiences think, a rank heresy in the land of the Philistines with its long-standing tradition of sweeping all unpleasant topics under the rug. As Harry Cohn, the revolting but highly successful head of Columbia Pictures, once said (and which has been repeated a good many thousand times since, I'm sure), "If you want to send a message, use Western Union."

Nor were all of Schary's message pictures financial failures. *The Blackboard Jungle,* a bitter exposé of big-city school systems, was a box-office success. Schary made this one despite violent opposition from nearly everyone in authority on the M-G-M lot which he then headed.

"Had it bombed," Schary admitted, "my ass would have gone, too. They were just waiting around for me to make a fat mistake."

His initial attempt to arouse public opinion against what he regarded as a widespread social evil was *Crossfire,* an attack on anti-Semitism in America. Dore made this for RKO in 1947 and to the surprise of practically everyone in the Industry as Dore claimed, the picture made money. In the long run, however, it probably was Dore's insistence that the studio produce sufficient message pictures to balance so-called purely entertainment films which brought about his ultimate downfall at M-G-M.

"With the kind of awful crap he was shooting, the son-of-a-bitch ruined RKO first," Miss Lana Turner said. "Then he went over to M-G-M and proceeded to wreck the greatest studio in the world. I predicted he'd do it in seven years; it took him only five."

Since Miss Turner informed me she didn't care who (including the subject himself) knew the way she felt about Dore Schary, I told him what she'd said. He smiled but without bitterness.

"Lana's not the only one."

I asked him whether he'd go back to Hollywood should they want him to take over M-G-M again, a rumor I'd been hearing almost from the first day I arrived in Los Angeles. He shrugged his shoulders.

"Go back to what? There's nothing left for me out there," he sighed. "But in its day it really was something and M-G-M had most of it. The actors, producers, directors! Cukor, Milestone, Jimmy Stewart, Walter Pidgeon, Irene Dunne, Wallace Beery, Lew Ayres, Robert Montgomery, Robert Taylor, Dame May Whitty, Judy Garland, Margaret Sullavan, Richard Whorf, Katie Hepburn, Charles Laughton, and so on. It takes your breath away."

He grinned.

"Even Lana, a woman with great talent although it's buried awfully deep. And I haven't mentioned Cagney, who was a fine performer, or Tracy, who was the best screen actor I ever knew in terms of versatility, or Cary Grant, a marvelous actor and a loyal friend. He could do comedy, drama, and anything else and be believable. You can't sell Gary Cooper short, either. He did some marvelous characterizations, in *Sergeant York*, for example.

"Nor can you dismiss Clark Gable, who did a superb job in *Gone with the Wind*. And Bogey, the anti-hero, who could make it today with the kids—the eighteens to twenty-eights, the ones who are so goddamned blasé about everything but Bogey.

"All these stars had something the rest of us haven't and they made Hollywood what it was once. As Josh Logan said, 'They brought their own lights with them, and they shone wherever they were.' It's a unique quality and it can't be superimposed and don't think it hasn't been tried. Remember Anna Sten?"

I nodded.

"Well," he said, "she was the classic example of how you can't build star quality into a non-star. Goldwyn spent a fortune on her promotion but she never got there. Another was Turhan Bey, the Turk. They tossed out millions for his buildup and ultimately it failed.

"These people, even those who never quite reach stardom, and I include Sten and Bey, have *some* acting talents but they are submerged because of what is loosely termed 'personality.' Something like Barrie's definition of charm. When you go over the careers of the true stars, those who made four or five successful pictures year in, year out, you'll discover that each possessed that unknown quality."

Sometime after this I had a couple of drinks with Arthur Mayer, who as a distributor and exhibitor has been an integral part of the Industry since 1907. He's one of the authors of *The Movies*, a pictorial history of Hollywood, and he shares many of Dore's opinions.

"At what precise moment and by what imprecise means a starlet or her nameless male equivalent graduates to stardom no one can say," he wrote. "The nature of the films in which he or she is cast and the quality and quantity of the publicity extended them are largely responsible. Yet all Sam Goldwyn's wiles and willingness to spend money could not sell beautiful Anna Sten to the American public, while a steady stream of mediocre stories could not stay Garbo's rise to glory. . . ."

Schary came to Hollywood for the first time in 1932.

"That was when the talkies were being accepted as a special art form and a way of life. When I arrived, it seems to me that the fan magazines' main function was to plead for a return of silent pictures. But they still were ballyhooing the stars and 'exposing' the secrets of their lives. And people from every city, town, and hamlet in the United States came to Hollywood and Vine, there to hope for a glimpse of their favorites.

"Whenever a star appeared, crowds of his or her adorers would be on hand, hours ahead, waiting and waiting and waiting. Unless you were present, you can't imagine what it was like in those 'golden' days. Whatever they said about Hollywood's glamor was true. It was as close as we ever came to creating American royalty. And the opportunities for self-indulgence offered the stars were limitless."

Dore paused to refill his pipe which he smoked almost incessantly until the air in his study was filled with a blue haze.

"Some members of 'royalty' fell by the wayside, drank, caroused, took narcotics, had lurid affairs which even Howard Strickling couldn't keep out of the papers. But the majority of those on top were hard-working men and women who took their jobs seriously.

"I often think of that trio of stalwarts—Cooper, Tracy, and Gable. Fine, decent, highly introspective gentlemen who

121

never succumbed to the blandishments of Hollywood—the thousands of weekly fan letters and the hundreds of indecent proposals they got. Not one of these ever was corrupted.

"I remember Gable's graceful answer when a woman he'd never seen accused him of fathering her child. Reporters showed him a picture of the plaintiff after she began a paternity suit. Clark looked at it for a moment, shook his head almost regretfully, and turned to his interrogators.

" 'I'm sure if I had ever met or had a romance with this very attractive woman I never would have forgotten her.' "

Although he came back to New York on frequent occasions to write, produce, and direct Broadway plays for the Theater Guild (*Sunrise at Campobello* was one of his most successful), Schary was a more or less permanent resident of Hollywood for twenty-five years.

"I hate to disappoint you," he said, "but I never was part of the glamor. With few exceptions I had no social contact with stars or executives. My friends were doctors, lawyers, writers, and social workers. I didn't even call for the services of the great Howard Strickling when I had press conferences, and that was almost unheard of."

During the three decades of his Hollywood stay, he was directly involved in the production of scores of outstanding films, including *Lassie Come Home, The Spiral Staircase, Lost Angel, Bataan, Mr. Blandings Builds His Dream House,* and *Bad Day at Black Rock,* the last starring Spencer Tracy. In 1938 he won an Academy Award for his story of *Boys' Town.*

Like Dave Friedman, Dore Schary has been in some form of the entertainment world most of his adult life. He was twenty-one years old when he made his first stage appearance as a bit player in summer stock. Although he has long since abandoned an acting career, Schary freely admits he is a "ham" and delights in public speaking, at which he is superb, as I have occasion to know.

Next to George Jessel and a few political personalities, Schary probably is one of the most sought-after speakers in the country. I don't want to create the impression that he makes speeches only when he gets paid. Upon many occasions he contributes his services to organizations engaged in the promotion of racial and religious understanding. To anyone who's ever heard Schary make a speech, it's obvious that from beginning to end he loves every minute of it. Of course, so do his audiences.

I, on the contrary, loathe public speaking; my legs tremble to the point of near collapse every time I'm called upon to address more than a dozen strangers. However, as anyone who's ever had a book published knows, there is far more to that craft than just writing. One of the unpleasant (for me at any rate) literary by-products is plugging your book. Consequently, when publishers' press agents make promotional dates for my appearances, I accept or bear the stigma of being non-cooperative. If the book doesn't sell it's my fault. Robbins, Irving Wallace, Cornelius Ryan, and a half-dozen other writers can and do get away with saying no to every promotional suggestion; their books will sell anyway.

Somehow I don't mind TV interviews, perhaps because I'm able to convince myself nobody is listening except the master of ceremonies and me, and possibly some bored engineer way off in the control room. About eight or nine years ago, shortly after one of my books came out, I was asked to speak at a dinner. The affair was held in an exclusive private club in New York and when I arrived I was horrified to find several hundred ladies and gentlemen waiting for me.

Right before I walked to the dais, the hostess gave me a printed program which I glanced at surreptitiously and to my terror discovered Mr. Dore Schary was the other speaker. What was even worse was the fact that *I* followed *Schary* whom I'd never met but I was aware of his reputation as a superb speaker.

Dore sat on the right of the M.C. and I on his left. I knew my ordeal would end in less than two hours but the intervening wait was unbearable. Schary, I could see, was completely poised, but I was so nervous I wished to hell I'd stayed in the newspaper business. I was half-tempted to fake a sudden attack of appendicitis but finally made up my mind I'd sweat it out if they'd switch the program around and I'd go on first.

During those few brief moments when everybody's head was supposed to be bent in piety while a rabbi intoned the blessing, I reached behind the cleric's back, tugged at Schary's coat sleeve, and hurriedly whispered my request. He grinned, nodded, and when the M.C. replaced the rabbi, the former announced that a last-minute change in the program placed me in the lead.

For post-prandial orators who dread the task as much as I, here is a word of advice. If more than one speaker is scheduled, insist on being first, or, if you're doing a solo, tell the M.C. you've got less than an hour before you have to be at the airport. The simple strategy behind this is that the cleric's "amen" is a cue for impatient waiters to swarm out of the kitchen, swoop down on guests, bank dirty dishes and silverware on metal trays, then swarm out again through noisy swinging doors. This is also the time when elderly gentlemen arise and make hurried trips to rest rooms and ladies retire to powder their noses.

During the twenty-minute period of mounting decibels it is customary for the president of the organization to announce that the regular meeting of the Hadassah is postponed or that choice seats are still available for the Ladies' Auxiliary production of *Springtime for Henry*. It doesn't make any difference what is said; guests couldn't possibly hear even if they wanted to. So, when I usurped the president's place, they couldn't hear me either; consequently, I drew a modest round of applause before surrendering the platform to Dore. By then the room was completely silent.

When dinner was over, our hostess, an impressive-looking, middle-aged lady whose fingers were encircled with diamonds, surreptitiously handed me a sealed envelope. I noted that she did the same thing to Dore who, with a nod to its donor, quietly slipped it into his coat pocket. I wasn't so naïve not to realize we were being given our "honorariums." Dore deserved his; I didn't and knew it. So I shook my head and returned the unopened envelope to my hostess.

Neither honesty nor ethics compelled me to act in this fashion. I never accept money for speaking because if I did audiences would have the right to expect more from me than I'm capable of giving. And besides, the agony I go through isn't worth the fifteen or twenty-five bucks I'm usually offered.

This lady refused to take no for an answer and thrust the envelope back into my hands. Again I returned it. Dore, who'd been observing the by-play, shrugged his shoulders, pulled me aside, and whispered, "Take it, kid, don't be a dope; it won't break the club." So when the would-be donor made a third attempt, I muttered my thanks and accepted.

After I arrived home the next day and unpacked my suitcase, my wife took one look at the tuxedo jacket and said she'd send it to the dry cleaner. She removed the junk from my pockets and came across the still unopened envelope.

"What's this?" she asked, and I answered that it was an honorarium she could use to buy a trifle for herself or our daughter. She slit the edge, took a quick look at the contents, and gasped.

"Jesus! A trifle, the man says. Do you know how much you got paid?"

I shook my head and she handed me the check; it was for seven hundred fifty dollars.

That evening in his apartment I told this story to my host.

"They short-changed you, bud," he said, grinning. "Should have been fifteen hundred bucks; that was the going rate in those days."

Chapter Fourteen

"IT'S NOT that I don't trust you," Frank McFadden, Lana Turner's press agent said apologetically, "but if I don't take you there, you'll never find the place by yourself. It's way the hell up in the hills. I promise to leave as soon as she's sure you're not a member of the working press. Newspapermen always gave her a hard time and she's scared to death of them."

He shook his head.

"You'll like her, I know. Everybody does; that may be her trouble. And I've one more admonition, or request, whatever you want to call it. Unless she brings it up herself, *please* don't discuss her marriages or her personal life; you know how loused up they are."

As we wandered up and down the hills and canyons surrounding Hollywood and its western suburbs, I assured Frank I hadn't any intention of talking about his client's many marriages (six or seven, I forget which), nor of the tragedies which beset her life, nor of the scandals which caused her to be known as Hollywood's "bad girl."

I suppose I should have looked it up first, but since I wasn't particularly interested I didn't know her current marital status. I was aware she was last wed to a nightclub hypnotist and, of course, I recalled the murder of an alleged boyfriend, Johnny Stompanato, in Miss Turner's mountaintop home to which Frank was driving me. I'd never followed this actress' career nor had I been one of her fans. But there were so many nasty headlines about her over the years that it was no surprise when reformers, trying to clean up the Industry, used to claim that "Hollywood," "sin," and "Lana Turner" were interchangeable words.

I don't know what I expected to see when Frank and I entered Miss Turner's house, but it certainly wasn't the slender, poised, attractive blonde who walked into her living room a few minutes after we were ushered there by a nondescript male secretary. I'd been informed by many that Lana's face is subjected to regularly scheduled lifts which may be true, but on her it doesn't show and, despite all she's gone through, she doesn't look past her mid-thirties. It may be that some unnoticed signal passed between client and agent, but to my great relief (I'm always uncomfortable when a third party is present during interviews) Frank left almost at once. I was to telephone him when I was ready and he'd pick me up if Miss Turner couldn't drive me back to my apartment.

The day was warm, I was thirsty, and before we sat down to talk, my hostess poured a tall gin-and-tonic for me and a short one for herself. We stood drinking at a bar in a corner of the huge living room which looked out on a formal garden and the usual, slightly-smaller-than-Olympic-size swimming pool. I guessed there were hills in the distance, but the smog was so heavy that late afternoon you couldn't see more than a hundred feet ahead.

Finally we sat down, a rickety old card table between us.

"I keep it for sentimental reasons," Miss Turner explained, but she didn't tell me what these were and Frank had inhibited me so much, I was afraid to ask for fear it had something to do with the murder that took place several years back exactly where I now sat. I didn't quite know how to begin the conversation and admit I was a bit awestricken being in such close proximity to the star of forty-five feature films and a bride of six or seven times.

But I needn't have worried. In a few minutes Miss Turner began to talk freely and intelligently, if not about her personal life, which I didn't expect to hear anyway, about her career, past, present, and future. She'd just completed a TV series, *The Survivors*, a prime-time soap opera from the pen of Harold Robbins. Not wishing to embarrass me as others might have, Miss Turner didn't ask if I'd seen any of the thirteen episodes. My answer would have been no.

"Too goddamned many directors, too goddamned many script changes, and too goddamned many writers," she explained. "So *Survivors* bombed. In addition to all those production problems, the opposition ran some of my old movies at the same time."

She shook her head in disgust.

"Television! What a *horrible* way to make a living. Working in that medium is like working in a jungle. Everybody's out to get you if they can, and there's no one around to provide you with protection. I'll tell you this, it's not like it was in the old days when I was with M-G-M. *That* was the way to live."

A faraway look came into her large brown eyes.

"It was an empire; we were princes and princesses and Gable was King. Every waking moment of our lives we were protected and cherished. Behind us was the prestige of the greatest studio in the world—that is, until Dore Schary ruined it. All of the other studios were imitators—Warners, where I made my first film for Mervyn LeRoy when I was fifteen years old—Paramount, Twentieth Century—they all tried but they never got within spitting distance of M-G-M.

"When I was driven through the gate there was the officer who recognized me. It was 'Good morning, Miss Turner,' and he'd wave me through. And all day long it was the same wherever I went on the lot or on location. Whoever I met was kind, respectful, and loyal. They watched out for us, shielded us, made us feel safe, and made us feel wanted.

"It was a giant umbrella which covered everybody from the humblest grips to stars who were under personal contracts—I, Shearer, Crawford, Robert Taylor, and so many, many others and, of course, Gable and Garbo. I *loved* that man Gable, but he frightened me, he was so *great*. I used to be so nervous and excited when he walked into the commissary, I'd drop my fork. And when I played opposite him, I was scared to death. And Garbo!"

Miss Turner gave a prodigious sigh.

"*There* was a woman. But in all the time I was with M-G-M, I caught a glimpse of her only twice. Each time she took my breath away she was so beautiful."

Rays of a late afternoon sun finally broke through the smog and shone directly on Miss Turner's face. She didn't wince, budge, or retreat into the shadows although she certainly had to be aware that I was taking a good look for signs of age, hard living, disillusionments, and more than one family tragedy. But I saw none; at fifty, give or take a few years, she's still an alluring woman and whatever ineffable quality a star's supposed to have to be a star, she's got. She waited patiently until I finished staring, then her eyes caught mine and she smiled.

"O.K.?" she asked, and I answered, "O.K."

I don't want to seem erudite—something I certainly am not—but when my hostess, who was wearing a satiny, tight-fitting gown, walked to the bar to refill our empty glasses, I was forcefully reminded of Herrick's lines concerning Miss Julia's "brave vibrations, each way free."

So I sat back and took a few swallows of the cooling mixture and listened while my hostess spoke about her advent into the Industry, thus shattering one of Hollywood's most publicized tales.

"I was fifteen when I got my start and I want to put one thing straight. I was *not* discovered sitting on one of those goddamned stools in Schwab's Drugstore, which they've been capitalizing on for a long time. What really happened was that I was a junior at Hollywood High—I was a teenager—and I heard there was a chance to try out for a part in a Mervyn LeRoy picture. I made it and Mervyn LeRoy gave me a contract which he later sold to M-G-M.

"I don't know what Mervyn saw in me; it might have been my looks, it might have been something else, but it certainly wasn't my acting experience. I had none; I wasn't even in my high school class play."

There is more than a fair chance that Miss Turner's physical appearance had something to do with LeRoy's decision.

"Sex is what this kid exudes mostly," reported *Screen World* shortly after Miss Turner made her first picture. According to the March 23, 1940 issue of *Collier's*, "Miss Turner has hazel eyes and a perfect figure. Weight 109, 22½-inch waist, 34 bust, 35 hips. . . ."

Without veering as much as a single degree from our subject, I hereby offer a few comforting words to men and women bedeviled by actions of their sons of the Class of '73, concerned with such troubles as student rebellion, draft evasion, sexual freedom, contempt for the Establishment, and pot. History, or at least that portion reflected in the same issue of *Collier's*, tells us that the Class of '40, too, had its problems. Kyle Crichton reported:

> If the parents of this country knew what their sons in college were doing, there would be a scandal that would stink up the nation. Are they drinking? Are they carousing? Are they carrying on? No! Are they studying? Alas, no! What they are doing, the young whippersnappers, is writing letters to Lana Turner.
>
> Instead of struggling with their differential calculus, they sit grimly at a desk and bite the end of a pen and write . . . to a young lady they have never even met socially.

I wonder which form their reaction would take—nausea, anger, contempt, or hysterical laughter—were members of the

Class of '73 shown what their fathers were alleged to have written when they went to college. At some risk I quote *Collier's* once again.

> Dear Miss Turner (they write):
> We fellows of the Phi Goofa Gamma house saw you in *Glamor Girls* and you were certainly swell; then we saw you in *Dancing Co-ed* and we thought you were the berries. We are having a dance on May 15 and last night we held a meeting of the chapter and decided it would be swell if you could be Queen of the Ball or something. You could also be Sweetheart of Phi Goofa Gamma. Just tell us when you're coming and we'll meet the train and every Goofa Gamma who can walk will be right down there.
> Enclosed find twenty-five cents in stamps for your picture. If you could sign it "To Dear Jake," it would make all the other fellows jealous and would make me feel swell. Ha-ha-ha!
>
> Jake Blots, '40.

According to those who were around at the time, it didn't take Miss Turner long to become an integral part of the Hollywood scene. The old school roommate of mine, Herman Hover, who bought Ciro's after a career as a song-and-dance man and later stage manager of Earl Carroll's *Vanities*, smiled broadly when he talked about Miss Turner. This was the evening before my date with Miss Turner and we were in Hover's Beverly Hills apartment.

"Jesus! What a swinger *that* kid was. A real sexpot, beautiful face and body, and a flounce that used to drive the boys crazy. She'd come into Ciro's pretty often like they all did then. She might be alone or with a date, but if she saw a guy whose looks she liked better than her escort's at another table, she was perfectly capable of ditching her guy for the new one.

"In her day I guess she was about the most popular kid in Hollywood. Didn't seem to give a damn about anything, and an enormous box-office success. Except for a couple of early bombs, and unfortunately some more recent ones, her pictures made money and so did she. She was a true Hollywood queen; whenever she went anywhere in the world, her fans stopped to gape and scream for autographs. In her day she was just as regal as Crawford, Stanwyck, and Bette Davis, although God knows none of that trio was wild—and Lana sure was. Here, let me show you a picture I have of her taken about twenty-five or thirty years ago."

He reached into a desk drawer and pulled out a glossy print showing Miss Turner dressed in an evening gown which exposed a considerable portion of her anatomy. It's obvious the photograph was taken in the front seat of a car; beside the star is a handsome, tuxedoed young gentleman. Both are being served platters of food.

"A drive-in, Herman?" I asked.

He gasped.

"A drive-in? Man, you *are* crazy. That's the parking lot in back of Ciro's, and don't forget Ciro's was the most elegant restaurant and nightclub in the world. I mean it."

I was properly repentant.

Herman continued. "At any rate, the picture you see was cooked up by my press agent. The idea was that Ciro's was supposed to be filled to capacity that evening; Lana and her date refused to eat anybody else's food, so they're being served outside in Lana's car.

"The guy is Bob Eaton, an actor. I think he married Lana, but I'm not sure. It's hard to keep up with her various grooms. I don't know what happened to Eaton, he hasn't been around for a long time."

He carefully examined the photograph, at the bottom of which was a date so faded it was hard to decipher.

"This was taken not long after Lana divorced Artie Shaw, the old-time band leader. The date, as close as I can tell, is December 26, 1945. What a hell of a lot of action Lana's had since then and she's still beautiful."

Now, as I looked at Miss Turner across the table, I had to agree. I asked my hostess if she thought Hollywood ever would stage a comeback. She shook her head.

"Never! Hollywood's dead. They don't know how to make pictures out here anymore and costs have gone so sky high they couldn't afford it even if they *had* the know-how. We used to make some damned good pictures for five or six hundred thousand dollars and now look what it costs to do one in Hollywood. Ten million? Fifteen million? Twenty million? No wonder the majors went broke.

"As for the actors, there's a new crop coming along from TV and elsewhere. These kids, and some of them are good, make one picture that pays off. But nobody knows if they're going to be able to do another; it's too soon to tell after one or even a couple of box-office successes. In the end, what counts is staying power; that's what the majors knew they had to have. These kids have no real training and nobody knows much about even the best of them. Today the story, not the star, is important; it was the public, not the studios, who made the stars.

"But you had to be brought along. If you were a true star they started you out into a 'low A,' then graduated up to 'A,' and finally when you got to work with Gable, you were in a really 'Big A.' If you proved your staying power, nothing was too good for you. It was the kind of life few people in the world ever get to live and none of us who was part of this is likely to forget. Now, with all the stinking, dirty films being made out here and elsewhere, there's no glamor left."

I asked my hostess if she'd accept a role in an X-rated picture.

"Absolutely not! I was offered the lead in *Angel, Angel, Down We Go*, a really filthy film. I read the script and turned it down fast. Poor little Jennifer Jones, who should have known better, accepted. The critics panned the hell out of it and naturally it bombed."

She sighed again.

"The saddest thing you can say about Hollywood today is that they've taken the romance out of sex."

Now I must tell you why I love Lana Turner. All during our interview we were quite formal; it was "Miss Turner" and

"Mr. Lewis." But as the pleasant afternoon drew to a close and I was about to take off (Frank was on his way to pick me up), my hostess quite unexpectedly kissed me good-bye.

"You may call me 'Lana,' " she said. "And may I call you Albert?"

Chapter Fifteen

ALTHOUGH ETHNIC origins, physical characteristics, cultural backgrounds, and an age gap of almost a full generation separate them, Lewis Milestone and Lew Ayres will be remembered as a team because of a single film they made together more than forty years ago. The picture, of course, was *All Quiet on the Western Front*, the first and, for nearly three decades more, the last Hollywood production with the courage to show that the face of the enemy was not unlike our own, and that the German possesses the same emotions which sustain the rest of mankind—love, pity, and, to use their own word, *Weltschmerz*. Unfortunately for mankind, as the Nazis were hell-bent on proving even while the picture was playing to sympathetic audiences all over the United States, the film's altruistic hypothesis was false. But at least for a short time *All Quiet on the Western Front* created an illusion that Germans are acceptable members of the human race.

To a World War I generation of Americans whose opinion of Germany was shaped by such films as *The Kaiser* and *The Beast of Berlin*, *All Quiet* was an unbelievable experience which I, for one, am never likely to forget. I saw the picture for the first time at Philadelphia's Chestnut Street Opera House where it was playing two performances daily. I can't recall the exact day, but I'm sure the month was June; I know the year was 1930, and it had to be a matinee because I was a police reporter on the Philadelphia *Inquirer*, working from five-thirty P.M. until three-thirty A.M., Monday through Saturday. The city's strictly enforced Blue Laws kept all places of amusement closed on Sunday, so it must have been during the week.

That afternoon, when my bride-to-be in a couple of months and I walked out of the Opera House onto Chestnut Street, we felt a great dimension had been added to Erich Maria Remarque's powerful best seller from which the film was adapted. The tortures and despairs of battle, the trench-born friendship, even love, developed among seven German school-boy soldiers, and their subsequent deaths, one by one, were agonizing, if only briefly heard, cries against war. It was Paul, played by Lew Ayres, who became the last one to die, and on a day when indeed it was quiet on the Western front except for an alert Yankee sniper.

The New York *Times* said:

All Quiet on the Western Front, released by Carl Laemmle's Universal Pictures Corporation, has produced a trenchant and imaginative, audible picture in which the producers adhere with remarkable facility to the spirit and events of the original stirring novel. It is a notable achievement, sincere and earnest, with glimpses that are vivid and graphic. Like the original, it does not mince matters concerning the horrors of battle. It is a vocalized screen offering that is pulsating and harrow-ing. . . .

Lewis Milestone . . . was entrusted with the direction. He has used his fecund imagination, still clinging loyally to the book. . . . One is as gripped by witnessing the picture as one was by reading the printed page, and in most instances it seems as though the very impressions written in ink by Herr Remarque had become animated on the screen. . . . Truth comes to the fore when the young soldiers are elated at the idea of joining up, when they are disillusioned, when they are hungry, when they are killing rats in a dugout, when they are shaken with fear, and when they, or one of them, become fed up with the conception of war held by the elderly men back home.

George Abbott and Maxwell Anderson . . . wrote the dialogue. Messrs. Milestone, Abbott and Anderson have contributed a memorable piece of work to the screen.

For his direction of *All Quiet*, Milestone won almost every possible motion picture award. Of the three hundred critics polled nationally by the magazine *Film Daily*, two hundred fifty-two put him in first place. Wesley Ruggles, the director of another prize-winner, *Cimarron*, for the 1930–31 season, wasn't even a close second.

Milestone is now in his seventies. He's a big, black-haired, handsome man who radiates that quality of masculinity the Mexicans admire and call *macho*. When I saw him for the first time—we met many times subsequently—he had only recently undergone major brain surgery for removal of a tumor, fortunately benign, and the following week was returning to the hospital for another operation. "Only a hernia," he said, "and I ought to be back in circulation within two weeks." He was.

Milestone, "Millie" as he insists on being called, lives at the Beverly Hills edge of Hollywood, within earshot and sight of Sunset Boulevard. Compared to Lana Turner's or Zsa Zsa Gabor's magnificent estates, his six- or seven-room cottage, with its small side and tiny front gardens, and single car garage, is modest, and the furnishings in excellent but simple taste. As far as I could tell he has only one servant, a polite little Puerto Rican maid. For one of the most financially successful moving picture directors, and one who, incidentally, is reputed to have saved his money, this unpretentious way of life is a rarity in Hollywood and its environs.

But then Lewis Milestone is a modest man, although his opinions are quite as strong and forthright as those expressed by his colleague and contemporary, George Cukor, who may be just as likable but who can hardly be termed self-effacing.

"I know you want to talk about Hollywood's past, present, and future," he said, "so let's begin with the future."

"O.K., Millie. What's Hollywood's future?" I asked.

He shook his head.

"It has none; all we have out here is a past; the town's got no future. And God knows it hasn't much present."

We were sitting, he and I, with our feet stretched up on either side of the director's desk in an alcove off the living room. On my right was a huge, old palm tree set in the center of the side garden. Although the house is on the corner of a comparatively quiet street, we could hear the dull, never-ending roar of traffic speeding along Sunset Boulevard, three and four blocks to the north. Millie noticed my annoyance when the rumbling sound of some truck momentarily blotted out some of his words. He stood up and shut the only open window.

He raised his hands, palms upward in a gesture of despair.

"Sorry that damned noise bothers you, nothing I can do about it. I'm used to it but I remember when Hollywood, well, this part of it anyway, was a hell of a lot quieter. That was in the old days.

"Let me tell you why I think Hollywood is finished as a center for the production of movies. If you've talked to others I suppose you've heard the story before. I've seen the whole picture change. I've worked around here for a long, long while."

Lewis Milestone has been a part of the Hollywood scene for more than half a century. He was born in Russia and received a degree in mechanical engineering there, but his first, last, and only professional love has been motion pictures. In 1918 he was a cutter, but by 1920, at the age of twenty-six, he became Universal's film editor and from there went on to direct the Industry's biggest box-office names, making the transition from "silents" to "talkies" with ease.

The first film to win acclaim for Millie was *Garden of Eden*, starring Corinne Griffith. He did this one on loan to

United Artists. On the list of his other credits are some of Hollywood's most successful and best remembered films as well as with the most durable and important stars. They include: *The Front Page* with Adolphe Menjou, Slim Summerville, and Pat O'Brien; *A Walk in the Sun* with Dana Andrews; *Arch of Triumph* (another adaptation from a Remarque novel) with Ingrid Bergman, Charles Boyer, and Charles Laughton; *The General Dies at Dawn* with Gary Cooper and Madeleine Carroll; and *Of Mice and Men* with Burgess Meredith, Betty Field, Charles Bickford, and Noah Beery, Jr.

I remembered some of these and rattled off the names of those I did. My host looked pleased.

"After a bit I'll tell you a story about *Of Mice and Men*," he promised. "It's typical of the honor and the faith you used to find here. For the moment let's concentrate on Hollywood's current plight and what I think are the causes of it.

"Basically, it's bad management. There's no reason why an area which still has the greatest concentration of experts, from electricians and cameramen to directors, couldn't still be the movie capital of the world despite those excuses I keep hearing. The point I want to make is that out here in a business as complex as this, there's no room for amateurs at the top. That's where Hollywood has put them.

"As an example, they pick a totally inexperienced man to head Warner Brothers. They brought this guy here from MCA, which is only a talent agency. As far as I know he did a satisfactory, or maybe even a phenomenal, job in *that* field. But what did he know about making movies? They imported Bob Evans to run Paramount and he knew little or nothing about making pictures. Can you imagine General Motors asking him to run *its* business?"

Millie's bright blue eyes sparkled as he warmed up to the subject. He leaned forward.

"The same thing's true at Fox and at M-G-M, all these majors bringing in people who don't know their ass from first base as far as the Industry is concerned. That's the tragedy.

Their theory is that if you're under thirty you're a genius if only because you've never done anything to disprove it. Ignorance is no longer considered a liability.

"I'm not claiming the old-time Hollywood tycoons didn't make mistakes. Of course they did and on a grand scale, too. One of their big faults was imitation and, if one studio produced a picture which made a lot of money, the rest followed suit."

He laughed.

"One I remember, and this goes back quite a while, was *The Miracle Man* in 1919. Frank L. Packard wrote the original story about a cripple who is temporarily 'cured' by a faith healer. George M. Cohan adapted it for the movies from his play. It opened up at his theater in New York and made a fistful of dough. And it made a couple of stars, too, like Thomas Meighan, Lon Chaney, and Betty Compson.

"Well, the point I want to bring out is that for the next year or two, everybody in Hollywood was pushing miracles. But the studios in those days knew something besides imitation. They knew *how* to make salable films and when they had a director they didn't cramp his style. Take Hal Wallis as an example. Hal's been here since the early twenties; he knows the business from every possible angle and he's produced so many great ones you stagger when you see his credits: *Anthony Adverse, Desperate Journey, My Friend Irma, The Rainmaker, Gunfight at O.K. Corral.* I could go on and on."

I was impressed.

"And if you think Hal Wallis is finished and can't compete with today's youthful 'geniuses,' think about his last one. That was *True Grit*—it made a fortune and won some Academy Awards besides. This is the kind of man who should be heading Warners or one of the other dying majors, not some inept young squirt. All I need to see is a single frame of his pictures and I recognize the Hal Wallis signature."

He nodded his head with satisfaction.

"Tell you something else about Hollywood's present plight.

They're ruining the Industry by continuing to turn out those X-rated pictures, each one vying with its predecessor to add more and more filth. Damned few of them are making money —there are exceptions like *Midnight Cowboy*—and audiences are getting bored.

"Hollywood today is a victim of myopia. There's only one company out here making money and the majors look the other way and ignore it whenever it's mentioned. Do you know who I'm referring to?"

For a brief moment I thought my host meant Dave Friedman's EVI but he didn't.

"I mean Disney. He keeps turning out those corned-beef-and-cabbage pictures and they all make money. They've become almost the only pictures you can take your grandchildren to see without embarrassment.

"The stupidity of the current crop of movie 'moguls' and their immediate predecessors is fantastic. Not only did they waste vast sums of money on such dull films as *Zabriski Point* and *Paint Your Wagon*, terribly expensive features that nobody paid to see, but they looked the other way when TV gave them a chance to recoup.

"Don't misunderstand me; I don't like TV or at least not very much. I tried it, directed six shows and got out. For me it's no good, which certainly doesn't mean it won't be substantially appealing to other directors and producers."

He paused in reflection.

"There've been some fine full-length TV features. For example, there was *Requiem for a Heavyweight*, which was highly entertaining, that is, if you can bear the proliferation of ads.

"Not that the major studios haven't tried to make TV but they've gone about it ass backward. Instead of calling upon the talents of first-class directors and producers, those who did successful early TV features, they used second-rate talents. You don't have to have sharp vision to see what's happened to television. It's mostly dreadful rot.

"When you consider the huge sums of money being lost

here as Hollywood dries up, you'd think the studio heads would change tactics. But they're so damned stubborn they refuse to alter the ruinous course they've set for themselves and their stockholders."

He shook his head, then chuckled.

"It reminds me of a poker game I once played in a long time ago. It was table stakes but the five or six of us who played were regulars, we knew the game or thought we did at any rate, so on a year-round basis none of us lost more than he could afford. Besides which, we played together so often we got to know each other's style and idiosyncrasies so we weren't likely to be outsmarted. Jock Whitney was a member of the group and on one occasion he asked if he could bring his sister along. She'd heard of our little game and was sure she could compete with the best of us. So we said, 'O.K., bring her.'

"Well, the first thing our guest did when she sat down was ask us to change the rules. She didn't like table stakes and wanted to set a hundred-dollar limit; in fact, she insisted on it. So we agreed, albeit reluctantly. The truth of the matter is she wasn't a very good poker player and she kept losing hand after hand. Suddenly she drew a good one and opened with a five-hundred-dollar bet.

"Jock protested. 'The limit's a hundred bucks.' His sister flared up. 'Who set that goddamned stupid rule?' she asked. So we went back to table stakes and she lost her shirt."

My host looked at me; I wasn't sure I got the point.

"What I'm getting at is that when you don't know the game, don't try to recoup your losses by tossing more cash in the pot. That's exactly what they're doing out here, throwing away money in an effort to get back their original dollars. It won't work.

"I'm not saying you don't have to spend a buck to make a buck, but you've got to know what you're doing. Let me give you an example. Not too long ago Billy Wilder decided there was money, lots of it, in a remake of *Ben-Hur*. The studio heads were dead set against it but Billy insisted and his track record is so great they couldn't say no. I won't go into his credits and Academy Awards, it would take too long. I'll just mention two: *Sunset Boulevard* and *The Apartment*. Well, I'll mention one more, *Some Like It Hot*.

"In *Ben-Hur* he starred Charlton Heston, who is one of the dullest fellows you're ever likely to meet. But Heston was just right for the role. To make a long story short, it cost the studio fifteen million dollars to make that picture. However, it was such a big box-office success, Billy's share of the producer's cut ran to more than a million dollars.

"Certainly Billy gambled with his reputation and the stockholders' money. Nobody knows for *sure* whether a picture will make it or bomb. But Billy Wilder's been around here for almost forty years and a success most of that time. Consequently, the risks were far less than they are for a studio which turns out such monumentally expensive failures as, for example, if you'll excuse me, your *Molly Maguires*. Part of the blame falls on my friend, Walter Bernstein, for a bad script. But the one really responsible is Marty Ritt, the producer-director. He's not a bad director but he had little or no previous experience as a producer, so costs and story ran away from him."

My host was beginning to look tired so I said it was time for me to leave. He insisted that I return the next day for another session and I did.

Chapter Sixteen

MRS. MILESTONE, a tall, handsome, white-haired lady, served us coffee in the same alcove and Millie and I resumed our conversation. The subject still was production costs.

"I must tell you one about Jack Warner," my host said and chuckled. "He *really* knew how to run a studio and when *he* was in charge of the show it was run right. Jack didn't mind spending millions on his pictures—*My Fair Lady* is a good example—but he used to practice small economies. I don't know if he did this to prove to everyone he was alert to waste wherever he saw it or because he was an eccentric. After all, I suppose most of us who've been out here for a while are a bit eccentric to say the least.

"I may have been working on the Warners lot at the time, I'm not sure anymore. But in any event Jack used to go crazy every time he'd see lumber or paint wasted. He was particularly upset when he spotted nails that prop men and carpenters left lying around.

"So he went out and had somebody design a nail-picking-up machine—I'm not kidding. I don't know how much it cost, but I'm sure it wasn't cheap. The trouble is it didn't work. One day Jack was walking over the lot as he often did, holding a sort of 'moving' conference with whoever was making one of his pictures.

"This was 1942, Warners was doing *Casablanca*, and the actors with Jack were Bogart and Sidney Greenstreet. But Jack wasn't able to concentrate; every time they'd get to some point in the production, Jack would frown, bend down, pick up a nail, and stuff it into his pocket."

Millie smiled at the recollection.

"Now these were expensive stars and every minute of their time cost a considerable amount of money. Finally Bogey got annoyed at the constant interruptions to their train of thought and asked Jack what the hell he was doing. The chairman of the board was then forced to explain that he was picking up nails and besides which he was counting them.

"When he got to fifty he couldn't stand it anymore, he was so upset. So he excused himself, left Bogey and Sidney standing, and dashed over to the head prop man and asked what had happened to his expensive nail-picking-up machine. Jack came back a half-hour later quite chagrined, the machine was a bust, he explained, and after a day's effort probably left three or four dollars' worth of nails on the ground.

"Bogey didn't let it drop. For the next half-hour, every time he or Sidney'd see a nail on the ground either of them would interrupt the conference, reach down to pick it up, dust it off carefully, and hand it to Jack."

I laughed politely but somewhere along the line I must have missed the point again. My host continued.

"I guess what I've been trying to say is that while Jack may have had his peculiarities he was entitled to them even though they cost Warners' stockholders a bit of cash. But because he knew how to produce pictures, he made money. *Casablanca* is a good example of his astuteness.

"Now all we have out here in Hollywood are poseurs who've nothing to justify their eccentricities. And they're pretty much without honor, too. Say what you like about the old-time moguls here or on Broadway but, generally speaking—there were exceptions naturally—they were men who kept their word. Let me tell you a story about one of them, Sam Harris, the famous producer."

I settled back to listen.

"I'd read Steinbeck's *Of Mice and Men* and I was absolutely mad about its picture potentials. More than anything else I wanted to do that movie. I was then operating as an independent, releasing most of my pictures through United Artists. I knew that if I did *Mice* I'd have to make it for a price because I had no major studio backing.

"First off I had to get the rights for a script. Annie Laurie Williams was Steinbeck's agent. I called her from the Coast and we made a deal. She called Sam Harris, who produced *Mice* on Broadway. It had opened up at the Music Box Theater and after a long and highly successful run there went on the road. Annie made a date for me to see Sam in his New York office which was in the theater.

"So I came east, saw Sam, and told him what I wanted and how much I could afford to offer. We finally agreed on terms and sealed the deal with a handshake; a written contract would follow later. I stayed around Sam's office for ten minutes or so talking about mutual friends in the Industry. I was halfway out the door when the phone on Sam's desk rang. He picked it up and motioned for me to wait.

" 'It's L.A. calling,' he said, 'and it's probably for you.' But it wasn't for me. It was Julius Laemmle calling Sam with an offer to buy the screen rights of *Mice* and offering him, as I discovered later, twice as much as I'd agreed to pay. 'It's not for sale, Jules,' I heard Sam tell Laemmle. 'I've just closed a deal with Millie.' And this on a single handshake."

Millie then told me he and Eugene Solo, one of his writers, went to Philadelphia where *Mice* was playing. After seeing several performances the pair returned to Los Angeles by train instead of plane so they could work on the script.

"We needed about three more weeks to finish so I rented Anatole Litvak's house in Beverly Hills where I knew we wouldn't be interrupted. We knocked it off in eighteen days, then Gene and I went to Los Gatos where Steinbeck was living at that time. Even though he had no legal right to make changes, I wanted him to see what we'd done to his book. I'm a perfectionist, you know, and was prepared to seriously consider any changes he might have in mind.

"While Steinbeck stretched out on a couch, Gene and I read the script to him although I felt all along he wasn't paying the slightest bit of attention to us. When we finished he said, 'Great, fellows; I like it.'

"So I turned to him and said, 'Listen, John, this is *your* book. I always want the author to be aware of what's in the script. So *please* listen this time.' We read it again and this time he heard us and made a few minor changes. That was because we'd copied his style completely."

Milestone told me he wasn't able to sell *Mice* to any of the majors and didn't have enough cash on hand himself to begin production.

"What I needed was what we called 'getaway money,' and the only way I knew how to raise that was to make a picture fast and cheap. I was having dinner at the Lambs Club in New York with Roland Young and Reginald Gardiner. Both of them were waiting for their plays to open and meanwhile were more or less 'at liberty.'

"I saw Donald Ogden Stewart sitting at another table. I went over to him and asked if he had any ideas for a movie. 'Sure,' he answered. 'I've got a good one I've been carrying around for a while. It's about a garbage collector who becomes a successful movie producer.' I wasn't sure if Stewart was kidding or not but he wasn't."

Milestone said they discovered another Lambs Club actor, Pat O'Brien, was temporarily out of work and induced him to join the other two stars. The picture was made in twenty-three days and gave Milestone his "Getaway money." However, by the time their script reached the final draft, the story turned out to be something quite different from Stewart's original idea. The picture was titled *The Night of Nights* and opened at Loew's Criterion Theater in New York, December 28, 1939.

Frank S. Nugent of the New York *Times* wrote:

> Almost anything goes at the end of a year, including the Criterion's trespassing in the field of drama. *The Night of Nights* is not the usual Criterion show; in fact, it is not a usual show at all, being a somewhat melancholy gambol at and around the Lambs.
>
> Pat O'Brien fits into it snugly as one of the fleeciest Lambs in Hollywood duress; so does Roland Young, who comes to haunt the place on Saturday nights. Somehow, although it is only a picture, we sense the nostalgia of its principal players. Theirs has been a labor of love and the film has profited accordingly.
>
> For *The Night of Nights*, written by Donald Ogden Stewart and directed by Lewis Milestone, is a film of the theater and some of the curious folk who inhabit it. Naturally it is sentimental, for it is the story of a playright-producer-actor whose life stopped when his wife left him; whose life began haltingly and fearfully eighteen years later when his daughter appeared and urged him to take up the theater once more.
>
> *The Night of Nights* is an uncommonly interesting study of a man's mind, subtly written and directed . . . and presented with honesty and commendable sincerity. . . .

A bit less than three months later Milestone began *Of Mice and Men*. It was completed, he said, in thirty-six days of shooting for a total cost of three hundred twenty-five thousand dollars.

"And this included Aaron Copland's fee of forty thousand dollars for doing the musical score," my host said. "A real steal; the man deserved ten times as much."

The film was released through United Artists and was an artistic and box-office success.

One of the last pictures Milestone directed was *Oceans Eleven*, starring Frank Sinatra.

"We shot this at Vegas in thirty-nine days," my host said. "I like working with Sinatra, he's a hell of a good actor, and despite his reputedly bad traits I find him an extremely interesting fellow."

Millie shook his head sadly.

"Not like some of the others, Gregory Peck to cite one. Mr. Peck is a gentleman of sterling character but a very dull fellow indeed."

I'm sorry to report that *Oceans Eleven* was a dismal failure both artistically and otherwise. Reviews of the film were generally bad.

Millie's hernia operation was scheduled for the following morning and since his doctor said he'd likely remain institutionalized for a minimum of three weeks I didn't think I'd be seeing him again, at least on this trip. But a few days later Mrs. Milestone telephoned to say her husband's operation was a success and, that while he was still recuperating, he was home and anxious for visitors. He told her he'd like to see me.

"Lewis instructed me to inform you he had a few more things he hadn't told you about *All Quiet*," Mrs. Milestone said. So the following evening I returned to the Milestones' for dinner. Millie looked a bit pale and had to support himself on a cane when we walked over to the alcove afterward, but he was in the best of spirits.

"I've been reading the manuscript of one of our mutual friends, Harry Kleiner. I'd consider doing it if such a big budget weren't required. Harry's got a great idea about a jewel thief who's so young he fails to make his getaway simply because he doesn't know how to operate a car which doesn't have automatic transmission. The one he's stuck with has a gear shift.

"The idea comes from an original story in *The New Yorker*. I gave it to Harry to read and see if he could come up with a story line. He did, all right, but what he has in mind would cost around fifteen million dollars and that's out. One of the reasons I've been considering it is that I think the time may be ripe for a return of films with a story, not just nudity and sex. And I'd like to aim for a larger audience than those god-damned eighteens to twenty-eights. I still think we could draw adults if we gave them something for their money."

Millie shrugged his shoulders.

"We'll see, we'll see. But meantime let's go back to *All Quiet*. I heard you've a date with Lew Ayres and maybe you'd like to know more background, not about Lew but about the picture. You may laugh when I say that, considering what goes on today in the theater, one of our major problems was censorship and I'll tell you the kind I mean. We were afraid, since so many nations were involved; none of them, even former Allies, were particularly friendly to the others. And that this would put a lot of pressure on me to make the picture so non-controversial that it would have lost all its meaning.

"A few years later with Hitler in power, there would have been no question at all; we'd never have made the film."

Millie said that a more serious problem was his intention to use inexperienced actors including Ayres because he wanted to give the film a freshness and spontaneity he believed he could not achieve otherwise.

"Even Ayres hadn't done a lot before I cast him, but at least he knew what it was all about. The others, with the exception of Louis Wolheim who played the part of Kat, and Slim Summerville who was Tjaden, weren't much more than amateurs. Slim was the only character I'd actually visualized for the role. I could see him as that skinny ex-blacksmith with the voracious appetite. He was the first one I hired.

"In making a movie, you know, unlike a stage presentation, we play scenes without regard to the continuity of the plot. In other words, if it's more expedient for us to shoot a scene which belongs at the end of the story instead of waiting for it to come along naturally, we shoot it. To an experienced actor this makes no difference, but to an amateur it does and we had a great many amateurs in *All Quiet*. I have in mind particularly six of the seven German civilian-soldiers.

"A good many years ago, forty-one of them to be exact, I was interviewed just after the picture was shown and asked how and why I developed this technique which gave *All Quiet* its strong sense of reality. I can't tell you anymore who wrote down what I said, but here it is. I think, but I'm not sure, it was syndicated by Hearst International."

My host produced an undated clipping from an unnamed newspaper. He had marked certain passages which I now read.

We could not expect . . . inexperienced youths to follow the conventional course of jumping from scene to scene without regard to sequence, governed only by physical surroundings as is usually done. Instead we started at the very beginning of the story and traced it with the same continuity as brought to the screen in the finished picture.

Consequently, three young boys grew into the story and became a part of it. They practically lived the lives of their German counterparts through a period of six months, and it was remarkable to note the changes they underwent in the process. They absorbed so much until they were equipped to reflect the thoughts and purpose of the author without the necessity of "acting." They had *become* those characters.

Thinking of Lew Ayres whom I was to see the next morning, I asked Millie if he had in mind any special questions he thought I should ask the star of *All Quiet*. Millie shook his head.

"Haven't seen him for years and years. He keeps to himself pretty much and unless you include some religious film I understand he's been making, I believe he's through with the Industry. They made it awfully rough for him out here in Hollywood for a time because of his antiwar scruples, you know. But I'm sure you'll find him a man of great moral courage and inner strength."

Chapter Seventeen

IF YOU'RE old enough to have been a 1942 World War II patriot, no doubt you shared the disgust of a hundred million or more Americans when word came out of Hollywood and Washington, D.C., that Lew Ayres was a slacker. Within hours of his refusal to bear arms, Ayres, for nearly a decade the handsome, enormously popular Dr. Kildare, was vilified and hung in effigy. Most theaters banned his films; the American Legion picketed those which did not, and a feature he'd just completed for Paramount was hastily called back from distributors and ordered remade with a new star to replace the fallen idol. Such a superpatriot as Frank ("I am the Law") Hague, mayor of Jersey City, New Jersey, took time out from municipal duties to lead an angry group of citizens through the streets of his bailiwick to a movie theater where someone claimed the owner defied decency and was showing *Dr. Kildare's Victory.*

As one contemporary columnist phrased it, "Lew Ayres blew a fifty-million-dollar career in one hour."

For Lew Ayres, now a handsome, gray-haired man in his early sixties, these are only unpleasant memories which he shrugs off lightly. The fact that soon after he was vindicated in the public's eyes by winning three Silver Stars for bravery under fire as a noncombatant did little to change this actor's philosophy—that war is evil, that all which counts is the brotherhood of man and, that, in the unlikely event he was called upon to bear arms again, he would refuse.

After only a few minutes with this shy, dignified gentleman, it's easy to believe he still possesses the same amount of moral courage which once enabled him to face down a hostile public. There is no physical resemblance between the two, but I felt a strong kinship between Ayres and the late Father John LaFarge, the Jesuit priest who, without fanfare or claims of intimate relationship with God, followed the dictates of his conscience regardless of the bitter antipathy he created within his own establishment in order to foster unpopular causes.

Despite marriages to a pair of glamorous women stars, Lola Lane and Ginger Rogers, both of which ended in divorce, Ayres is not now nor ever was a part of the Hollywood scene. I saw him at his very modest hilltop home in the Brentwood section of the city. I gave him Millie's regards, and the conversation began with a discussion of *All Quiet*.

"Everybody, I suppose, has at least one high point in his career," my host said, "and I had mine at the age of twenty-one in *All Quiet*. Everything else in my public life, at least from that point on, was anti-climactic. I'm speaking of my public career. My private one has had many, many peaks, one being the publication date of a book I wrote on world brotherhood and another the screening of a series of films I did on the world's great religions. One of these was called *Altars of the East*."

We were sitting in Ayres' book-filled living room which, in contrast to most of the Hollywood homes I visited, doesn't seem to overlook anything spectacular. There wasn't even a wading pool visible, although there could have been one for Ayres' son who was taking his mid-morning nap, according to his father.

"I don't know if you ever were told this," my host said,

"but the role of Paul in *All Quiet* was originally to be played by Douglas Fairbanks, Jr. I'm not sure what happened, whether he turned it down or wasn't chosen, but I'm lucky, the part landed in my lap.

"I'd just done a picture with Garbo, the last of her silents; Pathé dropped my option, and there was nothing ahead for me. Actually, it was a critical period for the Industry as well. It took a lot of courage for Hollywood to make a film where, in the end, the boy and girl don't walk out into the sunset hand in hand. This was unique in motion picture history.

"What a thing to do in those days, to show Americans that there was another world outside not realized here in this country. Carl Laemmle was the producer but the credit belongs to Millie, who's really one of the greats. Even though Carl had the final say, in any dispute he generally yielded to Millie, who had far more experience than either of us. Actually, Laemmle and I were nearly the same age, pretty young, wouldn't you say?"

I agreed.

"I'd read the book, of course, and when I heard they were going to do a movie about it I took a screen test hoping I'd get a bit part. I never dreamed I'd be chosen for the starring role which I got not because of my acting experience, which was limited, nor for my ability, which certainly wasn't terribly good, but because the casting director thought I looked like Paul. That was it and from then on I had no trouble getting work."

Ayres, who was born in Minneapolis, Minnesota, in 1908, made his initial appearance in Hollywood as a banjoist in Henry Halstead's then famous orchestra which played the Ambassador and other West Coast hotels. He wanted to get into the movies and after a screen test Pathé hired him, gave him a six-month contract, and used him for minor roles. Then came *The Kiss* with Garbo, followed by, as Ayres said, "near oblivion." But then came *All Quiet*.

His rise in *All Quiet* to national stardom and fame in the subsequent *Dr. Kildare* movie soap operas was phenomenal and his descent, after March of 1942, was precipitous. The contrast between Jimmy Stewart, the heroic fighter-pilot, and Ayres, the "conchie," was endlessly pointed out in thousands of editorials, newspaper stories, and by radio commentators all over the United States and Europe. For his actions Ayres had few defenders; the redoubtable Hedda Hopper was one and another was *The New Republic,* although that normally liberal magazine tempered its praise of Ayres with more than a hint of bitterness. One of the magazine's articles said:

> We are sorry to see the storm of denunciation that has descended on the unhappy head of Lew Ayres, the movie star who has been sent to a camp for conscientious objectors. This is the kind of thing we did in the last war; everyone with any sense was ashamed when it was over, and we should have learned our lesson well enough not to repeat it.
>
> We do not agree with Mr. Ayres' position; we cannot help remembering that, unconsciously, every non-resistant pacifist knows he is but one in ten thousand and also that his fellow countrymen will have to fight and die to protect him, no matter what he does.
>
> Nevertheless, it is clear that Mr. Ayres sincerely believes in his principles. It probably takes more moral courage to act as he has done than to obey the orders of the government and fight. . . . Democracy cannot be preserved if it is unable to tolerate the occasional sincere minority opinion, even on the subject of using force against the foreign enemy of democracy.

A more popular, if less erudite, publication vindicated Ayres some sixteen years later. *Look* Magazine said in its May 15, 1956, issue:

> *Look* applauds Lew Ayres. Many people talk about the brotherhood of man, but few do something about it. Lew Ayres is one of the few. During twenty-five years as a film star, he has quietly been a student of philosophy and comparative religion. Believing that spiritual understanding is one way to

promote peace among peoples of the world, he turned his back on an annual income of $250,000 from acting, and . . . has undertaken an ambitious program of making films about the world's great religions. . . . The films cover Hinduism, Sikhism, Parsism, Jainism, Buddhism, Confucianism, Taoism, Shinto, Judaism, and Islam.

To make the films, Ayres traveled 40,000 miles. . . . He spent eight months photographing shrines, ceremonies, and holy men, interviewing leaders on their ethical ideas and narrating the films—at a cost of $85,000 to himself.

There is little doubt that the role he played in *All Quiet* greatly influenced his later refusal to bear arms for his country.

"If you'll forgive a bad pun," he said, "it was a two-way 'Milestone' for me. First, it gave me the opportunity to work with a truly great director and, secondly, it enabled me to act out the philosophy of my grandmother, a liberal who was far ahead of her time."

Like his contemporary, Jimmy Stewart, Ayres had an early draft number. When his board called him he refused to go, claiming that to kill or wound a fellowman, regardless of cause, was in direct contradiction to his religious training. He was classified "1-A." He appealed and said he would be happy to serve his country as a member of the Red Cross or as a medic. While awaiting a decision, the actor enrolled in a Red Cross training program hoping he would be permitted to serve in a non-combatant capacity. But the board finally rejected his petition.

Ayres appealed to Washington which ruled in his favor and changed the actor's classification from "1-A" to "1-AO." Then, when word of the decision reached the press, all hell broke loose. From the matinee idol of millions, Ayres overnight became a detested figure. He was compared to Benedict ·Arnold and contrasted with Jimmy Stewart. Columnists who had heaped adulation upon him now competed with each other to find stronger terms of vilification. *Variety*, bugle of the entertainment world, editorialized on page one that Ayres was a disgrace to the Industry.

Ayres was removed to a "conchie" camp in Oregon to share a life of hard labor with two thousand other men having similar scruples about war. Friends, including Milestone, however, appealed to General Lewis B. Hershey, director of Selective Service, and asked that the actor be permitted to serve in the armed forces as a non-combatant. The general yielded and two months later Ayres was inducted at Fort Lewis, Washington, as a non-combatant.

Within two years a number of brave actions under fire reversed the anti-Ayres trend. Ayres himself will not discuss these, but Irving Wallace, best-selling author who knew Ayres well, told me that one of the actor's battlefield heroics occurred on the island of New Guinea.

"A Japanese bomb hit an ammunition dump at Pie Beach. Most of the GIs on Pancake Hill dove for slit trenches, but the wounded in a field hospital were unable to move. While the munitions were exploding around him, Ayres calmly strolled from tent to tent, kidding the men, soothing them, his own life endangered every moment.

"Another time, as the first wave of infantry was preparing to hit Leyte Beach, a call was issued for volunteers to set up an emergency clinic on the beach for wounded Filipino civilians. Ayres and thirteen others stepped forward and, unarmed, went in under fire."

Wallace asked me if I knew that General Carlos P. Romulo, then aide to General Douglas MacArthur and later President of the United Nations General Assembly, cited Ayres in his book *I See the Philippines Rise*. He pulled the book from his shelf and read this passage:

His own story was even more dramatic than any he had portrayed on the screen, for he was the thoroughly conscientious objector who would not kill. There was a spiritually remote look in the eyes of this handsome young actor who had known so much of worldly success and who had risked every-

157

thing rather than violate his faith in the divinity of man. He had made that protest bravely, and it won the respect of all. . . .

Immediately upon his return from the war in 1945, Ayres found himself a film idol once more and was besieged with offers from all the major studios. Subsequently, he made several dozen feature films playing opposite a variety of female stars including Jane Wyman, with whom he made *Johnny Belinda*, the tear-jerking albeit enormously popular story of a deaf mute. But never again was he to achieve the dramatic success he earned in *All Quiet*, or the financial success he won in the pot-boiling "family type" Dr. Kildare series. As a matter of fact, the first picture Ayres made after *All Quiet* was *Iron Man*, with Jean Harlow, Robert Armstrong, and John Miljan. Reviewers were harsh in their criticism not only of the picture itself but of Ayres' acting talent as well.

The last film of any importance in which Ayres had a part was *Advise and Consent*, a film based on the Allen Drury best seller. Ayres appears occasionally as a TV guest star where he is remembered only by an ever thinning line of oldsters not likely to forget his magnificent portrayal of Paul in the Remarque novel, plus a slightly younger generation which worshipped Dr. Kildare before he was ousted by Dr. Gillespie.

Yet, by some historic twist, this almost-forgotten star of Hollywood's glamorous past is in juxtaposition with a generation fed up with senseless war, and which never even heard of Lew Ayres.

"Paul," said Ayres more than four decades ago, "wasn't a soldier. He was simply a schoolboy who had started to write a play and who lived with his books when he was pressed into service. He never wished to be a soldier or to go to war.

"You will remember what thoughts Remarque attributed to Paul—'We were eighteen and had begun to love life and the world; and we had to shoot it to pieces. The first bomb, the first explosion, burst in our hearts.'"

The "exploitation" of films showing the universality of mankind and their production now occupies almost all of Ayres' working hours.

"I enjoy gardening, too, and I let off my excess steam that way."

Ayres walked me to my car.

"Give my best to Millie if you see him again, will you?"

I said I would. We shook hands and I was about to take off when Ayres raised his hand and smiled.

"We were talking before about high peaks in our lives, weren't we? Well, I think I should tell you there's a new one in mine, a son, just a little over a year old. Maybe it's wishing my life away, but I can't wait until he grows up so I can take him with me wherever I go."

Chapter Eighteen

SWATHED IN a tight-fitting hostess gown the color of which matched her blue eyes, her golden hair piled high, Zsa Zsa walked across the living room to greet me, looking better, if that's possible, than she had on New Year's Eve. But even at a distance of forty feet I could smell the perfume which swept along with her like an almost-visible sheath. I sniffed audibly.

"My own brand," she said, rather pleased. "Only thirty dollars an ounce. If you need any for your wife or some other woman, you can buy it at practically every good store in America."

There is one thing about an interview with Miss Gabor; you don't have to worry about starting the conversation.

"Every man in this world needs a Zsa Zsa," Zsa Zsa said for an opener. My heart beat considerably faster as she smiled and looked directly into my eyes. "Including you," she added, and I nodded my head in total agreement.

My hostess then glanced at me reflectively.

"You know," she said, "you remind me a little bit of Debbie Reynolds' husband, a fine gentleman, one of the men I'd like to make love with before it's too late."

I'm sure I blushed in appreciation. At least Marilyn Reiss, Zsa Zsa's beautiful press agent who came along with me and

A *tormented Lew Ayres in* All Quiet on the Western Front.—CULVER PICTURES, INC.

Joan Crawford dancing the Charleston in Our Dancing
Daughters (1928). *This scene was the highlight of the
picture.*—WIDE WORLD PHOTOS

Lewis Milestone directing All Quiet on the Western
Front.—CULVER PICTURES, INC.

With cameras grinding away, Joan Crawford and Zachary
Scott go into action for their love scene from Mildred
Pierce.—WIDE WORLD PHOTOS

Director George Cukor on the set of Undercurrent *with*
stars Robert Taylor and Katharine Hepburn.—CULVER
PICTURES, INC.

Joan Crawford poses for the M-G-M publicity department.—BROWN BROTHERS

In the Hollywood Victory Caravan, Cary Grant, Groucho Marx and Desi Arnaz rush on stage to retrieve the clothes Joan Blondell sheds in her striptease number.—CULVER PICTURES, INC.

Betty Blythe in the William Fox production of Queen of Sheba.—CULVER PICTURES, INC.

Chester Conklin surrounded by bathing beauties. (1925).
—CULVER PICTURES, INC.

Glenn Ford in a scene from The Blackboard Jungle.
—CULVER PICTURES, INC.

Zsa Zsa Gabor posing for a publicity photograph at M-G-M.—CULVER PICTURES, INC.

Zsa Zsa Gabor and Mario Lanza in For the First Time.
—CULVER PICTURES, INC.

Mrs. Mary Gish with her famous daughters Dorothy (at her right) and Lillian (at her left).—BROWN BROTHERS

Dorothy Gish appearing in The Beautiful City.—BROWN BROTHERS

*Lillian Gish as Anna Moore and Richard Barthelmess as
David Bartlett in D. W. Griffith's* Way Down East.
—BROWN BROTHERS

Mutiny on the Bounty *with Charles Laughton and
Clark Gable.*—BROWN BROTHERS

Without his moustache,
Clark Gable in Mutiny on
the Bounty.—BROWN
BROTHERS

Charles Laughton fighting
stormy seas in Mutiny on
the Bounty.—BROWN
BROTHERS .

Ramon Novarro and May
McAvoy in Ben Hur.
—CULVER PICTURES, INC.

The chariot race between Ramon Novarro and Francis X. Bushman in Ben Hur.—CULVER PICTURES, INC.

Edward G. Robinson in Little Caesar—CULVER PICTURES, INC.

Joan Blondell and Edward G. Robinson in a scene from Bullets or Ballots.—CULVER PICTURES, INC.

Movie tough guy Edward G. Robinson looks over paintings by Forain and Boudin. His collection is considered one of the world's finest.—UNITED PRESS INTERNATIONAL

Richard Widmark as Detective Madigan springs to apprehend a killer.—CULVER PICTURES, INC.

Location shot during filming of Bad Day at Black Rock. *Left to right: production assistant Herman Hoffman, Dore Schary, Spencer Tracy.*—COURTESY OF DORE SCHARY

Pete Smith after a hard day!—CULVER PICTURES, INC.

A glittering Barbara Stanwyck sings a saucy song in Lady of Burlesque.—WIDE WORLD PHOTOS

Humphrey Bogart and Barbara Stanwyck in The Two
Mrs. Carrolls.—BROWN BROTHERS

Lana Turner preserves her handprint for posterity at Grauman's Chinese Theater.—WIDE WORLD PHOTOS

Lana Turner in a scene from the 1953 movie Latin
Lovers.—BROWN BROTHERS

Jack Warner and friend Oscar.—CULVER
PICTURES, INC.

*Jack L. Warner, President of Warner Brothers Pictures,
visits director George Cukor and Audrey Hepburn on the
set of* My Fair Lady.—CULVER PICTURES, INC.

A *pensive John Wayne on location in
Mexico for* Rio Lobo.—UNITED PRESS
INTERNATIONAL

*The Duke scorns the use of a
double as he leaps into a haystack
for a scene in* McClintock.—WIDE
WORLD PHOTOS

*John Wayne in his
Academy Award perfor-
mance as Rooster Cogburn
in* True Grit.—WIDE
WORLD PHOTOS

Mae West and Cary Grant in I'm No Angel.—CULVER PICTURES, INC.

Aerial view of Warner Brothers Studio.—CULVER
PICTURES, INC.

*W. C. Fields delivers a fantastic excuse after having been
caught peeking into the keyhole of Mae West's room, in a
scene from* My Little Chickadee.—CULVER PICTURES, INC.

The main automobile gate to RKO Studios.—CULVER
PICTURES, INC.

*The huge entrance gates
at Paramount Pictures.*
—CULVER PICTURES, INC.

sat in shocked silence on a nearby sofa, claimed I did. Marilyn averred she was there for "protection" although she didn't elaborate.

"He's in shoes, you know," my hostess continued, referring to Miss Reynolds' spouse. So was I in shoes for that matter, but I realized almost at once that Miss Gabor was referring to a career.

Then she sighed.

"But unfortunately I know Debbie, so that's out."

I was deeply impressed by this display of character and asked whom else my hostess eliminated for similar reasons.

"Tony Quinn," she answered without hesitation. "A peasant, but every woman, including me, needs a Tony Quinn in her life. Some day, perhaps. . . . I never met him, but I know his wife. Clark Gable was another peasant, but a beautiful, beautiful man and terribly virile. Or so they say." At this point I was anxious to ask Zsa Zsa a couple of leading questions, but a warning glance from Miss Reiss deterred me.

Had Zsa Zsa ever had strong feelings about non-peasants?

"Oh my, yes! Spencer Tracy. He was the most elegant gentleman I knew and represented everything I wanted in a man. I think I'd better explain something so you don't get the impression I'm a snob."

I assured my hostess the thought had never entered my mind.

"What I mean is that there's nothing wrong for a *man* to be a peasant. He can't help it if he was born that way. But a woman *must* be a lady. Two actresses I can think of weren't ladies; the first was Marilyn Monroe. She had talent and lots of sex appeal but that was all. She was vulgar, well, at least half-vulgar.

"Then there was Jean Harlow; she was *all* vulgar. Do you see what I mean?"

I didn't want to admit I couldn't follow my hostess' reasoning so I kept silent. Zsa Zsa was reflective.

"Ask me, please, to tell you the name of a woman I *really* admire."

I obliged.

"It's Katharine Hepburn. She's a *genuine* lady, born and raised as a lady, and a typical one-hundred-percent American. Oh, how I admire that woman! So sure of herself; so sure of everything she does. You can tell just by watching her, the way she walks, the way she talks, the way she handles herself."

Our conversation was interrupted by the arrival of Zsa Zsa's uniformed chauffeur, hat in hand, as he approached Madame and gave her an envelope. I was afraid the message delivered to my hostess would end our interview and that Madame might take off. But fortunately for me such was not the case. My hostess excused herself politely, opened the envelope, scrutinized its contents with care, her lips moving silently as she did some mental arithmetic. Then she shook her head angrily.

"Outrageous! *Everybody* tries to take advantage of Zsa Zsa; it makes her blood boil."

She raised her hands, palms upward in a gesture of despair, borrowed a pen from Marilyn, initialed what obviously was a bill, and returned it to the chauffeur.

"Go tell Willy to pay it," she instructed, "but first make goddamned sure they did all the work they said they did and that it runs right."

The chauffeur thanked Madame politely and left. Zsa Zsa turned to me.

"Please forgive me, I do get upset once in a while. I should explain. My chauffeur brought in the bill they sent for fixing one of my Rolls'. If I don't check every penny spent around here I'll go broke. Everybody tries to rob Zsa Zsa. A woman must learn to fend for herself in this world. That's what I said to Conrad."

I knew enough about my hostess' affairs of the heart to assume she referred to an early husband, Conrad Hilton, the hotel magnate.

"I told Conrad I'd never take a cent of his money, no matter what. He begged me to come back but I refused."

She sighed once more.

"Too proud, I suppose. I was only seventeen years old then and it's hard to believe that was twenty years ago and I've had to make it on my own ever since."

I wondered why none of her four or five other husbands, including Burhan Belge, a Turkish gentleman, George Sanders, Herbert Hutner, and Joshua Gosden, didn't help their quondam wife in her struggles to succeed. But I felt this question might be interpreted as improper, if not by Miss Gabor at least by Miss Reiss, who was getting more and more nervous all the time.

"Now let's see, where were we?" Zsa Zsa asked, and I reminded her we'd been discussing the men and women she admired or scorned.

"I guess there's nothing else to talk about on that subject," she said, then, eyebrows raised, paused briefly before continuing.

"Oh, yes. I should include John Wayne. What a man! He's my hero; how *much* I'd like to make love to him. But I know *his* wife, too, so this will never happen. Now let me think, are there any others?"

Fearful, I'm sure, that her client would add potentials to the list, Marilyn, who hadn't uttered a word so far, suddenly burst out with a request for a glass of water or anything else Zsa Zsa might have on tap.

"Forgive me, dahlink, I'll have Francis bring us refreshments," she said, then pushed a button. I could hear a bell ring somewhere in the distance and a moment later Francis, attired in a morning coat and striped trousers entered, received instructions, and came back bearing a huge silver tray laden with all manner of tempting foods and beverages. It's not often I'm given an opportunity to munch genuine black Russian caviar, so that was *my* choice. Our hostess daintily spread some on a cracker and handed it to me. I was far more modest in my selection of a drink; fearful any alcoholic intake might dull my senses and make me miss or garble any of Zsa Zsa's words, I asked for plain ginger ale. Apparently neither

Miss Gabor nor Miss Reiss was worried about missing anything *I* might say, so they chose gin-and-tonic.

Francis poured drinks for each of the ladies, but when he put mine down on the table he failed to place a coaster beneath it, and as I raised the glass a wet ring was exposed. Zsa Zsa was furious and in angry tones ordered Francis to wipe the table and be more careful in the future. When he left she turned to us and sighed deeply.

"I pay that man five hundred dollars a month and he hasn't the slightest idea how to serve. I teach, teach, teach, but they never learn. I don't know what's happening to servants anymore, do you?"

Neither Marilyn nor I had an answer to Miss Gabor's question. Then Zsa Zsa, recalling her duties as hostess, asked if we cared for anything else. I shook my head; Marilyn, hands trembling slightly, requested a refill. Then, seeing an opportunity to change the subject, she suggested that her client talk about the Industry.

"She starred in thirty-one films, you know," Marilyn explained, "so I'm sure she has many interesting things to say about Hollywood."

Zsa Zsa smiled, accepted the challenge, and moved her chair closer to me. I found it difficult to concentrate on anything but Zsa Zsa.

"Yes, yes," she said. "I had some wonderful years at M-G-M, but they're crazy. They spent money like it was going out of style. Once I needed a pair of stockings, one pair, that was all. So how many do you think they gave me?"

The question was rhetorical.

"A dozen; I counted them. Once I needed a handbag for a picture I was doing. They sent over a hundred. 'Take your choice,' they said. 'Take as many as you want, be our guest.' No wonder M-G-M lost money. Once they tried to put something over, but they forgot they were dealing with Zsa Zsa and I wasn't so silly. I had to have a dress shortened and a bra put in. It was my own and I sent it over to Western

Costume. I almost fainted when I saw the bill. It came to *nine hundred and seventy-five dollars and sixty-five cents!* I refused to pay. 'Sue me,' I told them."

Did Miss Gabor think Hollywood ever would come back? She shook her head.

"Only if they start making pay-TV out here. It's their last chance. I think pay-TV is on the way, four or five years from now and maybe even sooner. I said so a long while back and put some money into it, money I lost, but I don't regret it. I was premature; the idiots who run the business here were stupid and bucked it. Now look what's happened to them; they're only getting what they deserve.

"The trouble with TV is that it's put together so bad technically; they never give you enough time to rehearse. But believe me, there are plenty of good people out in Hollywood who know their business and could make acceptable TV. But they don't get a chance. So many fools have taken over.

"Aouech!" [the spelling is phonetic] she uttered contemptuously. I translated the word as the Hungarian equivalent of our American "yeeuch." "Let's talk about something else. Let's talk about hippies. Did you know I am the first elegant hippie?"

I registered the proper amount of surprise although truth is that Miss Reiss had briefed me about her client's claim, originally made on one of the late-night TV talk shows on which Miss Gabor is a frequent and much sought-after guest.

"Well, I am," Zsa Zsa went on. "I like the kids today; we understand each other. They'll be O.K. once they get over all this nonsense about narcotics. After all, they're only doing their own thing. And they've got damned good reasons to rebel against the puritanism of their forefathers. I hate to think about that sexual hypocrisy they've been practicing here ever since the Mayflower. I loathe those phony Anglo-Saxon *mores*."

Zsa Zsa shook her head vigorously.

"What's wrong with sex?"

My reply was, I'm sure, what my hostess expected it would be. I asked Miss Gabor how she felt about the current crop of X-rated films.

"I detest them; I never see one and I'll never act in one. Furthermore, I think they're on the way out. Who but a *voyeur* wants to watch somebody else make love?"

A young man, wearing tortoiseshell glasses and attired in civilian clothing, timidly entered the room, approached Miss Gabor, waited until she finished speaking, then whispered something in her ear. Our hostess arose, said she was wanted on the telephone, and that she'd return in a couple of minutes. Marilyn then told me the young man was Miss Gabor's secretary.

"Why don't you take a look around the joint while we're waiting for Zsa Zsa," she suggested.

The house—I suppose it was French—wasn't on the same scale as some of Philadelphia's old Main-Line castles (now museums or private schools) with their two hundred rooms, but it was as luxurious as any of them and furnished in as excellent taste. Despite its elegance, I felt comfortable, a tribute to Miss Gabor's interior designer, whoever he or she was.

The view from my right took in the side of a mountain and a long, sweeping driveway which Marilyn and I had come through on our way to her client's house. Of course we didn't just drive in. First, my companion telephoned our E.T.A. from the office, then, as we reached a twenty-foot-high iron gate blocking the entrance to the Gabor estate, we announced our approach into a microphone. Once we'd been properly identified, the gate swung open and, before we parked the car, the gate was already closed.

The view through the tall windows on my left embraced a canyon, another mountain in the distance, a beautifully landscaped garden which seemed to stretch back for a quarter of a mile over velvety grass, evergreens, and fruit trees. In the foreground was the usual Olympic-size swimming pool and, as

I recall, a couple of tennis courts, none of which was in use.

"Not bad for a poor little kid from Hungary, is it?" Marilyn asked when I sat down again. "Wanna hear our agency's pitch?"

I nodded and Marilyn cleared her throat.

"Zsa Zsa has made a successful career out of being today's epitome of beauty, glamor, femininity, and exquisiteness. She has impeccable taste in furs, diamonds, gowns, coiffures, travel, and cuisines, and she has a blend of being unpredictable, angelic, Hungarian, clever, scandalous, generous, thoughtful, demanding, and patient. And not necessarily in that order.

"Wherever she goes, whatever she does, and whatever she says makes box office and headlines at the same time. Miss Gabor has appeared in motion pictures in this country and abroad. As far as TV is concerned, she appeared with the Beatles in *Night of a Thousand Clowns* and has been a favorite late-night guest for Johnny Carson, Merv Griffin, David Frost, and Joey Bishop.

"Men found her irresistible and over the years they would come from the ranks of princes, potentates, international celebrities, and millionaires to court her favor. Some she married. Some she didn't. 'The sexiest dress a girl can wear is black lace. With diamonds, of course,' she says. Her attitude on the subject of money: 'It's expendable.' "

I don't know what else Miss Reiss intended to reveal about her client but, suddenly, as I was about to sit down again, I discovered that a huge white cat occupied my chair and was eyeing me with disdain. I turned to the beast and hissed, "Get the hell offa my chair, you son-of-a-bitch!," a genetic impossibility, I realize, but I'm a known cat-hater and it was all I could think of at the moment.

"For God's sake, don't let Zsa Zsa hear you," Marilyn cautioned. "That's Endligh, her favorite feline."

I tried again but Endligh wouldn't move. Instead, she (or was it he?) placed one delicate paw over the other, leaned back and looked at me through cold, pitiless blue eyes. I gave up and had just reseated myself elsewhere when Zsa Zsa returned. At once I forgot all about the animal.

My hostess' face was radiant.

"That call was to confirm my engagement for tonight," she said. "He's a handsome Swiss gentleman, a doctor. He's taking me to dinner and a screening somewhere after."

Then Zsa Zsa put her hand to her face and, in consternation, said, "My God! I just remembered, he's a plastic surgeon. What if somebody thinks he's seeing me professionally?"

I offered what limited assurance I could that no one could possibly believe Miss Gabor ever needed a face-lifting. She smiled sweetly, apparently comforted.

"Save your pennies," she said, "and when you get seventy-five hundred of them, ask to take me to dinner. That's how much money's worth I usually eat."

I should have liked to ask if Zsa Zsa and I could somehow work it out with trading stamps which I know my wife collects. But on second thought I felt this would be a poor idea all around. It was on this note that my interview with Miss Gabor came to an end; Marilyn and I returned to Hollywood for the drink I needed.

"Please, please, as you are a gentleman," Miss Reiss begged, "promise me you won't use everything Miss Gabor said, will you?"

I promised I wouldn't and I didn't.

Chapter Nineteen

I'M CONVINCED that whatever Howard Strickling knows about the secret lives of the stars he both publicized and shielded from the press for over half a century will die with him. Either that or I must admit my own failure to extract those lurid stories I hoped to pull from this tall, shy, seventy-three-year-old press agent who recently retired as vice-president in charge of advertising and publicity for Metro-Goldwyn-Mayer.

I even talked to Howard's predecessor, Pete Smith, who surrendered the reins to Strickling back in the twenties and from that octogenarian received the same amount of inside dope on skeletons both gentlemen buried deep all over the lot. It was soon apparent to me that this pair regards its former profession in the same light as priests feel about the confessional.

Howard himself was my contact to Pete although it was Margaret Herrick who set up my date with Strickling.

"You won't get much out of him," Mrs. Herrick warned me, and she was right. Since his retirement, Strickling raises prize cattle on his farm near Encino, some thirty-eight miles from the now nearly vacant M-G-M lot. As my friend Herb Golden pointed out, "Strickling's retirement occupation is a natural. He was undoubtedly the greatest bull artist the world has ever seen."

Herb paused, then added, "But don't forget, he's the guy whose expertise developed the star system and it's the star system which made Hollywood."

Howard came to my Los Angeles apartment one smoggy afternoon a few days after I'd seen Lana Turner. He was extremely reluctant to talk about himself except in a general way and had nothing but good to say about the actors and actresses he once represented so well. However, he didn't mind discussing Hollywood's demise and the passing of glamor from the scene.

"It's all over now and likely to stay that way, and I'm glad I'm out of it. But it sure was fun while it lasted."

He shrugged his shoulders.

"It used to be an event when a star went anywhere," he said but didn't add, as he well might have, that most of the times it was he who made it an event by tipping off members of the working press beforehand. "There's so little going on around here anymore. Of course, this is nothing particularly sudden; Hollywood's been drying up for years. Do you know how many movies the remainder of the majors are making every year?"

I shook my head.

"Well, I'd say no more than five or six, that's all. When I started in this business, or at least after I'd been in the Industry for a little while, they were turning out fifty-two pictures a year, *each* of the majors, I mean. And theaters all over the country had to change marquees every week to accommodate the new features."

Strickling, who was born in St. Mary's, West Virginia, August 25, 1899, came to Hollywood at the age of twenty.

"I was a reporter on the old Los Angeles *Morning Tribune* when I met Rex Ingram. He had started out with M-G-M as an office boy about ten years before, but in 1921 he was directing *The Four Horsemen of the Apocalypse*, starring Valentino and Alice Terry, Ingram's wife. About that time I quit the

Tribune and went to work full-time for M-G-M. Pete was in charge of p.r. and I was assigned to work under Howard Dietz. I was sent to Europe in 1924 to do publicity out of M-G-M's office in Nice, France, and stayed there until 1928 when Pete Smith resigned. I came back to take over his job."

Howard's first major assignment under Ingram was to promote *The Four Horsemen of the Apocalypse*, a movie adaptation of Blasco Ibañez's enormously popular novel written in 1919. Strickling concentrated on the film's male star, Valentino, and built him up as the great Latin lover in the adoring and lustful eyes of American women.

Many claim it actually was Strickling who had a hand in selecting Valentino for the role after seeing a picture in which the actor played a very minor part. This, Howard denies as vehemently as he denies other attempts to credit him with more than what he says was simply "the execution of routine office procedures."

But the loyal opposition disagrees. A redoubtable trio of stars Strickling helped to create and keep in the public eye— Stanwyck, Crawford, and Turner—told me that Strickling, more than any one person in the Industry, was responsible for the glamor that once was Hollywood's. In any event, Strickling's great Valentino buildup shortly became only of academic interest to Metro which lost him soon after release of *The Four Horsemen*. It was for Paramount that Valentino made *The Sheik, Blood and Sand, Monsieur Beaucaire,* and subsequent films until the star's death in 1926. But the legends Strickling created about Valentino live on. One of these concerns the actor's astonishing virility and his hypnotic power to seduce any woman he chose merely by looking directly into her eyes for a second or two.

I'm not going to imply that the fertile mind of Howard Strickling was responsible for the legend's creation or promotion, but I should like to mention an advertisement which used to appear in such forbidden publications as *Captain Billy's Whizzbang* during my frustrated, acneed adolescent days. As I recall, the ad depicted a swarthy, sombreroed

171

hombre, obviously Valentino (a "dirty greaser," we envious male members of the Class of '23 called him to show our contempt), feet apart, arms akimbo, staring directly at a magnificent, high-busted woman in the last stage of swooning.

The cost of obtaining such power was minimal, twenty-five cents in stamps, I think, and a self-taught, easy-to-learn course in hypnotism would be sent by return mail in an unmarked envelope. Naturally I enrolled but, as I told Howard, who definitely denied responsibility for any parts of the commercial, it didn't work for me. Even though I stood arms akimbo, feet apart, and assiduously practiced in front of my mother's full-length mirror, nothing lustful happened. As a matter of fact, I had trouble summoning sufficient nerve just to *ask* Katherine O'Donnell for a movie date to see *The Sheik,* let alone attempt to seduce her.

To replace Valentino, M-G-M needed a new Latin lover. Ramon Novarro was the studio's choice and Strickling was given the assignment of popularizing this other, but equally awful, ham. Obviously my envy still shows after fifty-odd years, but in mitigation I add that my opinion of Valentino's acting talents was shared by no less an authority than Adolph Zukor. As Arthur Mayer reported, Paramount's chief executive once wrote that Valentino's acting "was largely confined to protruding his large, almost occult, eyes, until the vast areas of white were visible, and drawing back the lips of his wide, sensuous mouth to bare his gleaming teeth, and flaring his nostrils."

For Novarro's buildup, Strickling had little to work with except the strong physical resemblance between his current and erstwhile charge. It's hard to determine where fact ends and fiction begins in plotting Novarro's biography and his master press agent's immortalization of this obscure Mexican moving picture extra.

In any event, it's as good an example as any of Strickling's skill as a publicist. The pattern he followed with Novarro was typical of his later-day "creations" which, to mention only a few, included James Stewart, Wallace Beery, Hedy Lamarr,

172

Mickey Rooney, Greer Garson, William Powell, Van Johnson, Reginald Owen, Irene Dunne, Walter Pidgeon, Robert Taylor, Larraine Day, Robert Montgomery, Robert Young, and Esther Williams.

It would hardly be fair to lump all these and other M-G-M contract players together and claim none of them would have amounted to anything except for Strickling's wizardry. Many of these actors were stars in their own right, and while they probably wouldn't have reached the pinnacle of popular acclaim, or made out as well financially, such great talents as Laughton, Lionel Barrymore, Lewis Stone, Hepburn, Judy Garland, and even Lucille Ball, to cite several, would have gotten pretty far on their own.

Ramon Novarro, born Ramon Samaniegos, if you put your faith in the New York *World*, or Ramon Alberto Carmino, Alfredo di Samaniego, should you prefer to believe *Photoplay* Magazine, saw the light of day somewhere south of the border; of that there is little dispute. However, the city of his nativity is variously attributed to Durango in the state of Durango, Guadalajara in the state of Jalisco, or in the border town of Nuevo Loredo in the state of Chihuahua on the other side of the Rio Grande.

Novarro's year of birth was 1899, 1898, or 1897, and there's multiple choice about his family background and father's profession. The latter was either a dentist, an engineer-architect, or a wealthy ranch owner who lost all his land and money during one of the revolutions and was forced to flee the country for his and his family's lives. *Pictorial Revue* says Ramondo (*sic*) was the oldest of eight brothers and four sisters; an Associated Press dispatch reduced the number of siblings to ten.

I got no more than a shoulder shrug and a pleasantly enigmatic smile when I questioned Howard on these alleged discrepancies. As a result I am forced to leave all options to the reader. Besides, it's not easy to interview a gentleman so modest he disclaims credit for those promotions for which he is famous and refuses to be quoted on anything except trivia.

"All anybody needs to know about me and what I did in Hollywood is to be found in the *Motion Picture Almanac*," says Mr. Strickling. I digress to say that the great publicist's biography contained therein is restricted to four and a half lines, as compared, for example, to the sixteen and an eighth lines that publication devotes to Morton Sunshine. I didn't know who Morton Sunshine was, either, I just happened to pick his name out of the book because I liked its euphony.

Well, to return to Ramon Novarro and what Howard Strickling did for him. Prior to the actor's association with Rex Ingram, his career consisted of offering himself as a ball-room dance partner to unescorted ladies of uncertain age, and playing the very smallest of bit parts—walk-ons—in several Class "B" films. I forgot to say that, according to the *Ladies' Home Journal*, Novarro's greatest ambition was to be either a Jesuit priest or a Metropolitan Opera singer, although not necessarily in that sequence.

But sad to relate, his aristocratic family's poverty forced Ramon into other fields. It's quite a strain on both credulity and queasy stomachs to read an early M-G-M Novarro press release.

Upon me, the oldest son, fell the burden of my parents' and my brothers' and my sisters' support. However, I have always been inspired by deep family love which is characteristic of my race, so what others might consider a burden, I regarded as a joy.

I gave piano lessons, I sang, I danced, I even ushered in a moving picture theater—in fact, I performed any honorable though humble task which would support my family and keep it together. Yet I want no one to think of me as a martyr; what I did, I did for love.

Coeval with Ingram's selection of his Mexican protégé to star in such film classics as *The Prisoner of Zenda, Scaramouche, Where the Pavement Ends, Thy Name Is Woman,* and *The Arab* was Strickling's putsch to force the hitherto unknown Ramon into national prominence and to become a worthy successor to the aging Francis X. Bushman. I take a moment here to advise the younger generation that Francis X. placed an enormous strain on the corsets which tightly bound the heaving chests of movie-going grandmothers every time this handsome actor's profile was flashed on the silver screen. Senior citizens who have not yet become senile may recall Bushman as Beverly Bayne's Romeo in Hollywood's version of the Shakespearean play, thus becoming the male member of what Arthur Mayer termed "the first screen love team."

Obviously, once Novarro reached true stardom as he did when he played Ben-Hur against Bushman's Messala, the Latin lover needed well-publicized offstage romances if only to prove his virility, although in that era of innocence no one gave thought to the fact that a not inconsiderable portion of its matinee idols were homosexuals. Of course, in these more tolerant days, sexual deviation no longer is considered a handicap for a star and fans are able to regard, with complete aplomb, the passionate on-screen lovemaking between a known lesbian and an equally well-known homosexual. So be it!

It was no trouble at all for young Howard Strickling to distill adequate numbers of synthetic romances for his client and "leak" them, one by one, to the hordes of magazine writers then assigned from all over the world to cover the Hollywood beat. A recapitulation of M-G-M's pet Latin's life and loves is to be found in the November 1932 issue of *Photoplay* Magazine. Strickling's genius at force-feeding the American public anything he wanted them to swallow can be found in almost every nauseating sentence.

Katherine Albert, one of *Photoplay*'s Hollywood correspondents, wrote:

> Ramon Novarro was thirty-three years old last February and it's about time folks began to understand the boy.
> Ramon has moved, for the last eleven years, in a mist of misunderstanding. Fact and fiction concerning Ramon and

Ramon's character have become so intertwined that I'll wager not one in ten people can give you an accurate estimate of Ramon the man.

So, just for the fun of it, let's start picking Ramon apart and separating the false from the true to see if we can't find out something real about this amazing young man who has remained a star for ten years—thereby disproving the five-year star span of Hollywood.

I'll wager if you asked the average movie-goer to tell you what Ramon was like, she'd give you a picture of a saint-like, idealistic, poetic recluse; that would be as far from the real Ramon as caviar is from codfish. I can tell you how this idea grew. Ramon is religious and has always been. In Hollywood a man who admits deep religious convictions must, so the natives think, be lacking in humor and human understanding. Presto—Hollywood argued—Ramon must be set aside because he was religious.

Strickling reasoned that at this stage, if I may use another mixed metaphor plus an additional cliché, his client's manhood needed a public shot in the arm. This he gracefully provided.

Photoplay continued:

And so, when a couple of years ago a few parties that Ramon attended were highly publicized, Hollywood began to buzz with gossip. "Ramon has changed. He has become a good-time Charlie."

Although more than four decades have gone by you can almost hear Miss Albert gasp as she punches out the clincher.

It's because he's in love with Elsie Janis!

But Miss Albert has even more startling revelations to share with us.

One of Ramon's first Hollywood friends was Kathleen Key. And no man can be a recluse and a friend of Kate Key's. That friendship started when they worked together in the first picture, *The Lover's Oath*. And it lasted through *Ben-Hur* and even after Kate went to Paris. When Ramon went to Paris, he looked her up and they had some rousing times together.

Alice Terry [Ingram's wife] was his friend. Alice is another gay, madcap girl, who certainly would be no fit companion for a man of mystery. . . . Renée Adorée was another of Ramon's friends—and there were many more—you'll find that it wasn't Elsie Janis who drew Ramon from his imaginary shell.

Mind you, he was no hypocrite. He was, and still is, religious. And those gay [Oh, the wonderful innocence of that bygone era!] friends of earlier days respected his convictions.

For fans whose knowledge of Novarro's character might be subjected to question, Miss Albert concluded with a soupçon of inside information.

If anybody ever again asks you why Ramon, once a deeply religious introvert . . . suddenly blossomed into a good-time Charlie—you'll know the answer to that one.

But Strickling pushed his client into a really big-time (even if only on paper) romance with none other than the previously unobtainable, aloof Garbo.

The usually reliable International News Service reported:

Ramon Novarro came back after a vacation in New York almost ecstatic over an incident that occurred there.

Yes, it concerns Greta also. Ramon . . . or so the story goes, was alone in his suite at the Savoy-Plaza when there was a knock at the door. He opened it. A messenger stood there with a box of very lovely flowers. A plain little note was attached discreetly: "With sincere appreciation and best wishes." It was signed "M. H." Light dawned. But no—it couldn't be! Ramon thought a moment. "M. H." Ah, but it was. Greta was in town—she who had played the ravishing "Mata Hari" to his "Alex Rosanoff."

He immediately ordered three dozen yellow roses (her favorite flower) sent to her rooms at the Ritz-Carlton. He initialed the note that accompanied them "A. R."

By some strange coincidence *Mata Hari* opened the following night at selected motion picture theaters throughout the United States.

There was no doubt that the ladies loved Ramon. But Strickling wanted his star, if not to be adored, at least tolerated by members of his own sex. The great press agent surely was aware that a good many gentlemen in the audience, after seeing a Novarro film, were turning to their wives and asking, "What do you see in that greasy Spik bastard?" and perhaps adding, "What has he got that I don't?"

Consequently, Howard set about developing a kinship between Novarro and the male animal to prove that way down deep the star was just the same as all of his brothers. So many a husband, who for years refused to yield to a nagging wife's demand that he throw away a cherished, albeit moth-eaten, old sweater or a termite-ridden bat with which he used to drive in the winning run when Chillicothe High beat Marietta Academy three to two, found a formidable ally in "the greasy Spik bastard."

The United Press, in a widely syndicated article, stated:

One of Ramon Novarro's fondest possessions is a disreputable bathrobe he bought in Italy for $34 and wore in his dressing room during the making of *Ben-Hur*. Once it was green; now it is a muddy brown. He wore it when he received distinguished visitors backstage during his recent visit to France. And he continues to wear it whenever he feels like it, no matter who is present.

Other stories, with a strong male slant, followed.

"Who wants pheasant under glass, stuffed squab, and those

fancy salads when he can get a good beef stew?" Ramon Novarro told members of the Bakersfield Chamber of Commerce, according to the Associated Press. "I like food that puts hair on your chest," he concluded to a wildly enthusiastic audience. "Novarro's new film, *Ben-Hur*, will be shown tomorrow at the Bijou Theater here in Bakersfield."

But in none of the star's publicity photographs which displayed the subject's torso nude from slightly below the waist up is there a sign of any hirsute growth except upon his head. The caption, incidentally, according to Arthur Mayer, who used one of these photos in a book, read, "This picture proves rather conclusively that he has no intention of entering a monastery or taking up the profession of concert pianist." Mayer added that "Novarro's horde of feminine fans liked to see him as nearly nude as the censors allowed. . . ."

Due primarily to Strickling's genius, Novarro achieved a measure of success far beyond his acting talents, which, while certainly superior to his rival, Valentino, could hardly be categorized as more than adequate. His peak salary was five thousand dollars a week and, as a further measure of his enormous appeal, he is alleged to have received twenty-five hundred fan letters a day, some of which were addressed simply to "Ben-Hur, Hollywood, California."

According to the New York *Times*, "He [Novarro] was idolized to the point that he drew the normal star's complement of police protection when he went out in public." Novarro was able to make the transition from silent films to talkies. One of his co-stars was Helen Hayes in M-G-M's 1933 production of *The Son-Daughter*. As late as 1960 he appeared with Sophia Loren, although not as a star, in *Heller in Pink Tights*.

However, as the *Times* pointed out, "His [Novarro's] fame crested in silent films and he never achieved the height of popularity in talking pictures."

But there never was a need for Novarro to consider spending his declining years at The Country House. He was a shrewd businessman and, like George Cukor, invested his cash in Hollywood real estate which multiplied in value many times.

Except for a young male secretary, Novarro, a bachelor, lived alone in his one-hundred-fifty-thousand-dollar, Spanish-style Hollywood Hills home. It was there that the star was bludgeoned to death early on the morning of October 31, 1968. He was sixty-nine years old.

With few exceptions—Gable for one—Strickling never became particularly close to any of the stars he represented from Bert Lytel to Melvyn Douglas. For every name I mentioned, Howard had a kind word.

Irene Dunne? "A woman of great distinction." Mary Astor? "A great talent." Robert Young? "A fine gentleman." Lana Turner? "A beautiful woman, a nice person, and a good actress."

Whatever secrets Howard Strickling has will be carried to the grave, I'm sure.

"Every so often an editor or agent wants me to write my memoirs and 'tell all.' "

He smiled.

"I never will, so they can all breathe easy."

People who've worked with Strickling over the years say his most outstanding characteristic is loyalty, a much-admired but little-imitated commodity—in Hollywood at any rate. Herb Stein, the syndicated movie columnist, tells a story about Howard, one which Dore Schary should appreciate.

"It wasn't all gravy for Strickling with the passing of the Mayer regime some years ago. By all the laws of the town his closeness to Mayer made him the Number One target when Schary came into power, especially in the bitterness that developed. But even Schary had to recognize Howard's value—his loyalty to the company—and he himself profited by Strick's advice, although a bond of warmth never came.

"It is recalled that one time Dore complained that Howard was still seeing a lot of Mayer and that it was embarrassing to him. Howard was called by Loew's topper, Nick Schenck, about it. Instead of ducking or lying, Howard stood his ground, admitting, 'Yes, I still see Mr. Mayer. He is my friend. I would do the same for any friend as long as he didn't ask me to do anything disloyal.' Schenck never said anymore about it."

And, presumably, neither did Dore.

I saw Howard twice more before I left Hollywood and both times he came to my apartment. He drank nothing stronger than Coke and, when we were together, neither did I. Many times he said it was a great life while it lasted, that he'd do it all over again if given the chance, but he was damned glad it was all over.

Someone gave me the M-G-M press release that was issued upon Strickling's voluntary retirement. If what I was handed contained the full statement, I'm fairly sure I could pinpoint its author.

Howard Strickling has retired as vice-president in charge of advertising and publicity for Metro-Goldwyn-Mayer. Mr. Strickling, who is sixty-nine years old, joined the publicity department of the old Metro company in 1919. He was appointed vice-president upon the resignation of Howard Dietz in 1959.

Chapter Twenty

I PREFACE this chapter on Pete Smith with a statement that, while I think sports fans in general are a pretty gullible, if not an actually stupid, lot, I hereby promise them I will not urge my senator to introduce any measure banning this expensive form of humbuggery. Upon those very rare occasions when, in my extreme youth, I was forced to witness a so-called sporting event, a baseball game, for example, I used to wish I had the courage of the child in *The Emperor's Clothes* who said what every adult has been afraid to say then or now, "Why, the whole goddamned thing's a fake."

As far as I can determine, mine has been one of the few voices raised in protest against that monstrous hoax known as organized sports, a deliberate deception foisted upon generations of "fans" who've either deluded themselves into thinking they're having fun or, which is more likely, are scared to admit they are being taken. And so, *omerta*, the conspiracy of silence, has kept a sizable portion of the world's population from realizing it's a sucker.

Since September 22, 1926, when I was assigned by my newspaper to do a "color" story on the Dempsey–Tunney boxing match in Philadelphia's Municipal Stadium—as I recall, Tunney won—I have seen only two sporting events, one

182

exceedingly dull but financially profitable (to me), and the other quite funny. The latter concerns Pete Smith, but I'll tell you first about the former, only to prove my point. Both, by the way, were football games.

I have two close friends who, except for their inordinate and frequently outspoken enthusiasm for every conceivable athletic event including curling, seem reasonably intelligent. The first is Leo Weinrott, a distinguished Quaker City jurist, college athlete, and former football referee, and the other, Bernie Bergman, an editor of such diverse publications as *The New Yorker*, The Philadelphia *Daily News*, *The Jewish Exponent*, and currently book editor of the Philadelphia *Evening Bulletin*.

Bergie was our late breakfast guest one Sunday morning a few years ago. We were in the midst of our second old-fashioned when the telephone rang; it was the Judge.

"I got a pair of tickets on the fifty-yard line for the Eagles game this afternoon. Esther and I have to go out of town so you're welcome to use them."

It should be obvious that His Honor never has given up proselyting despite years of my rebuffs.

"How much will you pay me if I go?" I asked.

There was a moment's silence.

"How much will *I* pay *you?*" he answered in a fury. "Why, you son-of-a-bitch, these are worth twenty dollars apiece and it's a sellout, so you can't even buy them."

He hung up. Although Bergie'd heard only one side of the conversation, he reconstructed the Judge's part.

"How much will you charge *me* to go, Art?" Bergie asked, and without any hesitation I replied, "Two hundred bucks."

"O.K., I'll pay you the two hundred. Call the Judge back and tell him we'll go. On second thought, I'll call him; he probably won't speak to you."

Since Bergie can hardly be classified as profligate with his own cash, I asked what the catch was.

"No catch," he lied, then added, "all you have to do is write a short piece on the game for the *Bulletin*."

So Bergie and I trudged out to Franklin Field to watch the Eagles play somebody or other on a cold, dank autumn day which could have been far better spent playing poker or reading. During our twenty-five-block stroll, Bergie, who never seems to learn, was bursting with pride about "our" Eagles.

"What do you mean, 'our' Eagles?" I couldn't resist asking. "Are you trying to tell me the players are from Philadelphia, or went to school here, or that the team's owned by the city, that we all are gonna share in the proceeds?"

"No, and you *know* it," my friend snarled. "What's ownership got to do with it? Who cares? Don't be a piker. All it'll cost every taxpayer is fifty bucks to have the best arena in the country. Where's your patriotism? Where's your civic pride?"

A couple of guys walking ahead of us overheard the conversation. One of them, a typical hard-hat, turned around and shook a fat finger in my face.

"What's with you, bud?" he screamed, his face beet-red. "Don't you like football? What are you, a Commie or somethin'? Why don't you go back where you came from?"

Before we'd left, and unknown to Bergie, I borrowed a neighbor's stopwatch, and as soon as the umpire blew his whistle I put it to use. What happened was rather expected; my stopwatch showed a total of four minutes and twenty-three seconds of "action" during the entire first half, and three minutes and fifty-one seconds during the second. But you couldn't even see that much. Every time the ball was put in motion, each row of spectators automatically jumped up and blocked the view of those behind them.

A young fellow next to me didn't even bother to look down at the field; the whole time his head was bent low, ears glued to a transistor. At one point Bergie asked him how the Eagles were doing.

"Who knows, chum?" he answered. "I'm listening to the Packers play the Rams in Green Bay."

I knew I'd proved my point when Bergie asked me if he could borrow the stopwatch sometime.

"I want to take it to a baseball game next season," he said

with some embarrassment. "For scientific research, you know."

Bergie kept his part of the bargain and so did I, although I doubt that the piece I wrote for the *Bulletin* convinced a single sports fan to admit the truth.

And now to that second football game, the one I enjoyed. This must have been about 1933 or 1934 when it was hard to get fun out of anything anywhere. Bored by jigsaw puzzles and matchstick poker with the neighbors, my wife and I recklessly decided to blow a quarter apiece at a local movie one evening. I guess the management gave dishes besides.

When we walked into the Broad, our ears were pleasantly assailed by a sound nobody was hearing much during those deep Depression days—laughter. The audience was screaming with almost hysterical joy; the explanation, a Pete Smith short on the screen. There was that slightly ironic, albeit good-natured, wonderfully raspy voice coming from offstage poking wild fun at a professional football game.

I haven't the slightest recollection what the feature picture was that night, but I can remember quite a few of Pete's lines, one in particular: "Now isn't that too, too divine," was his comment when a monstrously large quarterback named Bronco Nagurski, after making a touchdown, delicately placed both hands on his hips, tilted his head to one side, and cast his eyes heavenward.

And here I was, damned near four decades later, sitting opposite Pete Smith in his modest Beverly Hills home and hearing that same, slightly ironic, good-natured, raspy voice coming to me from the other side of the desk which separated us. This was the first time I'd ever seen him "in person," as they say. He was wearing bright blue slacks, a maroon shirt, and a multi-colored neckerchief. Pete's at least eighty, a lean, lively, sharp-eyed gentleman who doesn't look or act more than sixty, and who's got all his marbles, his own teeth, much of his hair, and what's left is undyed black, and his ability to laugh at the world's antics.

"The wonderful thing about Hollywood and the Industry,

185

or the way it used to be at any rate," he said, "are the screw-balls you meet in it."

I was fearful my host was getting personal, but he cleared up that point.

"I was thinking of a woman who once, a long while back, brought her dog to M-G-M for an audition. And the reason I was thinking of that woman shortly before you arrived on the scene was that I just got a letter today from *another* woman who wants *her* dog to replace Lassie.

"The poor soul must still think I'm doing shorts, and I haven't made one for nearly twenty-five years."

Pete didn't tell me, Mrs. Herrick did, that one of the last series of Pete Smith shorts, *Quicker 'n a Wink*, made in 1941, received an Academy Award which was by no means his first. In fact, he's got a roomful of medallions, loving cups, and plaques from all over the world wherever his one-reelers have been shown. But he keeps the door closed and unless you know about this trophy room, as I did via Mrs. Herrick, and ask to see what's inside, Pete's not likely to open it for inspection.

"Must have been around 1934 or 1935," my host continued, "and I was producing and narrating M-G-M shorts. I was working on the lot one day when my secretary said there was a funny looking woman and an even funnier looking dog in the waiting room wanting to see me.

"All kinds of people used to come along itching to get into the movies and I never turned any of 'em away without giving 'em a chance. So I told the girl to send them along. A couple minutes later a tall, skinny female, must have been six feet tall and couldn't have weighed more 'n a hundred pounds, comes in with the oddest looking dog I ever laid eyes on, a long, clumsy, hairy, underslung beast with ears that reached down to the ground. It was a combination of beagle and Russian wolfhound, if you can imagine anything like that. By the way, this is not a 'shaggy dog' story, it's the truth.

" 'What can I do for you and your friend?' I asked, and the

lady answered, 'Wilbert's a talking dog; he can say anything you want him to say.'

"'All right, madam,' I said. I'd been through this kind of thing once or twice before, 'ask Wilbert to say "Pete Smith."' So the woman opens her big black pocketbook and takes out a hunk of raw hamburger. Meanwhile Wilbert had disappeared. Both of us searched all around the place and finally found the animal fast asleep and snoring under my desk where he'd crawled.

"She shoved him out into the open, held the meat high over the dog's head, and gave him his orders. Wilbert raised his long ears, opened his sad brown eyes slightly, and let out a couple of mournful howls, the sound of which in no way remotely resembled my name."

Pete chuckled.

"But his mistress thought otherwise and was so pleased she applauded loudly and tossed the hamburger to Wilbert who swallowed it in one gulp, curled up, and fell asleep again, this time on the rug in front of my desk.

"'All right, Mr. Smith,' she says, 'do you want to sign up Wilbert now?'

"'Well, madam,' I answered, 'you can't expect me to give a contract to a dog that can only say two words, do you?'

"The lady nods her head sympathetically.

"'I guess not, Mr. Smith, I appreciate your position. But I told you before that Wilbert can say *anything*. He has a simply enormous vocabulary.'

"With that, she removes some more meat from the pocketbook, prods Wilbert with the toe of her shoe, gets him to lean against the desk, and says to me, 'What do you want him to say now?'

"I thought for a second, then I said, 'Tell Wilbert to say "play ball."' She holds the hamburger over the dog's head once more, the animal unflaps his ears, wakes up, half-opens his eyes again, and gives out with those same two mournful bays. This time Wilbert's mistress was ecstatic with pride."

Pete smiled at the recollection, then went on.

"I had all I could do to keep from bursting out laughing and I had to turn around and look out the window a couple of times so she wouldn't see me. Well, we went through the same act four or five times more until I finally thought I'd better get back to work. But I wasn't sure how to get rid of the lady and Wilbert without hurting their feelings. She gave me the out herself.

" 'Wait till you hear this one,' she says. 'I *know* you'll be thrilled,' and out came those two howls.

" 'You *know* what he just said, Mr. Smith, don't you?'

"I was forced to plead ignorance; the lady looked down as though her feelings were hurt deeply, and that I was either stupid or deaf or maybe both.

" 'He said "Warner Brothers" as clear as a bell.'

"Then she paused.

" 'Isn't this Warner Brothers' studio?'

"I shook my head.

" 'No, madam, this is Metro-Goldwyn-Mayer.'

"The lady looked startled.

" 'Sorry, Mr. Smith, I've made a serious mistake. It was only Warner Brothers I wanted to give Wilbert his contract.' "

Pete told me that the lady then dragged the still-sleeping hound, this time from behind a couch, and the pair walked toward the door.

"She stopped, turned around, and glanced at me.

" 'You know, Mr. Smith, I still might be interested in giving you people a chance.'

"So I said, 'That's fine, madam. When Wilbert's been trained to say "Metro-Goldwyn-Mayer" clearly, bring him back and we'll give him another audition.'

"I never heard from her again, and for all I know Jack Warner might have signed Wilbert up."

Pete (nobody, not even his mother, ever called him by his duly authorized Christian name "Peter") was born in Brooklyn, New York, on September 4, 1892. After high school he went to work as a reporter on the long-since defunct Brooklyn *Daily Eagle* for which he covered amusements. He fell in love with the movies and about 1912—Pete isn't quite sure of the exact date—took a job as motion picture editor of *Billboard*. He remained with that publication until 1916 when he came out to Hollywood to head the press department of Famous Players–Laskey.

Famous Players eventually became Paramount and Pete was that studio's public relations director until 1925 when he joined M-G-M in a similar capacity. He stayed with that studio until his retirement twenty-five years ago.

"When you worked for M-G-M you worked for the best! We had a marvelous organization; you'll find almost everybody who ever worked for M-G-M is proud of the fact like I am. It's just too damned bad it's gone to hell, like the rest of this town. But my God! It sure was fun while it lasted."

He sighed.

"When I first started to work for the studio—I guess about 1918—there was nothing around Hollywood but orange and lemon groves. Our big social events were the Thursday night dances at the Hollywood Hotel, which was torn down a long time ago. Everybody in the Industry went there and the best ones came from M-G-M.

"Do you know that as early as 1926 M-G-M had seventy-two legitimate stars, those whose names came before the pictures they played in, twenty-nine directors, our own hospital, fire department, and a school. I don't mean a school for acting, I mean a regular school where kids got their three 'Rs.' And we had some pretty fancy graduates from that institution—Elizabeth Taylor, Mickey Rooney, Judy Garland, Deanna Durbin, and I don't know how many others.

"Well, what I'm only trying to say is that, if you worked for M-G-M, there wasn't a studio that wouldn't try to grab you. But most of us were loyal and we stayed where we were. No one else had anything as good to offer, and I'm not talking about money."

He shook his head.

"Oh, man! To be able to go back to that. But it's all over now. Wanna hear how I got into making shorts?"

I nodded.

"Well, ever since I was a kid, I wanted to be a writer. Not the serious kind, understand, just a guy with a chance to poke fun at all those things people were taking so seriously. You know, the state of the world, the monetary system which nobody understands a damned thing about although they pretend to, politics, channel swimmers, in fact, all kinds of sports, particularly football and baseball. The crazy emphasis people used to put on sports, still do, needed some kind of debunking."

With this statement Pete Smith won my heart completely.

"So, to go on with my ambitions to write for the movies and maybe, just maybe, do a little acting along the line. So I told them what I wanted to do; they brought Howard [Strickling] over from Nice, France, where he ran the p.r. for M-G-M's European operations, and I got my opportunity.

"This was soon after all the studios were trying to make the transition from silents to talkies. I volunteered to take the first test. After all, I knew what the hell my voice would sound like; I couldn't play any romantic leads with this kind of rasp, so what could I lose? But poor John Gilbert—the star they said never could do anything wrong. His voice came out harsh, high-pitched, and metallic, and it finished him at once. It was all over right then and there for John. Nobody could do anything about it; as the great lover he sounded ridiculous.

"Well, to get back on the topic. One day they found a lot of footage left over from a rodeo, so I asked if I could write and do a commentary. People used to take those damned rodeos very seriously then—maybe they still do—and I intended to debunk it. So I gagged absolutely everything, cowboys, horses, and audiences, and it went over big. From that time on I had it made and did exactly what I wanted to do and got paid for it besides."

He laughed.

"I almost killed it for myself, though. I was doing so well I thought maybe I ought to improve my diction and style and maybe do some serious films. So I hied myself over to the studio voice teacher, one of the greatest in the world, and told him I wanted to take lessons. He looked at me like I was crazy.

" 'Voice lessons, Pete? What are you talking about? Change your manner of speech and you're done. You want me to eliminate your "deses, doses, and dems?" That's what people like to listen to after all the cultured tones emerging from the talkies. Don't you know it makes them feel good to hear somebody who speaks even worse than they do?'

"So that was it for me. I never became a romantic star, but I sure was commentator for a hell of a lot of Pete Smith shorts, dozens and dozens of them. And I hope I brought some fun and a few laughs to the paying customers."

Question anybody past the age of fifty, or even forty, whether they got a lot of laughs from those wonderful Pete Smith shorts and you'll get a hearty "aye." He had plenty of imitators, but I can't recall a single one of them—if you'll forgive my use of a sporting term—who came within putting distance of the gentleman sitting opposite me.

I asked Pete what it takes to enter his profession. For an answer he opened a desk drawer, fished around for a couple of seconds, then handed me a yellowed newspaper clipping.

"Look it over while I freshen our drinks."

The clipping, headed "The Commentator's Art," was from the Brooklyn *Daily Eagle*, dated July 4, 1937, under a Peter Smith by-line. I quote several passages from Pete's sage remarks not with the object of luring the young into a craft as dead as the blacksmith's. Rather, my mission is to propose that the current crop of pontifical TV commentators (most of whom wouldn't know how to cover a strawberry festival at Zion Lutheran Church) do not look upon themselves as Pulitzer Prize winners. After all, they neither gather nor even write up the news they read so mellifluously from a tele-prompter out of the audience's sight. Nor am I about to suggest that they turn everything into a laugh; I just wish they wouldn't take themselves so goddamned seriously *all* the time.

So much for diatribes; here go a few wise words from the pen of Pete Smith.

A commentator is a man who profits by not knowing what he's talking about. He hides behind a soundtrack and flips quips and explanatory remarks at any and all subjects. He discusses the love life of tropical fish, wingbacks, halfbacks, and drawbacks, equestrian acrobats, and the proper method of stuffing ducks.

He claims his success is based on a total unfamiliarity with all the topics on which he discourses. If he were a sports expert, he would be talking about technical aspects of the games which would bewilder the average motion picture audience. If he were a devotee of Izaak Walton, his rhapsodies on piscatorial pleasures would be a dull lecture to the uninformed.

Until a man has battled his way through fifty pictures, he's not a commentator. With the fifty-first he finds his mind a haven for small, dark, and gloomy cubbyholes, housing considerable knowledge on a considerable number of topics that are totally useless. He makes a picture on a topic like inflation. He can speak freely, for no one else knows anything about inflation.

Pete was back with the drinks; I took a few sips and read on while my host watched.

Every time he makes a picture he studies his subject until he feels he knows nothing (the mark of an educated man!). . . . If he turns highbrow, it's for business purposes only, to get a laugh. Delving into scientific tomes to unearth mysteries about microbes, he remembers that he's crawling with them. He'll never get rid of the microbes but he'll put them to work *for* him, instead of *on* him.

Knowledge comes from books, from people, from experiences. . . . When he passes his twenty-fifth mile of film, a commentator is getting old. He has caught fighting fish, he has made spectacular broken-field runs through the greatest professional football team in the world, has driven golf balls out of sight, has sprinted, put the shot, run marathons, and pole-vaulted, has dodged dogs, and tossed tomatoes, has pushed throttles and traveled a mile a minute in outboard motorboats, has glided and power-dived, has trained dogs and gilded lilies.

In fact, he's lived a thousand lives, waged countless duels with death. If he's worth his salt, he has entered into the spirit of the thing and the conclusion of a picture [or a newscast, I thought to myself] leaves him tired and worn and a little older.

Pete asked me if I wanted to stretch my legs and maybe move to another setting, so we carried our drinks into the garden (no swimming pool as far as I could determine) and leaned back on beach chairs under an old shade tree. A certain amount of Hollywood history was made in the Smith house.

"Wesley Ruggles, the director, used to own the joint," Pete said. "In fact, he married Arlene Judge in front of the fireplace in the living room we just passed through. Then Judy Garland bought it and lived here for a while when she was married to that composer, David Rose."

My host paused and shook his head.

"Speaking of roses, I've got to tell you a story with a moral, or maybe it's only a lesson in economics, moving picture economics, I mean, and why I believe Hollywood is doomed. I want to say first that what really murdered the Industry and drove picture makers away to Mexico and Europe and other parts of the world were union demands and the ridiculously high salaries stars asked for and got—some of them still do. Imagine an actor or actress getting paid a million bucks for a picture that they're pretty sure beforehand isn't going to make any dough.

"But my story's about unions and the way they've been operating, not just recently but for a hell of a long while. This goes back to around 1947 and I was making a short subject called *I Love My Wife* for the opening of National Laugh Week."

He shook his head dolefully.

"We sure could use that one nowadays, couldn't we? Well, to go on. In one of the scenes we were doing, the director, or cinematographer, I forget which, wanted a cut rose in a vase moved from one side of the table to the other. So I picked it up myself and started to place it there.

"Up jumps a property man screaming, 'Hold it, Mr. Smith. You're not supposed to do that, we have to call the greenhouse man.' So we all sat around waiting, getting paid, naturally, while they sent out for the greenhouse man. I'm the producer and I have a budget, but we're all standing around waiting—director, cameramen, grips, electricians, property men, and a half-dozen others and, of course, getting paid.

"Well, about a half-hour later, they locate the greenhouse man who comes in, takes one look at the job, and shakes his head. 'Sorry, gentlemen, you're asking me to remove a cut flower and under union regulations I'm not permitted to. Unless you want to have trouble you'll have to call in the cut-flower man.'

"So we sent for the cut-flower man and he gets there in another hour and finally moves the vase from one side of the table to the other. Can you imagine how much this silly rule cost M-G-M? Finally, of course, this is the sort of hidebound stupidity which cost about seventy-five percent of the people in the Industry in Hollywood their jobs."

I'd heard similar tales of union high-handedness, including Dore's one about the stagehands, so I wondered if perhaps Pete's wasn't apocryphal. He must have sensed my doubt.

"I didn't invent that one, Art. I saw it happen."

Then he smiled.

"Now I gotta tell one on myself and how *I* wasted some of M-G-M's dough." He took a few swallows, cleared his throat, and began.

"Remember an actor named Dave O'Brien?"

I vaguely recalled the name.

"Well, Dave was from Texas; he was a very funny man, a damned good actor, and I used him in a hell of a lot of my pictures. He always played the role of the clumsy bungler; everything he did turned out wrong, if you know what I mean."

I nodded.

"We were doing a nine-minute short in the middle of which somebody suggested we have a bumblebee crawl into Dave's toupee. It sounded like a good idea, so all of us dropped what we were doing and ran out on the lot to catch one but nobody had any luck. I'm sure everybody who saw us thought we were crazy. Then it dawned on me that this was winter and bees would not be flitting around the flowers until spring, and we couldn't hold up production that long.

"M-G-M had a million specialists on the lot, but no apiarist. The closest one we could find was located in a town called Indio which is around a four-hour drive from L.A. I called the guy, made a deal, and asked him if he could send us a pair of bees in a hurry. I thought I'd better buy two in case one of them died. I asked him if he had any suggestions on how to keep the bees healthy at least until six o'clock the next morning when we'd start shooting and use one of them. After that, since we weren't renting the animals and didn't have to return them in good condition, I really didn't give a hoot what happened."

Pete paused once more to refill our empty glasses, a task he performed himself since I saw no hired help in the vicinity. Then he went on.

"Well, the apiarist said his bees were a pretty healthy species and all we'd have to do was keep them at a seventy- to seventy-five-degree temperature and they'd survive. So we sent the studio limousine out to Indio with instructions that whoever went out with the driver was to make sure the bees were kept cozy and warm.

"They'd be in a wooden container which he was to put on a table in the studio where Dave, Jack Cummings, the director, and the rest of us were shooting. Next morning, promptly at six o'clock, we were all assembled and ready to go to work. I listened for those buzzing sounds M-G-M had paid a lot to get, but I didn't hear a damned thing. Then I took a look around for the container. It was there all right, on top of an electric hot plate we kept handy to make coffee.

"The hot plate was turned on, the box was singed and, when I opened it, I saw the bees. Whoever did it not only kept the insects warm, he'd fried them. Well, I figured this was the end of the bee sequence even though it seemed like a good idea. We were sorry but we knew we'd have to substitute another sight gag and were trying to think one up. Dave opened a window to let out the stink of burned wood and fried bees. Will you believe me when I tell you what happened then?"

I suggested that Pete try my credulity and he did.

"Art, I swear to Christ that when Dave opened the window a bee, which must have been waiting outside, flew into the studio. There were eight or nine of us and you can imagine how out of our minds we looked running around trying to catch that bee, yet scared to death if we did we'd get stung.

"Dave finally succeeded; he threw his hat on it when the insect landed on Dave's toupee which was resting on a chair, and we finished the short right on schedule. Never did another one on bees, though. You say you've seen a lot of my films, so you know most of the subjects were every kind of sport. My theme usually was to caricature their overemphasis and prove how really dull they can be, with so damned little action there unless the commentator puts it in."

I felt I'd taken up enough of Pete's time. I thanked him for his hospitality and assured him, "I agree with you completely about the boredom of all sports, professional and amateur."

He frowned.

"Not *quite* true," he said slightly annoyed. "Ever play golf?"

Out of politeness I was forced to tell a near falsehood. The only form of that activity I ever indulged in was known as "Tom Thumb" golf, which I played upon several occasions with my daughter until she reached the discriminating age of seven. Of course I didn't mention that to my host.

He shook his head as though not convinced of my veracity.

"Great game! I'm going to play a couple of rounds later this afternoon. Never miss a day. Now *that's* a sport with plenty of action every minute of the time."

I've never used a stopwatch on a golf match but I will someday, and I'll bet the ball isn't in action more than one one-hundredth of the time it takes to go a round of eighteen holes. When I make this experiment, I'll send the results to Mr. Pete Smith of Beverly Hills, California.

Chapter Twenty-One

FIVE MINUTES at the most was all it took me to fall in love with Barbara Stanwyck. I guess it began when I made an abortive attempt to reform her. Let me tell you how and why this came about. I used to be a chain cigarette smoker but quit—cold turkey—on September 25, 1940, after an evening of poker during which five of us finished a full carton of Camels. By two A.M. we were groping among the ashtrays for usable butts.

Ever since, I have been what is known in polite society as a crashing bore every time I see somebody I like puffing away madly, and earnestly warn them about the evils of tobacco. As a footnote I should say I do not feel that way about alcohol. Well, to return to Miss Stanwyck. She's a friend of Howard W. Koch, the producer, he's a friend of Herb Golden, and Herb is a friend of mine. I called Herb, Herb called Howard, Howard called Barbara, and Barbara called me, and there we were at a choice table for two in the Brown Derby.

The last time I'd seen Miss Stanwyck she was playing the role of a tough, sexless, middle-aged widow in a TV Western called *The Big Valley*, a horse opera I watched while I baby-sat for my six-year-old grandson who preferred it to *Bonanza*, which, in truth, isn't saying much. So what I expected to find in Miss Stanwyck was an unhappy combination of the late Marie Dressler, Marjorie Main, and Lorne Greene. But the stunning, silver-haired woman who was already in the restaurant waiting for me (and I was early) was as physically attractive as, for example (and may I be struck dead on the spot if I'm lying), Zsa Zsa.

Another quality about her, one I discovered almost immediately, is that she is completely unphony, says exactly what she thinks and, so I'm told, never tries to impress anybody. She certainly made no attempt to impress me, that I can vouch for.

We hadn't even glanced at the menu and I was already lighting Barbara's third cigarette. I coughed delicately and was about to launch into the reformed smoker's usual lecture on the evils of nicotine when the actress looked me squarely in the eyes.

"Look," she said, and she wasn't smiling, "I know damned well what you're going to say, but please don't. I smoke a lot, I know, I like it; it may kill me someday, but in the meanwhile I'm a son-of-a-bitch if I want to quit and nobody's going to make me. So let's drop the subject before it starts and spend a couple of hours together pleasantly."

I promised, and that's what we did. I mentioned the fact that I'd met Maurice Evans the previous afternoon and the actor told me he'd come to the United States to do a television show for CBS. I'd done my homework and knew the English actor once played opposite Barbara in a Western. I mentioned her name to him; he had told me he held Miss Stanwyck in great esteem, that she was a real pro, and that I should extend his warmest regards, and ask her what she once called him. I think Barbara was pleased; her face lit up when I told her this.

"What a great guy *he* is!" she said. "That's a real pro for you. Let me tell you what I know about Maurice Evans. You're familiar with the parts he played in London and New York—Romeo, Macbeth, and so on, all the plays for the Old Vic and Broadway. And how about those wonderful films he made, *Dial M* and *Rosemary's Baby*, which he hadn't done yet when we worked together. At any rate, you appreciate the type of dignity that man possesses.

"I'm sure when they asked him to make a Western he regarded it as a kind of lark, but he was so thrilled he was like a child. I'm not going to try to tell you the script for our Western was anything like what Shakespeare might have written; it was *not*. But Maurice took it all in stride and, even so, did as professional a job as he knew how and that's saying a lot."

She smiled.

"I used to call him 'Maury baby,' and he loved it. In a couple of scenes he had to climb aboard a wagon and, unless you're used to doing this, it can be damned rough. He'd be struggling along, trying hard, sometimes actually falling flat on his face. I'd be aboard and I'd sing out, 'Get your ass up, Maury baby,' and he did. That man's a real pro; he never once complained or tried to put on an act. Nothing fake about him."

She shook her head.

"If there's anything I hate it's a goddamned phony and Hollywood's filled with 'em, pretending to be what they're not and some of them never were. You know who I'm talking about—these ex-stars who claim they could go to work any time they felt like it, turning their noses up at TV because they say it's beneath their dignity.

"All they do is sit around talking about the good old days. Well, I have news for them, the good old days are gone forever and they better realize that if they want to work they'll have to get off their fat asses. Don't they understand that out of twenty-five thousand S.A.G. members, only around two hundred are working today? That's a pretty small percentage. As for me, I'm in this business to work, I love it, and I'll work at anything I can whenever and wherever they call me. Believe me, it's not the money."

She sighed.

"Of course, I miss the way it used to be when we were all

there on top working for the majors. I'm not going to claim I didn't enjoy those beautiful dressing rooms they gave me, and the maids all around to serve me, and my own chauffeur to drive me in a limousine every place I wanted to go, even if it was only five hundred feet from one set to another. Don't misunderstand me, I loved it all just as much as anybody else, but when it was gone I adjusted; so many of them don't.

"I learned to get along without all those wonderful trimmings. If you're a performer, the most important thing is to be able to perform, and that's something those phonies never learn. All I want, all any of the real pros want, is a decent script, a competent cast, and a good director. The rest is a crock of shit."

She chuckled.

"And while we're on *that* subject, let me tell you what every dainty young lady who ever acts in a Western has to learn. We use real horses and the lovelies better watch where they step or they'll do what I did during the first few Westerns I made.

"I used to laugh when these haughty, phony young ladies used to come on the scene to work. They refused to listen to anybody's advice and went their own way. It was a pleasure to see them, noses tilted to the sky, eyes up in the air, suddenly put down their dainty little feet into a heap of manure. Did they scream? You can bet your sweet ass they did!"

The waiter brought our order, Barbara doused her cigarette, and for a few minutes we ate in smokeless silence. A trio of girls in their late teens or early twenties, sitting at a nearby table and eyeing my companion ever since we sat down, now walked over to Miss Stanwyck and asked for her autograph.

"We saw you on the Late, Late Show last night, Miss Stanwyck," said one of them, a tall, slender, well-dressed girl with a Midwestern accent.

Barbara looked at her.

"What was the picture?"

"*Sorry, Wrong Number.* It was good, Miss Stanwyck."

Miss Stanwyck appeared pleased.

"Any of you kids ever see *Executive Suite?*"

"Yes, *I* did, ma'am," one of the other girls answered. At this unexpected display of politeness I almost gasped.

"Did you like it?"

The teenager shook her head.

"No, Miss Stanwyck, it wasn't plausible. Executives don't act that way. I'm a secretary for one of them back home in Chicago, so I kind of know."

The young ladies got their autographs and thanked Miss Stanwyck graciously. "God bless you, kids," Barbara said, and the trio left. My companion looked at me.

"Well, I asked for it, didn't I? I had a point, though. That's one thing I like about today's kids. They'll spot fakery every time and don't hesitate to call their shots. That script *was* phony and I knew it then."

Then she smiled again.

"I hope you didn't mind the interruption; I didn't. When they stop asking me for my autograph then I'll fold my tent, but meanwhile I love it and won't pretend I don't."

While we were on the subject of youth, I asked Barbara what she thought of the recent crop of X-rated films.

"I detest them; they're for *voyeurs* only. If there's any sex around, I want to enjoy it as a participant; sex just ain't a spectator sport. But I do believe there's going to be a change in the trend once the limit's been reached. The public finally will put an end to them; it always does when it gets weary of something. I've been around Hollywood for a long, long time, you know, and I've seen this happen before."

Indeed, Miss Stanwyck has been around Hollywood for a long, long time, and in the entertainment world even longer.

"I'm an old broad," she told Ezra Goodman of the New York *Times*, and this was back in 1965.

Barbara was born in Brooklyn, July 16, 1907, and, as far as I know, never tried to conceal either damaging fact. Her name at birth was Ruby Stevens. Legend has it that Willard Mack, the playwright and producer for whom Ruby was working, thought this wouldn't look good on a marquee. He happened to spy on the wall of a theater in which Miss Stevens was playing an old handbill reading: "Willard Mack presents Jane Stanwyck in *Barbara Frietchie*." He turned to his eighteen-year-old ingénue and said, "Hello, Barbara Stanwyck."

It's not impossible that there is a modicum of truth in this one, even if a number of "authorities" have substituted Buck Mack for Willard Mack, thus downgrading the tale. Buck was an old-time song-and-dance man who played Keith's subway circuit and frequently was on the same bill with Ruby Stevens. It doesn't really matter much which (if any) reason you believe.

Barbara began her career at the age of fifteen or thereabouts as a dancer in New York's nightclubs. Shortly after, she went on the Keith circuit, then got into the Ziegfeld Follies' chorus. A few walk-ons followed; then came her big chance, the starring role in Arthur Hopkins' hit play *Burlesque* which opened at New York's Plymouth Theater in 1927. A year later Barbara went to Hollywood and has been there ever since.

Her first film, *Locked Door*, bombed, and Barbara's contract was dropped. Then Frank Capra starred her in his enormously successful 1930 movie, *Ladies of Leisure*, and Barbara was on her way. Five years later she was getting fifty thousand dollars for a picture. I need not point out that in 1935 fifty thousand dollars was a hell of a lot of money; for most of us, I guess it still is.

In the intervening years, and until she went into TV because she wanted to work, and she says she couldn't get a job in the Industry, Barbara has made more than ninety major films, including such box-office successes as *So Big, The Bitter Tea of General Yen, Annie Oakley, Stella Dallas, Two Mrs. Carrolls, B. F.'s Daughter, Sorry, Wrong Number, Double Indemnity, There's Always Tomorrow, Walk on the Wild Side,* and *The Night Walker.*

Despite all this, and considering the fact that with Crawford, Wayne, Davis, and a few others, she's one of Hollywood's true "survivors," Barbara never has won an Academy Award. That, many of those in the Industry say, is a rank injustice. Herb Golden says it's "dirty pool."

Barbara's been married twice, the first time to Frank Fay, the Broadway star whom I remember best for the role he played in *Harvey*, the show, not the movie, which substituted James Stewart for Fay. Fay died of acute alcoholic poisoning. Miss Stanwyck's second marriage was to the late Robert Taylor, whom she divorced and who subsequently remarried. The latter's name was mentioned only in passing, although I got the feeling she still cared deeply for this onetime matinee idol who died only a few years ago of cancer attributed to excessive smoking.

We also talked about Hollywood's future, which Barbara claims there isn't much of.

"We're going to have to adjust to the cold, bloody, unsentimental world of television. The majors and all they offered—protection, *esprit de corps*, and all the other wonderful fringe benefits—have gone or are fading away, one by one. At best they're folding in what was left of their glory. At worst they're being absorbed by janitor-supply companies, car-rental agencies, or glorified gasoline salesmen."

Her smile was bitter.

"I was at the 'Farewell Dinner' they gave Jack Warner recently. It wasn't funny, but I laughed when he talked about Warner Brothers' past and wound up saying, 'Someday somebody's going to have to figure out a way to give a farewell dinner to a conglomerate.'"

She was thoughtful for a moment.

"I wouldn't want to leave you under the impression that all was fun at the majors. It sure wasn't. We worked very hard, got up at six A.M., and frequently worked right through until ten o'clock at night. But if you're a pro you do it and you don't complain, and I'm not complaining now, believe me. That's part of those 'good old days,' too.

"I can't say television is any easier. If you take your job seriously, in fact, it can be considerably tougher. When we

204

were shooting *The Big Valley*, I had to get up long before dawn to get to the studio by five A.M., when we started. But there are none of those pleasant fringe benefits the major moving picture studios offered; they just don't exist for TV. Damned little glamor, I can assure you. But I was performing, that's what I want to do, and, besides, they pay you well for your efforts."

She sighed.

"The old niceties they practiced at M-G-M, Warners, and Fox and all the others were pleasant but they weren't important. What was and *is* important is acting. I've a word of advice for those who fail to see what's been happening. 'When the dynasty falls, adjust. Don't let *your* head fall, too.'"

The word "pro" and Miss Stanwyck's obvious admiration for all who fall into that category kept cropping into much of the actress' conversation. Howard W. Koch, somewhat of a professional himself, told me that Barbara is known as the most dependable actress in the entire Industry.

"When she says she'll be where her director wants her to be, wherever it is, he can count on it, right on the button. And she'll know her lines, too, no fumbling. She sets one hell of a good example."

There's another story about Barbara, one which has been going the rounds out in Hollywood for years and is part of the Stanwyck legend. During the production of *Annie Oakley*, Miss Stanwyck, its star, was thrown from her horse but refused to leave the set until she completed the scene. Then she collapsed and was taken to the hospital where doctors discovered she'd broken her leg.

No breath of scandal ever touched Barbara's life, nor did she permit studio p.r. men to create synthetic romances for her.

"My private life is my own," she said. "It's *completely* private; it always was and it always will be, even if I live to be a hundred."

A fairly thorough combing of scores of movie fan magazines

which used to clutter the newsstands (and are now largely replaced for better or worse by soft- and hard-core pornography) reveals only an occasional attempt to tie Miss Stanwyck to her male co-star of a forthcoming production. This actress must have been anathema to the Warner Brothers' department of public relations.

Even when she went through one divorce with Frank Fay and two with Robert Taylor, the press found little pay dirt in court proceedings since neither gentleman spoke disparagingly about his libelant. From an anticipated overkill of juicy fan-mag fodder, only a few items appeared in the press. These concerned custody of the Fays' adopted son, Dion, whom the judge finally awarded to Miss Stanwyck with visitation rights for the father.

Loyalty is another quality Barbara possesses, according to those who've been in or around the Industry. Jim Tully, the well-known novelist of the late twenties and thirties who used to do a frequent hack piece for the fan mags when he was broke, which was often, once wrote, "Barbara Stanwyck is a one-man woman in a five-man town."

Barbara led our conversation back to TV and *The Big Valley*, her last important role, and one which survived fierce competition for four seasons from 1965 through 1968, until Nielsen and the other ratings killed it the following year.

"I talk about television a lot because of course you know it's the only hope Hollywood has. There's no basic difference between talents required for the movies and for television. In fact, the latter medium is considerably harder; don't let anybody kid you otherwise. For example, the TV director has only four days to prepare everything, and I include scouting for location.

"God knows it wasn't that way in the old days when time didn't matter. Then time was your friend; on TV it's your enemy; the pressures are tremendous. They may even be worse for me. I'm the kind of actress who has to memorize the whole damned script before we even start shooting and I have to sit up all night studying. I simply can't work otherwise, learning my lines in bits. It's damned back- and mind-breaking work. The trouble with so many of my colleagues, the ex-stars I mean, who keep harping on the way things used to be and actually look at TV with secret envy, is that they're just too goddamned lazy. They had it so good with the major studios they've forgotten how to work, that is, if they ever knew.

"Another trouble with television, so far at any rate, is, except for a gifted few, it hasn't attracted enough good writers. I don't know why, it certainly pays well. Hollywood no longer is important; you can make films all over the world. But writers *are* important and without them you're dead. The writer is the real structure and, even if you could somehow resurrect Duse or Bernhardt, their pictures would bomb; the stories, in the eyes of today's audiences, are awful."

Barbara admitted she'd counted a great deal on *The Big Valley*'s success.

"I knew the medium well, I'd guest-starred lots of times with Jack Benny and Joey Bishop, in *Rawhide*, with Bob Stack in *The Untouchables*, and a lot of others. I even had my own show for one disastrous season, ten years or so ago.

"I get lots of scripts all the time and I'd been reading them carefully trying to find one I liked. *The Big Valley* was it. I needed a part without romance—after all, I'm past sixty and I doubt that I'm the lover type anymore."

She smiled.

"I mean, if I ever was. I liked *Big Valley*'s story line and I just hoped it would hang on for a respectable five years. As you know, it missed. The reviews when we premiered weren't too bad, were they?"

I noted the disappointment in Barbara's voice. The fact that the series lasted as long as it did could hardly be attributed to the New York *Times* review of the show's premiere.

Anything *Bonanza* can do, *The Big Valley* would like to do better, which is not too likely. Miss Stanwyck is cast as the matriarch of the Barkley family, living in California in the

1870s. The entourage includes three sons of her own and an additional masculine offspring resulting from her late husband's broadmindedness. Indeed, the weakness of the flesh is acknowledged in the show with a candor that could make interesting conversation in some viewing homes.

But if compassion for illegitimacy is TV's latest twist, the show is not without conventional problems. The premiere was too crowded with a plot about the nasty railroad, uprooting settlers in the San Joaquin Valley. And the heirs of the versatile sire looked and acted so much alike that on the basis of a single viewing it was difficult for a viewer to keep a coherent scorecard. The Barkleys will need a while to get adjusted before one can judge whether they have opened a viable annex to the Ponderosa of the Cartwrights on *Bonanza*.

The public, at least that portion of the population which watches television as much if not more than once went to the movies—just because it's there—as usual paid scant attention to the *Times* or other newspaper critics.

"I'll tell you one important factor in presenting a finished TV product, and why some of them I've seen look raw," Miss Stanwyck said, and I think she was referring to a few members of her original *Big Valley* cast. "You've got to give your all during rehearsals, something those damned non-pros can't be convinced of. I do. True, I may not shed as many tears in a rehearsal as in the actual shooting. You've got just so many tears to shed, but otherwise I give it my all.

"Talk to any of us 'old survivors,' John Wayne, Eddie Robinson, for example [I did, a few days later], and you'll discover we all operate in the same fashion. To us a rehearsal has meaning; we're not there merely to fill in time and get paid for it.

"I told you this before, and I'll tell it to you again. Good, professionally produced TV shows, whether it's pay-TV or the other kind doesn't matter, are Hollywood's only hope. But shoddy, inept direction, poor scripts, and actors unwilling or unable to take their jobs seriously, working only for what they can get out of them, are killing this last potential. And it's a damned shame because many of the finest craftsmen in the world are still around this town—actors, producers, directors, and technicians, the true professionals. They're waiting to go to work and give everything they've got.

"Before you go back east, try to catch a TV rehearsal, the right kind, I mean. If there's a good director and a competent cast, you'll know what I've been talking about and where Hollywood's future, if any, lies. Let me know if you have any trouble getting into one and I'll try to work out something for you."

As we arose from our seats, an elderly couple approached Miss Stanwyck. The gentleman had a pad in his hand and asked for the actress' autograph.

"We're lucky, Miss Stanwyck," the lady gushed. "We've been here for almost a week and you're the first star we saw in person."

"We're extra lucky," her escort said. "You played the lead in the best movie I ever saw."

Barbara smiled.

"What was that?"

"*Double Indemnity*. I'm a retired insurance agent and I *know* when a person's faking. And you sure acted natural in that picture."

Chapter Twenty-Two

ALTHOUGH I'M sure she meant it, I didn't have to ask Miss Stanwyck for help to arrange for my admission to a TV rehearsal. This was a good one put on by such professionals as Maurice Evans, Dean Jagger, and Glenn Ford, all of whom were familiar names to me and I'm sure to most of the public. Their director, a former Philadelphian named Paul Wendkos, is one of the new breed of TV directors, and at about forty-five seems to be able to bridge the gap between the movie capital as it once was and the Hollywood of the present, and possibly the future. Incidentally, he is convinced there is a future for Hollywood.

I reached Wendkos through Glenn Ford and I reached Ford through Harrison Carroll, the nationally syndicated movie columnist who retired a few years ago after covering the Hollywood beat since 1923 for Hearst and King Features, the Los Angeles *Times*, the Los Angeles *Herald Examiner*, and the Central Press Association.

"I was getting a little old, I guess," Carroll said, "but that's not the main reason I called it quits. It was just getting too damned tough to fill a daily column, let alone five a week. Nothing going on out here anymore."

He shook his head sadly.

"I knew them all, from Gish to Gable and lots of the ones who followed—Paul Newman, Rock Hudson, Joanne Woodward, Loretta Young, and the rest. But after I retired only one of them ever came to see me or even ask how I was doing. These were the same actors whose press agents used to give me handouts all the time and plead for space in my columns for their clients. And many of the clients themselves were after me constantly, pretending we were close friends."

Naturally I asked who the one exception was; Carroll didn't hesitate to inform me.

"Glenn Ford. He never fails to give me a ring and ask how I'm doing and how things are going for me. One of the kindest, nicest, most decent guys you'll ever meet. And a hell of a good actor, too. He's one who made the transition from moving pictures to television with ease. If there's any hope for Hollywood's future—and I doubt that—it's with performers like Glenn.

"If you want to see what's going on now, watch Glenn work out. Call him up, I'll give you his number. You tell him I said it was O.K."

It was O.K., Ford told me, and, if I didn't mind sitting around the set for an extra hour or two, he'd be glad to talk to me between scenes. I answered that I didn't mind at all, so he said he'd leave a pass for me at the CBS Studio City gate the following morning at nine o'clock. Next to John Wayne, Glenn Ford happens to be a favorite actor of my grandson, Patrick. Pat went mad over *The Courtship of Eddie's Father* in which Ford starred. In fact, we stayed to see the picture twice, making this somewhat of a sacrifice for me because the theater was playing a sort of double feature and the top (or lower) half of the bill was a half-dozen assorted Woody the Woodpecker cartoons. I'm rather fond of Woody but twelve of his pictures in a single sitting is a bit much.

Naturally I was pleased to be welcomed by Glenn Ford, but the truth is I'd have much preferred to be welcomed by his ex-wife, Eleanor Powell, the beautiful, long-legged tap dancer of the 1930s. As Dave Friedman would have expressed it, "She turned me on." While I'm at it, I confess to two major disappointments during my last Hollywood hegira, and not seeing Miss Powell was one of them. It wasn't for lack of effort, though. I knew she'd staged an unsuccessful comeback several years ago in a Las Vegas saloon, but no one I asked seemed to know where she'd gone from there and she's no longer even listed in the *Motion Picture Almanac*.

I cannot imagine anyone caring very much about learning what my second disappointment was but, in order to dispel even the illusion of secrecy, I will name him. It was Joe Venuti, the greatest hot fiddler in the world. I consider his rendition of "The Hot Canary" comparable, if not superior, to anything Elman, Heifetz, or Menuhin ever assayed. I used to play a fairly hot fiddle myself, and once I worked with the Scranton Sirens, so I consider myself somewhat of an expert in that field. A friend of mine told me Joe was performing at the Ambassador Hotel, but I was misinformed. Joe wasn't there or, as far as I could determine, anywhere else in Los Angeles, so I gave up the search, albeit reluctantly.

Glenn Ford is one of the people you have to like right away. I can't imagine anyone being envious of his ability to remain fully employed in Hollywood since 1935, an achievement only a few fellow survivors can honestly claim. I make this statement without prejudice since I never was a Ford fan—Glenn, Ernie, Edsel, or Henry.

Glenn was born in Quebec, Canada, but I don't know when, although my guess is somewhere around 1915, give or take a couple of years. A high percentage of the one hundred thirty films in which he played are Westerns and his serious mien, firm jaw, bright blue eyes, quick draw, and rapid disposal of "baddies" are well known to three generations of American movie-goers and TV viewers. He's never won an Academy Award although many critics say he should have gotten one for his fine performance in *The Blackboard Jungle*, a message picture which also happened to make money.

Reviews of *The Blackboard Jungle* were excellent and Ford won considerable praise for his acting.

> Evan Hunter's *The Blackboard Jungle,* which tells a vicious and terrifying tale of rampant hoodlumism and criminality among the students in a large city vocational training school, was sensational and controversial when it appeared as a novel last fall. It is sure to be equally sensational and controversial now that it is made into a film.
>
> . . . In telling how one young teacher (Ford) goes into a vocational school and pits himself against a classroom full of nothing less than hoarse and heartless "hoods," this picture begins with the feeling that the classroom is a bloody battleground, and then proceeds to present a series of episodes that bear out this grim anxiety.

This was my initial visit to the old Republic Studios which used to turn out nothing but "B" pictures. Its new owner, CBS, is maintaining the tradition for television viewing. There are occasional exceptions to this rule of mediocrity or worse and Paul Wendkos, with the aid of a first-rate cast, a good script, and a million-dollar budget, hoped to be making one of them.

Glenn Ford was busy on the set when I arrived, but he'd left word and a lot cop escorted me to the stage where *Brotherhood of the Bell* was being made. I was stationed in the midst of cables, cameras, and crews, and, after being warned not to move an inch, watched my host, Dean Jagger, and Maurice Evans get a workout ten feet away at a simulated press conference. A megaphoneless Paul Wendkos sat nearby quietly giving directions. Since I wasn't briefed beforehand I didn't understand what the hell the plot was all about and I never did learn exactly, but I gathered it had something to do with a secret right-wing organization preparing to take over the country. The portion I watched didn't appear to be a bit far-fetched, unfortunately.

I know so little about film production, I wouldn't dare offer an opinion as to the quality of direction, acting, or the camera work I saw. All I know is that everyone involved seemed to do his job efficiently, without displays of temperament and, in short order, following a couple of retakes, the scene was completed to the director's satisfaction.

Ford walked off the set, saw me standing by, introduced me to his colleagues, then led me to a temporarily unused set where he poured coffee for each of us.

"I'm not in the next scene," he said, "so we'll have at least a half-hour. If you've got the time you can watch us do another one, and then I'll come back and we can talk some more."

I nodded and Glenn (you reach a first-name basis with him immediately) gave me a canvas chair with "Director" stenciled on the back and he sat in another which I noted was labelled "Glenn Ford." He looked at the printing a little self-consciously, then grinned.

"They used to do this all the time in the old days, but I didn't ask them to do it here," he said, and I believed him. Ford seems to have no affectations.

"How'd you like what you just saw?" he asked, and I answered noncommittally.

He smiled.

"I didn't expect an expert opinion. Harrison Carroll told me you're an ex-newspaperman and this was your first visit to Hollywood."

I nodded. He was right on the first count, but I didn't bother to correct him on the second.

"I don't want to put you on the spot," he continued. "What I really wanted to ask you was if you realized that the scene you just saw shot was done in less than an hour. In the old days it probably would have taken a day.

"Currently, with modern techniques we can make a good full-length television feature in around five weeks and it'll have the same quality which used to take the majors one hundred twenty to one hundred fifty days of shooting to produce. The point is we're in a new media and we're not hidebound by studio tradition. We have directors and producers who aren't afraid to experiment; they've got the courage to do it."

He paused.

"Do you understand what I mean?"

I told him I wasn't quite sure; he explained.

"I guess what I'm trying to say is that this new crop of directors, fellows like Wendkos, allow an actor the luxury of imperfection. Here's an example. Suppose the scene calls for me to light a cigarette. I strike a match and it doesn't flicker the first time, so I try again. At Columbia or Warners, or any of the majors where I used to work, the scene would have to be shot all over again until the match flared on my first attempt.

"But not on television, which figures life isn't perfect either and it just *might* take me two strikes to light the match. So the scene is played out with no retake for my imperfection. On the majors it used to happen all the time—things like the match failure. There's a constant striving for bigger-than-life perfection, a sort of unreality which has no relation to things as they truly are."

He shook his head.

"And the shocking extravagance! The wasted footage! Scenes, well done, tossed to hell for a normal 'mistake' which would have added to the picture's sense of reality instead of detracting from it."

This time I knew exactly what Ford was talking about. I remembered looking at a whole series of these "luxuries of imperfections" one evening a long while back. One of these practically duplicated the story Glenn had just told me. This must have been in the early fifties when McCarthyism was poisoning the country and Canada Lee, the great Negro actor, couldn't get work because he was on the producers' blacklist. The accusation, by the way, was completely false; Lee was totally apolitical. The late senator figures in my story only because it was in Canada's apartment where these very funny clips were shown.

Lee lived in a railroad flat, the rooms, seven or eight of them, stretched out like cars on a passenger train so that you couldn't get from one to the other without walking through the room that adjoined it. The place occupied half of an upper floor in an old red-brick building which once stood on Sixth Avenue in the Fifties. The furnishings must have come from the secondhand salesrooms of the Salvation Army or Volunteers of America.

As I recall, except for Canada's living quarters, the rest of the space in the building was occupied by small and possibly shady businesses—massage parlors, carnival supply houses, numismatists who probably dealt in counterfeit coins, public stenographers no doubt with skills other than shorthand and typing. I used to be fascinated by the names and occupations listed on the building's directory while I'd wait in the dimly lit lobby for Canada or one of his guests to come down for me in the elevator, the operator of which had long since gone off duty.

I don't know who paid his rent—Canada was broke most of the time—but I suspect the money came from Tallulah Bankhead, with whom the Negro actor played in the film *Lifeboat*. I was aware that Miss Bankhead had great respect and sympathy for Lee and tried to get him work, but the pressures against him were so great she couldn't. I'd met Canada a few years before when I helped with the publicity of an unsuccessful Broadway play, *On Whitman Avenue*, in which Lee starred.

At any rate, on the evening I'm talking about there were seven or eight of us gathered in the Sixth Avenue apartment. An actress, Ruth Mundy, Herb Golden and his wife Trudy, and a couple of others whose names escape me, were there. There wasn't anything stronger than coffee in Lee's apartment. Canada, who used to box professionally, never touched the stuff himself and, for reasons which I discovered later, didn't even like to see it around. So if any of his guests wanted a drink, he'd have to get it in the Great Northern Hotel bar across the street. But the building's elevator situation made this too much of an effort except for one whose thirst was overpowering.

About ten o'clock that very stuffy, warm July evening—naturally there was no air-conditioning in the apartment—I decided I had to have a cold glass of beer and, with Miss Mundy, who felt the same way, descended to the lobby, there to be greeted by Al Capp, the cartoonist, on his way up to Lee's apartment. He knew where *we* were headed.

"Don't go," he urged. "Come up with me. I brought a whole bunch of cutting-room clips and some of them are hilarious."

So Ruth and I decided to forgo the beer and rode back to the apartment. Herb set up Lee's projector and the rest of us sat back to watch. The first clip flashed on the screen was a military session depicting James Stewart, in a high-ranking air-force uniform, briefing a group of serious-looking fliers on a mission they were about to undertake. Stewart, a long wooden pointer in his hand, was showing his pilots, bombardiers and navigators their targets for the night on a large wall map.

They all looked so brave it was quite disillusioning to see the heroes leap from their chairs and scream with fright when the map suddenly snapped closed and twisted around the roller, knocking the general's briefing stick right out of his hand. There was another short clip—none of them ran for more than half a minute—this one showing Jean Harlow in a scene with Wallace Beery. As I recall, the picture was *Grand Hotel*, but I wouldn't swear to it. Beery is leaning over the partially clad Miss Harlow who is in bed.

"For Christ's sake, Wally," Miss Harlow shrieks, "button your fly, will you? Your dingus is showing."

There were dozens of clips gathered over the years from cutting-room floors, but the one apropos of Glenn Ford's story about lighting a match on the first try comes from another war picture. What it was I no longer remember. The clip involved a young blonde actress whose name I've forgotten, and a handsome youth whose name I never did know. The young man is in uniform and the young lady is bidding him farewell before he's off to the war. She looks wistfully into his eyes and says, "Let's have one last cigarette together," and he offers her one from a pack.

Togetherness is what she really means, because it looks as though she intends to share the single cigarette with her boyfriend. With his one free arm—the other is draped around the girl's shoulders—he reaches into his pocket again and removes a silver lighter. With a sophisticated gesture he flicks the wheel, but either the instrument is out of fluid or the flint is no good and nothing happens.

Considerably abashed, he tries again, although you can see the young girl is getting impatient; her bust is beginning to heave in anger. When, on the second try, he fails again, in fury she wriggles her shoulders free from the youth's arms, grabs the lighter from his hand, hurls it to the ground, smacks his face, and screams, "You stupid son-of-a-bitch!"

I don't know whether Glenn would have been willing to apply his "luxury of imperfection" theory to this situation, but, since I was interviewing him and not the other way 'round, I didn't say anything about Al Capp's cutting-room clippings. Should he ever read these lines, he's welcome to let me know then.

I watched Glenn and the others do another scene which certainly didn't take more than an hour to complete. Then Ford came back for some more talk.

"I guess you've been hearing talk all over that Hollywood is dead without hope for a future."

I nodded. Glenn shook his head thoughtfully.

"Maybe not. There's a good chance it's going to stage a comeback of sorts. Not like it used to be of course—the majors as they were constituted are gone forever and so is the star system. But I don't think Hollywood's gone beyond resuscitation. The shot in the arm, or artificial respiration, or whatever you want to call it, may very well come from pay-TV, and that's what a lot of people out here are hoping.

"But whoever's going to make the grade in the future will

have to be aware that you can no longer fool the public. People have been becoming more and more sophisticated as the years go by. Let me give you an example of what I mean. Say there's got to be a shot beneath the Arc de Triomphe. This one *must* be authentic and to do it authentically you must shoot it on location. Too many potential viewers have been there and they'll know if you're faking.

"However, when the hero moves from the Arc to a bistro, then it should be done in Hollywood where you have more control. That's what I mean. And this is going to come about, you mark my words. Part of the films will be done on the spot and part will be done in Hollywood."

He shrugged his shoulders.

"I'm not saying this is going to come tomorrow or the next day; it may take as long as five or even ten years, and meanwhile an awful lot of S.A.G. members are going to be out of work. The sad part is that a good many of them, and I won't mention names, could be working now in television but they think it's beneath their dignity.

"Believe me, and I'm not being boastful, I could go to work on feature films any time I wanted to. I'm referring to those which are shown in moving picture theaters. But I actually prefer television; it's so far ahead of the old-time studio films, you can't imagine unless you've done both, and God knows I have.

"They'll still make a few big-budget pictures out here and some of them, like *Airport*, are going to make money, but most of them will not. At last, I believe, the majors learned their lessons although you never can tell for certain. But what they found out came too late and not many banks are willing to gamble ten million bucks anymore."

He left me for a couple of minutes and returned with a fresh pot of coffee, filled my cup and his, then went on.

"It takes an awful lot of guts to produce a picture, that is, if you're thinking of costs and want to keep them under control. You're always fighting the battle between making the scene as

219

good as possible and then again settling for less because of the money involved in retakes. I know because I produced a feature film some time back. It was from a Runyon story called *A Pocketful of Miracles*. Turned out all right, financially at any rate, even if it didn't break any records.

"But it was like sitting in a big-stakes poker game, holding three aces and willing to draw for the fourth. But *not* like willing to draw to an inside straight, if you know what I mean. Of course, a hell of a lot of producers and directors don't care how much their pictures cost. They're not spending their own money so they can laugh at runaway budgets. As for me, I'll stick to acting."

He smiled.

"Funny thing is I never consider what I'm doing to be work, and I'm constantly amazed that I get paid for it. You have to pay five bucks an hour to ride a horse in the valley and here they pay me to ride one. It's damned nice. And I'm crazy about working and living in Hollywood, too. I don't want to make my home base anywhere else in the world. I've had it up to the ears making pictures all over the world."

A few months ago when Ford was in Philadelphia promoting *Brotherhood of the Bell,* he told Rex Polier of the *Evening Bulletin* he never intended to travel again except for pleasure.

"I've been home in California only four months a year for the past ten. I finally have decided I want to stay home even though I'm not married. I have friends and I have a son, and that's the way I want it."

There was another intermission while Glenn and Jagger met for a brief conference with Wendkos. Then Ford continued.

"I really like to work for this new crop of directors, fellows like Wendkos who were able to make the transition from movies to television. And mostly we all cooperate with them because they know their stuff."

He sighed.

"But don't think I didn't love the old breed just as well. I still have stars in my eyes for Bette Davis, Joan Crawford, Fredric March, and all the other greats. They were wonderful in their day, too, and I don't forget it."

Somebody called a two-hour break; Glenn had some business to attend to in town; Jagger and Evans said good-bye to me and went off somewhere, and Wendkos asked me to join him for a sandwich and a glass of beer in a restaurant around the corner from the studio.

Chapter Twenty-Three

You NEED a tape recorder or a working knowledge of shorthand to conduct an interview with Paul Wendkos. I never could conquer the mechanics of the former and haven't tried the latter skill since high school. Consequently, I'm afraid I missed much of what was said by this ebullient, enthusiastic, and articulate gentleman. According to Wendkos, himself, and a claim made also by those who work with him, this director represents a new school of movie making and, given the opportunity, will bring back to Hollywood a fair portion of her former glory.

In the opinion of such experts as Glenn Ford, Dean Jagger, and Maurice Evans, Wendkos has the talent, vitality, and creativity necessary for the revival of the world's erstwhile movie capital. But, as Wendkos said, "Hollywood won't be run the way they once ran it."

Many, including one of the medium's earliest critics, Harry Harris, who, God help him, has been looking at television some six hours a day, seven days a week for the past twenty years, beg to disagree. But, of this fault-finding, captious or justifiable, more later. Meanwhile, for the benefit of S.A.G. members, as well as other unemployed Hollywood movie makers who some day expect to get off relief rolls and go to work again and are counting on Wendkos to perform that miracle, I present the "Wendkos Story." I will thus let his potential beneficiaries decide whether to stick it out a while longer or start looking for jobs in more secure fields.

There wasn't any opportunity for me to speak with either Jagger or Evans for more than a minute but, while they were waiting for a car to take them into Los Angeles and I was waiting for Wendkos, I asked each actor how he felt about working on television. I already knew what Ford believed. Jagger answered first.

"It's satisfying when you've a director of Wendkos' caliber. He knows exactly what he wants and, furthermore, how to get it with a minimum of confusion or delay and he gives an actor a chance to expand. Paul's got some fine ideas on how a film should be made, and he's not afraid to experiment."

Jagger has been in almost as many pictures as Ford or anyone else in the Industry for that matter, and he was a 1949 Academy Award Winner for his supporting role in *Twelve O'Clock High*, so his opinion should carry weight. As for Evans, he'd spent only a few hours on *Brotherhood of the Bell* and had not known its director beforehand.

"I can tell you this, sir," the British actor said, "the man has quality; you sense it at once. I think it's going to be a privilege to work with him." As an internationally famous actor who achieved great success on the stage, in the movies, and on television, his opinion of Wendkos must be considered important. As for myself, I admit freely I'd never heard of Wendkos, although I saw and liked *Gidget*, a picture he made in 1959 for Columbia with Sandra Dee and Cliff Robertson in starring roles.

Because of Wendkos' potentials in the Industry, plus the fact that CBS chose him to direct its first million-dollar-budgeted television film, I report briefly on what three leading critics had to say about *Gidget*.

Variety said:

A class teen-age comedy in which the kids are, for once, healthy and attractive young people instead of in some phase of juvenile depravity. . . . Direction is ingenious in delineating the youthful characters, not so easy in presenting normal youngsters of no particular depth or variety. Direction could have been more fluid, however, particularly in the musical numbers. . . .

"For what it is, easy entertainment for the younger set, it is uncomplicated, frisky, and reasonably diverting," declared the New York *Herald Tribune.* The New York *Times* reported the film as "a mild little frolic. . . . Has a relaxed air befitting its nice young people and some random, knowing observations about growing up . . ."

We talked about *Tarawa Beachhead*, another of Wendkos' successes, albeit less so than *Gidget.* This was a semi-documentary of the United States Marine's invasion of Guadalcanal. Wendkos made it for Columbia using a little-known cast.

"I didn't have much money to work with," he said, "so I had to improvise. For example, we shot most of it on a couple hundred square feet on the studio back lot. We created the illusion of being on the beach by carefully integrating stock footage. I used the same technique when I directed *Battle of the Coral Sea.*"

In its November 5, 1958, issue, *Variety* said in its review of *Tarawa Beachhead:*

Wendkos emphasizes the action, properly so, to hold interest, but he is also adept at making the story's thought content palatable.

Wendkos' first film was a documentary about Matthew Brady, based on the works of the famed Civil War photographer. Among other credits are *The Burglar,* made on the streets of his native Philadelphia, *The Case Against Brooklyn,* and *Angel Baby.* The last-named film opened simultaneously in many of New York City's neighborhood theaters on October 5, 1961, as part of a double bill.

Neither *The Burglar* nor *The Case Against Brooklyn* was deemed worthy of notice by any major critic, while *Angel Baby* was. This cast included two veterans of the Industry, Joan Blondell and Mercedes McCambridge, and a comparative newcomer, George Hamilton.

The New York *Times* said:

. . . the best of the players and the most interesting directorial job were in evidence in *Angel Baby*, but the film itself is only a cut-rate *Elmer Gantry*. It is mainly notable for the debut performance of Salome Jens, the strange and sensitive young actress who dazzled off-Broadway as the horse girl in *The Balcony*. Miss Jens plays a psychosomatic mute who is shocked into speech by a fervent young . . . evangelist. This odd event gives her the call to preach the gospel herself. . . .

As eccentrically directed by Paul Wendkos, the drama generates some excitement . . . but it ends in cheap contrivance when the disillusioned heroine performs a "real" miracle for an easy solution. A pair of vivid actresses, Joan Blondell . . . and Mercedes McCambridge, also do what they can to bring the script to life.

The other half of the double bill fared far worse. This one starred such stage and film notables as Joseph Schildkraut, Keenan Wynn, William Demarest, Mickey Rooney, Jack Carson, Dianne Foster, and a host of others.

"Unfortunately," said Eugene Archer of the New York *Times*, "the film is as long as its cast list, and Joseph Newman directed it with more force than style."

Wendkos is an interesting-looking man in his middle or late forties. He's slender and tall, at least six feet, and his forehead is high and crowned with a thick crop of gray hair. There's an intensity about him which is almost hypnotic; I had a hard time taking my eyes away from his long enough to reach for my glass of beer. My host drank nothing except coffee, and not even a full cup of that, and he took only a few bites out of his sandwich, so intent was he on showing me the reason for Hollywood's demise.

"The goddamned trouble with the majors was the stupidity of those fatheads who ran them, their entrenched methodology, their bureaucracy, and their unbending rigidity. The 'important' producers were—still are—old men who've lost touch with audiences and hadn't—still haven't—the slightest idea of what people want to see. It's as simple as that.

"I'll tell you something else which may or may not shock you. These foolish, extravagant old men never went to theaters that showed their films; they saw them only in their studios' screening rooms or in the privacy of their homes. So how in the hell would they know what the public was willing to buy or what it thought about products being turned out so profligately?

"I worked for them so I know whereof I speak. With few exceptions there was no *one* man to say *what* should be done. The entire Hollywood operation was based on the 'committee system.' "

Paul explained.

"This was how decisions were made. The whole hierarchy got together—producers, studio heads, everyone involved, and naturally a chorus of 'yes men.' Their role was important. The artistic director didn't have a chance; he had to please so many men with different senses of values, nothing really satisfactory could be worked out.

"What this meant was that the picture was reduced in strength to the lowest common denominator. The film was brutalized. It took a very powerful director with contractual strength to beat the system, and not many of them had it. Then, too, you had to contend with a philosophy of making motion pictures.

"For many years the studios equated excellence with size and not with value. Their reasoning—a ten-million-dollar picture was ten times as good as a million-dollar one. They were oriented to bigness and had been almost from their very conception. And the fools are still looking at feature films in the same myopic fashion.

"The ridiculous part of it all was that with the kind of operation they were doing, and the way they were handling films, they still made a lot of money. Sure, as long as there was no other form of mass entertainment they did better than just get by. Then along came television and they collapsed. The entire Industry fell apart at the seams."

He blew a long breath of air through his lips.

"When I think of the patronizing attitude the majors had toward television I could throw up. They regarded it as an interloper, and a temporary one at that; when the public realized television was a fraud, they told themselves and anybody else who would listen, all those nice people would start coming back to see *real* movies. Well, I don't have to tell you how wrong they were.

"What they didn't realize and never have is that this new medium offered something different in values. Not all TV is good, of course, and much of it is dreadful. One of the reasons for the medium's frequent failures is the director's inability to understand what he's doing. This applies particularly to those who've worked, and successfully, too, with the majors and have not been able to make the transition.

"They're still trying to make pictures the old-fashioned way, forgetting they no longer have a big screen on which to project. What they don't grasp is that television does its best when it deals with the character—the nuances of the actor's emotions. Because our screen is so small, we must concentrate on faces."

He paused for a moment.

"This is what gives quality to the medium—this concentration on character rather than setting. This is why directors such as Howard Koch and George Seaton, highly competent in the ancient Hollywood fashion—aren't going to make it in television. Their method and their methodology are antiquated.

227

"The old-time directors, those now in their sixties, even the giants who made memorable films in their day, have completely lost touch with their audiences. They, too, were oriented to bigness. They couldn't comprehend just why in 1969 alone there were ten successful pictures made, not one costing as much as a million dollars. *Midnight Cowboy* was one. I think great directors like Billy Wilder and Fred Zinnemann understand what it was all about and I don't doubt, given the chance, they'd have made the transition."

He took a few bites of his sandwich and a swallow of coffee, then went on.

"And the generation gap between Koch, Seaton, and company, and audiences is not only in content and methodology, but also in terms of the actor. The films they made were produced in what I can only say was a lethargic manner. Here's what I mean. It took ninety to one hundred twenty days of shooting to make these big-budget pictures. During this time the poor actor, whose adrenalin was up and ready to go, had to cool down and wait, and wait, and wait, while the technicians went to work on the lights and all the other things. This meant that for an interminable length of time the actor's emotions ran down. Consequently, the scenes became suffocatingly boring."

Wendkos smiled.

"It's as though the actor were a boxer who did his best fighting in the gym. Understand what I'm getting at?"

I nodded. Paul continued.

"Then along came television, and in this medium there's no need to let the actor's adrenalin fall. We've no complicated set of ancient rules, customs, and traditions to follow. And we don't have to work with Cecil B. De Mille's twenty thousand elephants. We're allowed to use our imagination and our skills. When you get that rare, wonderful script, actors are able to perform unbelievably well. Fine actors like those you just saw on the set—Evans, Ford, and Jagger—do marvelous jobs when they're given freedom to act.

"Glenn, as you know, has been around Hollywood for a

long time. The other afternoon he and I were talking about the rapidity with which *Brotherhood* was progressing. We covered seven pages of dialogue in a single day and I asked Glenn how long this would have taken to do in former years. His answer? At least two weeks—fourteen shooting days. There isn't an actor, no matter how great he is, who can sustain his emotions for that length of time."

He shook his head.

"Just compare the costs of what we're doing to what M-G-M, Fox, Warners, or any of the other majors would have spent to handle the same job. Chances are it wouldn't even be as good. Hollywood's potentials were once great; the tyranny of the executive suite with its self-righteous values and taste-lessness finally destroyed the Industry."

He frowned.

"And yet there is a chance for a Hollywood comeback. It's a marvelous place to work because here we have the greatest collection of moving picture technicians in the world. Given a chance to use their skills, anything can happen. I'm not referring to the majors—they're dead as the proverbial doornail. But good films for theater showing are going to be made out here; they'll be made in what I call 'accommodation' studios. And they'll be good because those who make them will have learned new skills through television.

"I'm not denying that much of the vast quantities of stuff now being shown on TV is utter crap and, if they're old-fashioned, they'll fail. This is a medium which can either teach you or obliterate your spirit. For a maverick like me, the only hope is pay-TV, and I think it's going to be here a lot sooner than anybody realizes. Then we'll be able to eliminate those awful ads which foul up everything. Now all we can do to counter them is try for six peaks, one before each scheduled interruption."

I think a couple of really trivial incidents I witnessed, one on the CBS lot and the other in the restaurant, are worth mentioning because they reveal something of the director's character, self-control, and patience. Copybooks from Mc-

Guffey to Dale Carnegie claim these qualities are the marks of successful men in every field, although I don't believe it. The only self-made multi-millionaire I know well is an impatient, irascible son-of-a-bitch with absolutely no control over his foul tongue or temper.

Well, so much for disbelief in my very own Establishment's tenets. I was standing in a corner of the studio watching them shoot *Brotherhood of the Bell* and saw Wendkos back off the set, turn around, and ram his shin into the sharp edge of a heavy glass-topped table a property man put there a few minutes before.

Had this happened to me, I know what I'd have said and I'm almost afraid to imagine how the villainous-tempered millionaire would have reacted. But all Paul did was wince, grit his teeth, limp over to a chair, pull up his trouser leg, and wipe off the blood with a handkerchief. Meanwhile, filming of *Brotherhood* proceeded without interruption.

Afterward, in the restaurant, our waiter didn't get one single thing right. First of all, he handed out breakfast instead of lunch menus and, apparently trusting to memory, wrote nothing down on his pad. He mixed up the orders completely, we had to ask him several times to bring us silverware, and finally he made a mistake on the check. He was a mean-looking bastard besides and I don't think I'd have left him more than a token tip. But Paul has more guts; he glanced at the check, pointed out an error made in the restaurant's favor, gave our waiter the cash and, while the latter watched greedily, Paul looked him right in the eye, counted the change carefully, then put every cent of it back into his pocket. That's character for you!

Some weeks later I watched the premiere television performance of *Brotherhood of the Bell*, which I enjoyed immensely. The following morning I read what my friend and fellow Philadelphian (Wendkos' as well) Harry Harris wrote in *TV Week*, a publication syndicated by the Knight chain of newspapers.

. . . *Brotherhood* was bizarre, but continuously interesting as it described the efforts of a member of a "WASP Mafia" (Glenn Ford) to break away from and expose the organization.

During the unequal contest—the covert *Brotherhood*, it was noted, *is* the Establishment—Dr. Andrew Patterson, a top researcher at the Institute for the Study of Western Civilization, lost his job, his father, his wife, and his reputation. His situation seemed hopeless until at the very close he thought of an effective ally.

The story required wholesale suspension of disbelief . . . but it was slickly told by Ford & Co., including Rosemary Forsyth, Dean Jagger, Maurice Evans, and William Conrad.

Harris is, in point of seniority, one of the oldest television reviewers in the world and is considered one of the most able. He is also a Founding Father of "Critics' Consensus," an organization comprised of approximately twenty of the nation's top professional television reviewers. Its purpose, Harry claims, is to improve the quality of the medium (obviously a hopeless task) and grant annual awards of merit for what members agree have been the four best TV productions of the year.

I was surprised to find no mention of *Brotherhood*'s director in Harry's critique. I managed to pry him away from his standard equipment of three screaming television sets long enough to ask why, and a couple of other questions besides. Naturally, I didn't dream of invading Harry's working hours; consequently, the interrogation took place after midnight when all three channels in my host's living room seemed to be showing Lana Turner movies on their late shows. Even so, it was hard to keep Harry's eyes from straying over to the trio of screens, although he said he had no intention of reviewing twenty-year-old films, one of which was an early Dr. Kildare. (I wondered if Lana, too, way out in her Beverly Hills home, was watching the same thing.)

231

"An occupational hazard," Harry admitted when I had to snap my fingers in order to get his exclusive attention.

"Why didn't I mention Wendkos' direction in my review?" he repeated and shrugged his shoulders. "I guess because I didn't think the direction deserved mention; it wasn't that good, you know."

Did Harry believe Wendkos had talent, creativity, and imagination sufficient to salvage what's left of Hollywood and bring the city back to its former glory? My host shook his head.

"Somebody's sold you a bill of goods, Art. Wendkos is quite a competent director—I'll say that—and he does melodrama extremely well, better than most. But you must remember that melodrama is not a serious art form, and Wendkos never has been able to reach beyond that.

"Sure, he's done quite a few good things in feature films— *Gidget*, for one—and even more for TV, the FBI series for example; they are tightly plotted and very well directed. However, he's never earned a Critics' Consensus Award; in fact, he's never even been nominated."

He grinned.

"You know, this reminds me of that hypothetical question they're always supposed to be putting to a gourmet after he's tasted some chef's *potage*. My answer about Wendkos is the same: 'It's a good soup, not a great one!'

"Not that there aren't some great ones around—directors with the potentials of bringing television to a high level of entertainment, and probably capable of making damned good feature films for theatrical presentation as well. John Frankenheimer is an example. Ever hear of him?"

I nodded. Only a week or so after I came east from Hollywood and was plugging a book on "Long John" Nebel's midnight to five A.M. talk show, I had a chance to talk to another guest, Khigh Dhiegh. Khigh was the villain in *The Manchurian Candidate*, which, among myriads of other subjects, we discussed. Dhiegh gave credit for the picture's success to John Frankenheimer, its director. I mentioned this to Harry.

"Well then," he said, "you've seen what John's capable of doing. He also directed *Birdman of Alcatraz* and *Seven Days in May*, to name only a few. But that was after he left TV where he did some first-class shows, many for "Studio One," "Playhouse Ninety," and "Sunday Showcase," almost invariably the best in the series. There's a guy you should have interviewed."

I'm sure I should have, but, even so, I'd probably find other TV "gourmets" who believe Frankenheimer is only "good soup."

"No!" my host continued, "if you're searching for a really 'hot shot' director, you'll have to look beyond Paul Wendkos."

I now quote from a column written by another member of the Critics' Consensus, Marvin May, one of Harry's distinguished colleagues of *TV Week*. It appeared August 8, 1971.

> The name may not be familiar to many TV viewers, but one of the hottest properties among Hollywood's directors-for-television-films these days is Paul Wendkos. A native Philadelphian and a graduate of the University of Pennsylvania, Wendkos is one of the most sought-after directors in Cinemaland. Even before finishing an ABC Movie of the Weekend: *A Little Game* (starring Ed Nelson and Diane Baker, it will be aired in the fall) at Universal, Wendkos had been signed by Metromedia to direct *A Tattered Web*, for the New CBS Friday Night Movies.

Like they say, "You pays your money and you takes your choice."

Chapter Twenty-Four

My FONDEST recollection of Edward G. Robinson is not his *Little Caesar*, whose hero I couldn't identify with, but the aging romantic in *Middle of the Night*. The first, a motion picture, I saw at the Strand Theater in New York in 1931 on our first wedding anniversary. A pair of tickets for the second, at Philadelphia's Locust Street Theater, was my wife's present on my fiftieth birthday, a quarter of a century later.

Both film and stage show were memorable occasions not merely because they represented highlights in my own life, but also because they were damned good entertainment and that's all I want, and seldom get, when I go to the theater or to the movies. I'd like to jog the minds of my contemporaries who may have forgotten what a truly great actor Edward G. Robinson was by quoting several professional opinions of the day.

This is what the New York *Times* critic Mordaunt Hall had to say about *Little Caesar* and why it became a movie classic:

> *Little Caesar*, based on W. R. Burnett's novel of Chicago gangdom was welcomed . . . by unusual crowds. The story

deals with the career of Cesare Bandello, alias Rico, alias Little Caesar, a disagreeable lad who started by robbing gasoline stations and soared to startling heights in his "profession" by reason of his belief in his high destiny.

The production is ordinary and would rank as just one more gangster film but for two things. One is the excellence of Mr. Burnett's credible and compact story. The other is Edward G. Robinson's wonderfully effective performance. Little Caesar became at Mr. Robinson's hands a figure out of Greek epic tragedy, a cold, ignorant, merciless killer, driven on and on by an insatiable lust for power, the plaything of a force that is greater than himself.

The film, incidentally, was directed by Mervyn LeRoy; others in the cast included Douglas Fairbanks, Jr., Glenda Farrell, Sidney Blackmer, and George E. Stone.

In the quarter of a century elapsing between *Little Caesar* and *Middle of the Night*, it is apparent from reviews of the latter show that Robinson had lost none of his skills, in fact, undoubtedly added to them.

"Robinson is superb," said Coleman in the New York *Mirror*.

"There is great tenderness in Edward G. Robinson's playing of the distraught lover. He succeeds in being deeply poignant without ever ceasing to be a figure of dignity and stature," said Watts in the New York *Post*.

"Mr. Robinson is precise, honest, warmly affecting. He gets an opportunity to do something he does almost better than any other working actor. It's a beautifully controlled, absolutely direct, performance," said Kerr, of the New York *Herald Tribune*.

Finally (well almost), "Mr. Robinson gives a winning and skillful performance. No one could give the character more warmth or tenderness," declared Atkinson of the New York *Times*.

Possessing a typical Quaker City sense of cultural inferiority, I don't suppose anybody elsewhere really cares that they loved Eddie Robinson in Philadelphia, too. Even so, I quote briefly from the *Inquirer*'s Martin.

"Mr. Robinson truly is one of America's great actors. His performance in *Middle of the Night* was superb."

And now, another fifteen years piled on top of that, I sat drinking Scotch-and-water with Edward G. Robinson in his Beverly Hills house, listening to this white-bearded gentle old man talk about *Little Caesar* and *Middle of the Night*, about his long and successful stage and movie careers, about the Industry and what it used to be like, about television, and about the future, his own and Hollywood's.

"I can go back much farther than *Little Caesar*, if you'd like." He puffed on his identifying cigar and his voice sounded like it always did, a clipped baritone which from one moment to the next can be pleasantly soft or turn into a harshly commanding bark.

"Ever see *East Is West*?"

I nodded.

"The stage show or the movie?"

"Both."

"I remember lines from the show. That was about 1920 or 1921; Fay Bainter played the lead. I thought then it might make a good movie; never dreamed I'd be in it, but I was, in 1930. Universal made it with Lupe Velez, Lew Ayres, and a Japanese actor named Tetsu Komai. I was San Francisco's chop suey king."

"Sure," I added. "You were Chollie Young."

"I was Chollie *Yang*," he corrected me with a smile.

" 'And nobody knows Chollie Yang like Chollie Yang.' I'm pretty sure I was in your hometown, Philly, on a promotion tour when the picture premiered. Stayed at the Bellevue, too."

I let pass the fact that my hometown is not "Philly," but a hard-coal-region city with the unpronounceable name of "Mahanoy." Instead, I complimented Eddie (he insisted at once that we address each other informally) for his excellent memory.

"Oh, I can do better than that."

He stood up and for the next ten or fifteen minutes he *was* Chollie Yang. When he sat down again I applauded.

"I may have missed a few words here and there, but no more than that, I'll bet you."

I wasn't in a position to question Robinson's claim or bet against him, but I'm sure I would have lost anyway.

"And how long ago did we say I saw Fay Bainter in *East Is West*? Fifty years, wasn't it. Not bad if I do say so myself. But I never did have trouble remembering my own lines and everybody else's besides. I had good training, you know.

"Started acting when I was only a kid, in vaudeville at that. I always loved the theater. Come to think of it, even before I acted I used to ring the curtain. I guess I must have done over a hundred movies and appeared in at least half that many stage shows ever since. Some were hits and, believe me, some weren't.

"One of the plays which wasn't, I wrote myself. It was called *The Bells of Conscience* and it was a big flop, or as they'd say these days, it bombed. I was at Townsend High School, or maybe I'd finished and was at CCNY then. Around 1914, when I was twenty-one, I was auditioned for the road company of *Kismet* when Otis Skinner gave notice. I got the part and played it until shortly before World War One."

He sighed.

"Man! That was a hell of a long time ago when you start thinking about it. The company folded and I went back to New York to finish my studies at CCNY and get my degree. But I lasted there only until my junior year; then I enrolled at the American Theater Academy. The war came along and I couldn't get an acting job so I went to Columbia, thinking I'd take some courses in pedagogy and teach literature at high school or college level.

"Teaching wouldn't have been too bad a profession; I

237

always liked it next to acting, but it was a very poor second. I was saved by the bell. Selwyn was casting for a show, *Under Fire*. I auditioned and got the part.

"I guess what shaped my future Hollywood career was acting in a sort of documentary play about crime in Chicago. Appropriately enough it was called *The Racket*. We played all over the lot, every major city except Chicago where Al Capone wouldn't let us in because the play was about him, and I suppose that's understandable.

"Come to think of it, I've never had any real trouble getting work. Maybe because I speak German and French and even a bit of cockney."

He laughed.

"And you just heard me speak Chinese. Maybe it was my linguistic ability that helped me along rather than the acting. I don't know. At any rate, I left Broadway for Hollywood in 1929.

"A couple of Hollywood producers saw *The Racket*, liked me, and offered me a part in a pretty bad movie called *The Hole in the Wall*. This was in 1929 and by that time I was thirty-six years old since I was born in 1893. I finished the film and went to San Francisco where I did repertory for ten weeks. I got called back to Hollywood by First National to do *The Widow from Chicago* for them."

He stroked his neatly trimmed beard.

"Seems like I'm always being identified with Chicago because the next role I got was in *Little Caesar*. An author named Bill Burnett wrote the book and the script as well."

I mentioned the fact that Burnett and I had adjacent studios at Paramount a few years back.

"It was a good book," Robinson went on. "Bill's a very able writer and, as you're aware, the picture was an enormous success; started a whole trend in the Industry. But in a sense it's haunted me ever since and, though I've had so many roles other than portraying gangsters, people still think of me as a cigar-smoking, cold-blooded, murderous racket chieftan. It's an easy character to impersonate so I'm always finding *Little*

Caesar included in the repertoire of half the TV and night-club comics."

He rolled the cigar over to one corner of his mouth, stared at me, then lapsed into a gangster vernacular and snarled, "O.K., you guys. I'm the boss around here, see!"

Robinson grinned.

"All kidding aside, *Little Caesar* was a good picture and one of the reasons was it had a good script. This is a problem actors must face—lack of artistic control over their lines. In other words, they don't get story approval.

"That's always bothered me. On the other hand there are methods, unofficial naturally, of getting what you want or eliminating what you don't. You just swing your weight around a bit at story conferences."

For Eddie Robinson this no doubt worked, but there are few American actors or actresses who can swing nearly as much weight as he could on Broadway, in Hollywood, or on television. For one thing, his screen credits are long and include such well remembered films as *Five Star Final, Kid Galahad, The Amazing Dr. Clitterhouse, Dr. Ehrlich's Magic Bullet, A Dispatch from Reuters, The Sea Wolf, Destroyer, Double Indemnity, Key Largo, The Glass Web, Cincinnati Kid,* and *A Boy Ten Feet Tall.* There are more than one hundred others. His last major film was *Song of Norway,* which was neither an artistic nor financial success.

With few exceptions, his stage performances have been in plays which ranged from moderately successful to smash hits. He appeared in *The Goat Song, Peer Gynt, Androcles and the Lion, The Brothers Karamazov, The Man with Red Hair,* and *Middle of the Night.*

"I had a marvelous part in that one," he said, referring to the last-mentioned play. "If you remember, it's the story of a middle-aged man who falls in love with a woman much, much younger than himself."

He smiled.

"And he marries her, too, against strong opposition."

Despite the fact that he never won an Academy Award

(except for a recent "honorary" one), other laurels Robinson collected over the years are impressive. Members of his own profession held him in high esteem and a couple of years ago he received the annual Screen Actors Guild award "for outstanding achievement in fostering the finest ideals of the acting profession."

The plaque was presented to Robinson by president Charlton Heston who might have added, but didn't, that the recipient was still one of the few S.A.G. members who could do the kind of work he wanted to whenever he wanted to, a statement which, unfortunately, Mr. Heston himself is unable to make.

Not too long ago, one of Robinson's alma maters, CCNY, honored him with a medal.

The New York *Times* said:

> Edward G. Robinson, famous for his gangster movie roles, yesterday played the cultured, college graduate before 150 City College students.
>
> However, he bowed to student demands for a glimpse of the tough, cigar-stomping Little Caesar.
>
> "So you want to be an actor?" he asked one sophomore, with a finger jab in the chest. "Well, stick to your schooling, kid."
>
> Mr. Robinson, who graduated from college in 1914, returned to accept the first James K. Hackett Medal for "excellence in oratory or drama." . . . The Hackett Medal is named after an 1891 graduate of the college, a Shakespearean actor at the turn of the century who founded the school's dramatic society.

In 1952, as a belated acknowledgment for his World War II efforts, the Republic of France made Robinson a *Chevalier de la Legion d'Honneur*, and in 1963 he received the National Humanitarian Award in Washington, D.C.

On December 17, 1968, five days after the actor's seventy-fifth birthday, twenty thousand men and women gathered in New York's Madison Square Garden to honor him at a sellout performance of the Hanukkah Festival for Israel Bonds.

"Congratulatory telegrams from President Johnson and Premier Levi Eshkol of Israel were read as part of the festival's birthday salute," said the New York *Times*.

"As a special gesture, one of the four new ballets presented at the festival by the Sophie Maslow Dance Company was dedicated to Mr. Robinson."

The following month Robinson received another type of "honor," one he shared with a colleague.

"The Minister of National Guidance of the United Arab Republic has signed an order banning movies in which Eartha Kitt and Edward G. Robinson take part," said the New York *Times* under a January 21 Cairo dateline.

"The reason given was they have shown pronounced pro-Israel sympathies and have helped collect donations for Israel."

I mentioned this dispatch to my host. Robinson, a normally refined, cultured gentleman, whose splendid vocabulary is far more than adequate to express himself without the use of four-letter words, uttered his first one in my presence.

"———the Arabs," he said, and I could not have expressed it better.

Robinson, a short, squat man, walked over to a corner of the large living room to get a refill for our glasses. From the rear, at any rate, he didn't give any impression of age or infirmity, even though he had had a serious heart attack in 1962 while doing a film on location in Africa, and an automobile accident on a Hollywood street which nearly cost him his life that same year.

He walked crisply and when he poured the drinks his hands didn't tremble at all. I soon discovered he was more than slightly hard of hearing, but he compensated for this deficiency by looking directly into my face and listening carefully to what I was asking. I had to repeat my questions only a couple of times during the three or four hours we were together. When he sat down again he talked about television, which he, like others, felt would play a large part in whatever future Hollywood has.

"It's not a bad medium; tells a story well although it forces an actor and director to make compromises. And, of course, there's been far too much violence. But you must consider that a picture is a picture whether it's shown on television or in the theater and it *does* speak a universal language.

"Look, I've done quite a few things on TV. As a matter of fact, I'm an alumnus of radio. Remember *Big Town?*"

I nodded.

"Well, then you know. I didn't consider I was denigrating myself doing shows on radio, and I don't feel I'm lowering my dignity when I appear on television. When I'm offered a good part I accept. Of course, I prefer the theater, but that sure is in bad shape—in this country at any rate. I suppose that's because we've allowed films to dominate the entertainment world. In England they didn't and they still have marvelous theater in London. Eternal verities are always eternal.

"But coming back to TV. Sure, you can go slightly crazy with the commercials. But I figure they're a necessary evil. Otherwise, how would I get paid? Naturally, in the good old days of the majors life was easier; everything was handed to you on a silver platter. You were a star and you were supposed to act like one and they gave you what it took to play the role.

"I think there's a fair chance Hollywood will exist if only to make films for television and perhaps an occasional small-budget one for the theater. Lots of good people still out here, and also a lot of them are out of work. I, for one, will be sorry to see the era pass as it's doing. I've worked for quite a few of the majors, you know. Never did much for M-G-M because I had a disagreement with Irving Thalberg; he wanted me to sign a five-year contract. I refused, not because of money differences, but at the time I thought I'd take a break in between movies and go back to Broadway. Thalberg never forgave me for this although he was not a vindictive man.

"Generally speaking, though, despite some grievous disappointments and serious problems, I've had a pretty good life in Hollywood and I've been here for a long, long time. As a matter of fact, I've been in this same house for nearly forty years."

He paused to take a few swallows of heavily watered-down Scotch (mine was purer) and shook his head.

"If I have one regret it's that I didn't make more of an effort to combine my movie career with the theater instead of returning to Broadway only occasionally. But three thousand miles wasn't covered so easily in those days. Like the rest of us who left New York in the late twenties, I came out here because this is where the money is, or rather, I should say, *used* to be. If you look around at my walls, you'll see I've not done too badly."

This description of the scores of art treasures which were on his walls must be put down as a masterpiece of understatement. In the opinion of experts—and I hasten to repeat I am not one—Robinson's French moderns comprised one of the greatest private collections in the world. The actor himself, these same experts say, was an extremely discriminating buyer who was respected in art circles of every nation.

With an understandable air of pride he escorted me on a tour of his "galleries" which stretched for nearly the entire length of his home, filling the walls of every room and the passageway to the second floor as well. It took us no more than an hour to complete the rounds. I'm sure that with his colleagues of the art world this would have taken days. What made me like my gentle, unassuming host even more than I had was his kindness. He did not talk down to me, a temptation others with less reason have not been able to resist.

When we were seated again he revealed, although only in passing, one of the "grievous disappointments" he'd mentioned before.

"A lot of what you just saw are fairly recent purchases; my ex-wife got half of my old collection."

A gentleman, this was all he said about the bitter court battle in 1957 when he and his wife, the former Gladys Lloyd, were divorced. Under California law where the suit was instituted, the collection was considered community property shared equally by both husband and wife. As part of the divorce settlement it had to be liquidated and Robinson did not have sufficient funds to buy out his wife's share. The sale itself attracted worldwide attention.

On February 26, 1957, Sanka Knox wrote in the New York *Times:*

The largest and most important part of the Edward G. Robinson art collection was sold yesterday for between $3,000,000 and $4,000,000.

Fifty-eight paintings—predominantly impressionist and post-impressionist—and a bronze Dégas changed hands in a complicated transaction that, for value and size, dwarfed any other art deal of this generation. . . .

Thirteen paintings and a second bronze Dégas are still left to Mr. Robinson. . . . Under California law his carefully brought-together collection had to be liquidated in a divorce settlement between the sixty-three-year-old actor and his wife.

"There was no way I could buy the part we had to sell," he said. "I'd put everything in pictures."

According to reports, however, the actor did purchase fourteen of the works of art from the collection by paying the going market price for them.

For Knoedler's East Fifty-seventh Street [the art dealer where the sale was held] the transaction was the biggest since 1931. . . . For Mr. Robinson, a collector for twenty-five years and more, the sale means that picture buying has begun all over again. "No sum of money can compensate for the collection," he said. "But," he added, "the pictures are still mine; they can't take my love away. I could never be anything but their custodian anyway."

B. A. Bergman—"Bergie" to most people who know him— once an editor on *The New Yorker* magazine, currently book editor of the Philadelphia *Evening Bulletin* and a very old friend of the actor, told me that an art book with color prints from the Robinson collection would soon be published.

"I heard about it this past June at the National Book Sellers Association convention up in Boston. I ran into Eddie at the same time; I hadn't seen the old son-of-a-bitch for at least fifteen years; the last time, if memory serves me, was when he played the lead in *Middle of the Night.*

"At any rate, they asked Eddie, who just *happened* to be in Boston at the time, to make a talk before the assembled salesmen, newspaper reporters, press agents, and so on, about a thousand of them. He told us how his wife, the former Jane Bodenheimer whom he married shortly after he and Gladys were divorced, went about gathering material for the book.

" 'At certain times, over a period of several months,' Eddie told his audience, 'I'd notice one of my paintings missing from its customary place. First it was a Renoir, and my wife Jane saw I was looking around for it with a puzzled expression on my face. She smiled and said, "Don't worry, Eddie, it's not been stolen. The frame was cracked and I sent it out for repair." '

" 'Well, this kept happening and my wife always had a plausible excuse. What I didn't know was that every time a picture had been removed, it was being photographed for my new book. I can tell you honestly that I had no idea the book was being prepared. It was quite a shock.' "

Bergie added that the booksellers and publishers may be in for quite a shock themselves when bound copies are offered for sale. The suggested retail price is expected to be around sixty dollars. He continued.

"Eddie wound up his talk with a good punch line. 'I don't collect art; it collects me.' Well, spontaneous or not, in my opinion this was the best speech the convention ever heard. When he finished he got a standing ovation. If you knew how difficult it is even to keep the booksellers awake, you'd realize that anything that gets them up on their feet must be regarded as a major achievement."

Bergie told me a couple of other stories in which Robinson figured when he and the editor, who are approximately the same age, were both young men.

"Shortly after Eddie made his big hit in *Little Caesar*, a few of us had dinner together in New York where he was promoting the film. Of course you're aware Eddie'd already had a reputation on the stage for at least fifteen years. But this was something different; the kind of national adulation that only Hollywood was able to give. Compared to the fifty or more million viewers who used to go to the movies, audiences which see even a long-run Broadway play are minuscule.

"Well, after we finished eating and had a few more drinks at the Algonquin where he was staying, Eddie suggested we go down to the Village and see Sam Jaffe. Sam was a close friend of both of us; he had a tiny apartment on Sullivan Street."

Bergie looked at me.

"You ill-informed bastard, Lewis, you know who Sam Jaffe is, don't you?"

I nodded vehemently.

"I'm not sure you're not lying," my friend said [I wasn't] and went on. "Sam was—still is—one of the great American actors of both stage and screen. But I'm talking now about the period during which he hadn't quite made it yet, around 1930, before he became a huge success on Broadway in *Grand Hotel*. And before he scored in Hollywood as the High Llama in Hilton's *Lost Horizon*.

"He was 'at liberty,' a fairly long one between jobs and he was respectably broke, not completely busted even if he didn't have much cash to play around with. Not like he'd be later on when Joe McCarthy had Sam blacklisted and those cringing superpatriots out in movieland wouldn't give him a job; in fact, they were so scared they wouldn't give him the sweat off their balls.

"At any rate, the doorman at the Algonquin got us a cab and what happened five minutes later was my first experience with movie-man madness. We got stopped by a red light at

Forty-third and Sixth, a little more than a block away from the hotel, when some woman walking along the street looked up and spotted Eddie.

" 'There's Edward G. Robinson!' she screamed at the top of her lungs and rushed over to the cab. Of course everybody all around heard her; they couldn't help it."

Bergie looked at me.

"Ever see a mob in action?" he asked, and before I could answer he went on.

"It's a terrifying experience, I can tell you. That was a howling, yelling swarm of insane people. They jumped up on the radiator and the running boards. Yes, they had them—running boards—in those days. They even climbed on the roof. Drivers were beginning to abandon their cars and rush over to join the mob and create one hell of a traffic jam.

"They yanked at the door handles, but between the driver and ourselves we'd managed to lock them. We didn't get one window closed completely and some maniac reached in, yanked at Eddie's coat sleeve, and tore a cuff link out of his shirt. I can't say it was a good-natured crowd, either, no uncontrolled mob is, I guess. They wanted to get to their hero, Little Caesar, and they didn't give a damn how, even if they had to trample old ladies who got in their way.

"Meanwhile, Eddie's sitting back calmly taking it all in, puffing away on one of his foul stogies, and grinning.

" 'For Christ's sake, Eddie, I'm scared,' I said. 'You're laughing and our lives are in danger. Is this what you want?'

" 'Sure,' he said. 'This is what I want. When they don't come 'round anymore that's when I'll be scared.' "

Finally, Bergie told me, a pair of mounted policemen came by, broke up the mob, and got the cab through, but not before Robinson gave both cops his autograph.

"Well," Bergie went on, "that's what it meant to be a Hollywood star in the so-called 'good old days.' "

I was a witness to an experience similar to the one Bergie described. As a matter of fact, I was the culprit because I had no idea what happened when an orderly group of men, women, and children are suddenly put within touching distance of a Hollywood star.

This one occurred in 1949 when I was doing p.r. for the late Senator James H. Duff, then governor of the Commonwealth of Pennsylvania. On October 23 of that year I ran a one-day pageant on the outskirts of a tiny village in the dead center of the state. The theme was racial and religious tolerance, and in those naïve days all of us thought these ideals were achievable, at least in America.

Local talent furnished authorship, direction, and cast, while music was provided by the famous Penn State University Blue Band. But we needed to import a narrator of some renown and my friend Herb Golden, motion picture editor of *Variety* at the time, offered to help. He came up with an acceptance from Cornel Wilde who agreed to make the trip from Hollywood without a fee, in fact without the three-hundred-dollar honorarium I timidly offered. As I recall, he refused to accept any out-of-pocket expenses.

Jim Duff, a Republican, would be running for the United States Senate the following November, so I wanted to make the celebration as big as I could in a predominantly Democratic area of the state. As it turned out, the venture achieved stature way beyond partisan politics, although I readily concede that the credit for this upgrading belongs to forces far past my control.

To prove that the governor had acceptance beyond the Commonwealth's borders and thus would make a better United States senator than his opponent, I arranged for a nationally distinguished group of citizens to share the speakers' platform with Duff. Their assignment was to preach the same "brotherhood" gospel as the pageant depicted. They were not asked to praise Duff (although they did); their very presence in this nearly inaccessible Pennsylvania village in itself offered proof of the governor's eminence.

So I loaded the dais with dignitaries, including the late United States Justice Felix Frankfurter, General William I. "Wild Bill" Donovan, Ralph J. Bunche, and Sir Muhammad

248

Zafrulla Khan, then vice-president of the United Nations General Assembly. There were a half-dozen others of equal importance, but this ought to be enough to demonstrate the caliber of Duff's quondam colleagues and their international reputations.

By some inexplicable combination of perfect weather (a warm, sunny day in late October), for which I claim no credit, and tremendous national publicity, for which I was at least partially responsible, fifty thousand men, women, and children gathered that Sunday afternoon in the tiny farming village of Aaronsburg, a community of three hundred twenty-one souls and a dozen hastily erected comfort stations.

For the most, the audience was composed of conservative, white-skinned, middle-class Christians from farms, villages, and small towns of central Pennsylvania. A deeply felt sense of religion—not the tempestuous uncontrolled fervor generated at camp meetings, but rather the quiet kind achieved at Quaker meetings—permeated the atmosphere. The huge crowd, with obvious albeit subdued pleasure, witnessed the pageant with Wilde doing a beautiful job of narration; then all listened attentively to the speakers. When Jim Duff wound up the day with an appeal for racial and religious understanding, the crowd began to fade away from the scene in a thoughtful mood.

All of a sudden someone spotted Cornel Wilde walking alone toward his car, parked a few hundred yards away, and then hell broke loose. Within seconds the actor was surrounded by a howling mob which only moments before was an audience of well-behaved, self-controlled ladies and gentlemen.

"It was a horrible experience," Wilde told me later. "I thought they were going to tear me apart and frankly I was frightened to death. They ripped my coat and shirt and closed in on me so tightly I could hardly breathe. But, thank God, a couple of your state troopers saw what was happening and broke through to rescue me."

I'd arranged police escorts for General Donovan, Justice

Frankfurter, and the other speakers who really didn't need any, but for Wilde, who certainly did, I'd failed.

Bergie told me that the evening at Sam Jaffe's wound up with Robinson KO'd by a heavy leather cushion one of the guests playfully hurled at another.

"Eddie was an innocent bystander; he was between the two guys and got knocked so hard he landed on his ass and was actually out for a couple of seconds. When he came to, always the ham, he looked up and said, 'Was I convincing?' "

One last Bergie-Robinson story.

"When Joe McCarthy finally put the skids to Jaffe," Bergie concluded, "poor Sam really was broke, didn't have a dime or a place to hang his hat, and everybody was afraid to hire him. Eddie Robinson got him a place to live, paid his rent, and gave him eating money. I think I know why, but that's not important. The point I'm trying to make is that Eddie didn't forget old friends when *he* had it and they *didn't*."

Chapter Twenty-Five

You would indeed be hard-put to find a more unlikely place for the collection of data about Hollywood's romantic old days than New Castle, Pennsylvania. An even more improbable spot, if possible, is the town of McKeesport, a larger and measurably dirtier community than the former, and located in the very same state fifty-odd miles southward.

Yet it was in New Castle that the great Warner brothers got their start; in McKeesport, a female resident became one of ten winners in what its sponsor, *Photoplay*, modestly proclaimed was "the most unusual, interesting, and successful artistic competition ever inaugurated in America."

While both cities thus would appear to have contributed equally to our nation's cultural history, the balance, in my opinion at any rate, was tipped in favor of New Castle when I learned it was there that Bob Hope, comedian, intimate of presidents, and hard-line philosopher, got his start.

For the accumulation of this impressive information I am indebted to Mr. Bart Richards, New Castle native, long-time member of the working press, distinguished state legislator (three terms; he was trounced in the fourth campaign), current director of Lawrence County civil defense, collector of trivia, and my old drinking companion.

I extract the following paragraphs from a letter Bart sent to me during my recent Hollywood sojourn.

I hear from our mutual friend and former fellow Capital Hill political correspondent, Lefty Lush, that you are engaged in writing a book on the movie industry, or what's left of it at any rate. If true, you must have heard the name Warner Brothers, a firm which at one time stood for something in film land.

Ergo, I hasten to advise that no authoritative history of Hollywood can possibly be written without including New Castle. Believe me, this statement is made not out of civic pride, although I admit I am chairman of the New Castle Chamber of Commerce Publicity Bureau, but rather because I know you are a seeker of truth wherever found.

I certainly would not want to waste the time of such a busy journalist as you and bring you to New Castle (even though it *is* the Garden Spot of Pennsylvania) without an offer of proof that a visitation to my diocese will yield untold riches for your project.

I list in evidence:

Item One —A photograph of the Warner brothers standing in front of their first theater on South Mill Street, not a thousand feet from the desk upon which mine rest.

Item Two—A picture of the late Harold Rostheimer, New Castle's 'understanding' funeral director. (As our grandchildren might say, 'Rostheimer digs you.') Mr. Rostheimer supplied the Warner Nickelodeon with chairs.

Item Three—A faded but still legible program bearing the name of Tod Sloan, 'Jockey Extra-ordinary now appearing at the Warner New Castle Nickelodeon.'

Item Four (and this should knock you right on your buttocks)—My own personal reminiscences of Bob Hope, who made his first appearance as a comedian in 1926 on the stage of the Bijou Theater for which I was moonlighting as press agent.

So pad your generous expense account, fly to New Castle

(well, not directly, you'll have to take the bus up from Pittsburgh), hoist a couple with me in my humble kitchen, and I'll ply you with fascinating recollections of the movie world as seen from Lawrence County.

Your friend,
Bart 'Olivier' Richards

So here I was hoisting a few at Bart's house in Pennsylvania's Garden Spot, a city surrounded by automobile graveyards, abandoned strip-mines, and twenty-four sheet-billboards. This is a tough town where children are weaned on boilermakers. But my friend has gone a giant step farther—he drinks a deadly admixture of Bass's Ale and Guinness Stout laced with a full ounce of one-hundred-proof Old Overholt. I am sorry to say I went right along with Bart and not until noon the following day was I able to hold my head sufficiently high to gaze at what's left of Warner Brothers' first Nickelodeon.

The sum total of what I learned authentically about the Industry from Mr. Bart Richards forced me to renounce all expenses I incurred coming to this Garden Spot of America. True, the night before while I was still able to function, I did learn something of slight value about the brothers Warner, but not much.

"During the war, I mean the Second World War," Bart had said, "a USO troupe came here to entertain the boys at Deshon Army Hospital Annex right outside the town in Cascade Park. With them was a patent-leather-haired youth who averred he was the troupe's director of public relations, by which he meant their press agent.

"He'd come over to the *News* with handouts. I said I might have to rewrite them, but we'd get them in the paper in some fashion or other. Then he invited Ed Buchanan, the publisher, and me to lunch. I was then city editor. I liked the idea of a free lunch; we don't get many such in these parts.

"In a rather grandiloquent fashion he asked me where the best place in town was to eat. 'That's where I'll take you,' says he. I knew *he* wouldn't be lifting the tab, that'd be on us taxpayers, so I suggested the Castleton Hotel dining room. They used to serve excellent food at fairly high prices. However, that's beside the point."

I begged Bart to please go easy on the Overholt this time, but he paid no attention.

"At any rate, there we were with Mr. R. Wallace Finker—that was the name on his business card, so help me, and I've never forgotten. In fact, we've made a family joke out of it and whenever any of the Richards tribe gets snooty we take him down by calling him 'R. Wallace' or '*Mister Finker*.' You can see the poetic potentials.

"Our host brought with him a half-dozen lovelies and, believe me, they *were* lovelies. We were all enjoying the ambience (I think that's the right word) when R. Wallace turned around and, addressing no one in particular, but obviously trying to impress everybody, said, 'Did you know that Warner Brothers founded their empire thirty miles from here?'

"I was more than a little puzzled, not that I questioned the empire bit, but I'd always been under the impression their careers began right within New Castle city limits. So I asked our host where he meant.

"'Youngstown,' Mr. Finker replied, and he seemed that sure of himself I didn't want to argue. Besides, it might have embarrassed him in front of the young ladies so I let the statement go unchallenged. However, the following day I began to do some research on my own."

Bart put down his glass long enough to reach into a drawer, extract a photograph about ten-by-twelve inches in size, and hand it to me. Even though the picture had faded somewhat, the subjects, five men standing in front of an open storefront, were still sharp. Above was a marquee reading "Matinees Daily" with electric bulbs visible clearly outlining every letter. Below that was a cardboard sign upon which was printed quite unprofessionally, "Matinee Today at 1:30 P.M."

I'd seen the picture before, or one much like it, in Arthur Mayer's *The Movie*. But Arthur had neither identified the place where the picture'd been taken nor the subjects other than to say they were the Warners. Bart stood next to me.

"The guy in the center wearing a derby is Albert; to his left that's Jack, he's the one with the funny mustache. The short, skinny guy in the far corner is Sam, and the hefty young man who looks like he's wearing gloves is Harry. I don't know who the fat guy standing in back of everybody is, except that he's not a member of the family.

"Let me give you an unpublished story about Harry Warner. He was only a kid when he and his brothers came over here from stinking old Youngstown to open up their first Nickelodeon. And goddamn that smart-assed jerk, Finker, I get mad every time I think about the son-of-a-bitch. That's what it was, their *first* one, right here in New Castle. Don't argue the point with me."

He almost snarled although I hadn't said a word. I learned long ago that when a man's civic pride is at stake, it's fool-hardy to question *anything* he says. You can't win. It so happens in this case I have every reason to believe the truth is that Warners' *very first* Nickelodeon was in the rear of Kaier's Brewery in my hometown of Mahanoy City. Someday I'm going to prove it and make Bart eat his words. This, however, was neither time nor place for the confrontation.

"Let's see," my host continued after he simmered down, "where was I? Oh, yeah. I was telling you about Harry Warner when that lying little bastard, R. Wallace Finker, interrupted us. Harry had played end for Youngstown High a couple years back and he was good, much too good for those cheap Youngstown goons. In 1906, which is when that picture was taken, New Castle High started out badly and got swamped first game of the season.

"Sharon beat us fifty-four–nothing. Nobody but Frosh on N.C.H.S., and *they* had eleven seniors; must have outweighed us by fifty pounds a player."

Bart shook his head angrily at the recollection.

"It was an outrage! Totally unethical, too, even if it *was* legal. Well, seems our coach heard about Harry Warner being in town so he gave him a proposition to go back to school and play for us. He wouldn't have to attend classes or anything like that, just come out every Saturday for the game. 'Ringers' they called them in those days, but what else could we do?

"In any event Harry looked young enough to still be in high school, so some public-spirited citizen—I won't mention names; even though this happened sixty-five years ago, his grandson is still alive—offered the kid quite a few bucks under the table and he took it. From then on we won every game but the last; we tied that with Greenville. Should have beaten the bums but I found out later the referee's wife's brother was on Greenville's faculty. I bet the thief taught ethics or something."

Timidly, I mentioned to Bart that we seemed to be veering from the subject. He appeared astonished.

"What do you mean, veering? We're right on target. The *dough* Harry got paid took care of rent for his brothers' Nickelodeon. And if this doesn't prove their first moving picture was right here in New Castle and not in Youngstown, I'll eat my hat."

Bart and I were now, you might say, back "on location," standing in front of Lipkin's Quality Food Market, two hundred feet south of the corner of Mill and Washington streets in the heart of New Castle's main business block.

"Well, Art, you're looking at history," my guide said with great pride as he unbuttoned his jacket, placed a thumb in back of each suspender strap, and drew it out just like Mr. H. L. Mencken of the Baltimore *Sun* used to do when he showed Barbara Frietchie's house to visitors.

"If you want," Bart went on, "I'll take you inside and introduce you to Morris. To tell you the truth, though, he doesn't known a damned thing about the Warners and the store itself was built in 1928; nothing left of the original building, although you'd never think so the way Morris shows them around and talks to those movie buffs who come every so often to see where the *world's* first Nickelodeon was."

256

Bart looked at me out of the corner of his eye to see how I'd take that, but I made no comment. I declined an invitation to meet Morris and instead asked my companion about "Item Two," that picture of Harold Rostheimer, the friendly undertaker. I wasn't sure I'd get much more out of this man than I had from gazing at "Item One" and Lipkin's Quality Market. But it was worth the try; after all, I'd detoured a considerable distance just to get *into* New Castle.

"I'll do better than that," Bart promised. "I'll introduce you to his son, Walter, who's been carrying on the same good work since his father passed on in 1944."

The current Mr. R's establishment was less than a five-minute walk and when we arrived, the proprietor himself, a pleasant-enough-looking gentleman in his early seventies, stopped spraying rose bushes as Bart and I approached the well-kept lawn.

"Art Lewis, shake hands with Walt Rostheimer," Bart ordered. I've always had strong feelings of revulsion every time I'm forced to shake hands with a mortician, not knowing where these might have been last and imagining the worst. However, since I'm not one to shirk an unpleasant task if necessary, I obeyed. Walt's hands were, as I'd expected, moist, caressing, and soft as a baby's ass. I commented on the beauty of Mr. R's flowers; he beamed with pleasure and admitted modestly that he had a green thumb.

"Tell Art about how your father used to lend chairs to the Warners for their Nickelodeon," Bart said as soon as the three of us were settled on a bench beneath an old shade tree. Walter followed instructions.

"This was back in Dad's day, 'round 1905 or so, and I was only a young squirt then, just out of undertaking college in Philly."

Bart interrupted to add that I was from Philly.

"Well, what do you know?" Walt said. "Small world, isn't it?"

I agreed that it truly was a small world and Mr. R, the younger, continued.

"Those Warner brothers were from Youngstown, Jewish boys, you know, but they were all right, honest as the day is long and with lots of initiative, like most of their countrymen. Felt their own town wouldn't give them any kind of opportunity to get places so they came over to New Castle and opened up here.

"They scraped up enough cash to rent the store and buy a motion picture camera, but when it came to seats there was no money left. You fellows have no idea how much chairs cost, even in those days, and now they're *really* sky-high! Well, anyway, one of the brothers, I think it was Albert, came over to my Dad and gave him a proposition.

"What they wanted was to borrow chairs and after each performance pay only for those that were used, at so much rent per chair. There was no way to say which ones went idle and which had somebody sitting on them. But, like I said, the Warners were honest and Dad agreed. He never regretted it. It so happens they used *every* chair for *every* performance; even matinees were sellouts. People in town and all 'round were anxious to see the movies. They were quite a fad while they lasted, weren't they?"

I wasn't sure that Mr. R's reference was to what had become the world's first Nickelodeon or to moving pictures in general. However, I had no desire to enter into a discussion of the Industry with our host; I kept silent.

"There was one hitch, though," Mr. R went on. "There'd be times when Dad had a big funeral to handle and we'd need all the chairs we owned for viewings. So on those days we'd have to bring 'em all back; use 'em for whatever length of time it took, then it was my job to run them back to the Warners in the hearse."

I asked whether the Nickelodeon was able to operate without chairs to accommodate the customers. Bart answered.

"The show went on. All Warner Brothers did was put up a sign, 'Standing Room Only.' And for that, you can chalk up another first for New Castle."

Mr. R's wife, a sprightly lady about the same age as her husband, emerged from the large white home-cum-undertaking parlor, bearing a tray with three glasses and a pitcher of lemonade on it. It was a warm day and I was thirsty, but I didn't like the color of Mrs. R's beverage; it was a very, very deep pink, almost red. I refused politely and said I was allergic to lemons.

"Item Three" in those offers of proof, the program showing Tod Sloan headlining four acts of vaudeville, was as Bart described it and offered an equal amount of substantive evidence in support of New Castle's claim to movie fame, as had Exhibits One and Two.

My friend, however, did have one comment to make about this jockey.

"Tod was the Bill Hartack of his day; developed the idea of riding the stirrups for a finish, actually standing up in them."

"Very interesting, Bart," I said, and waited for a further comment. It was soon forthcoming after my friend gave it some thought.

"You know, you could almost say it was right here in this town where Tod got the idea. So chalk up *another* first for New Castle."

We disposed of the last item.

"Bob Hope was playing dramatic roles for a stock company he was traveling with during the winter of 1926," Bart said. "I was making an extra buck or two press-agenting for the Bijou and, of course, got to see all the shows for free. One night something happened backstage between the first and second act; they needed time to straighten whatever it was and the manager sent Bob out to do a monologue.

"He made it up as he went along and cracked a few jokes besides. I was behind the curtain and it sounded like the audience was enjoying the performance. When Bob finished and came backstage again, he looked at me and said, kind of surprised, 'Well, whadaya know? They actually laughed. I may try the same stuff again.'

259

"With the fame Bob Hope began to win as a comedian from *that day on,* don't tell *me* this isn't another first. New Castle's always been a great movie town."

At the moment, Bart admitted reluctantly, the only movie house in the area is a drive-in six miles west of the city.

"We used to have four theaters in New Castle; last one closed a year ago. I remember when I was a kid it was hard to figure out which one to go to on Saturday matinee—John Bunny, Flora Finch, or Wally Reid. And later on, Rin-Tin-Tin; he was a Warners dog, you know. Those were the good old days, weren't they?"

I nodded.

"You tell me the Warner lot is like a cemetery now. I wonder if they didn't price themselves out of the business, all the studios I mean, paying Liz Taylor and actors like her a million bucks a picture and a percentage of the take besides. I wouldn't give her *half* a million even if they threw in a set of dishes."

Bart had to hurry off for a Lion's Club dinner to which he cordially invited me, but I begged off even though I knew both Mr. Lipkin and Mr. Rostheimer would be there.

"While you're around checking up on what other great contributions we made to the movie industry in this neck of the woods, why don't you hop down to McKeesport. They had some kind of national movie beauty queen contest when I was around fifteen years old. A girl from McKeesport was one of the winners. She came up to New Castle for a personal appearance and naturally I and every other kid my age fell in love with her."

I asked Bart if he remembered her name and if she subsequently was a success. He shook his head.

"Could be she made it big all right, but perhaps she might have changed her name to something else, you know, like Spangler Arlington Brugh, the actor who married Barbara Stanwyck."

I wasn't rising to that bait; I knew *those* answers.

"You could stop into the McKeesport *Daily News*," Bart advised me as we said good-bye. "If Don Fox is still city editor, mention my name and I'm sure he'll be glad to help."

I rented a car and drove down Route 19 headed for Mc-Keesport. Six miles outside I passed the drive-in Bart had told me about. By coincidence, *The Molly Maguires* was playing there; I'd never seen the picture; I was out of the country when it opened and by the time I came back less than a month later, it already had been withdrawn from first-run theaters and wasn't even playing in neighborhood houses. I just couldn't accept the fact that a feature film costing as much as this one did, and with a cast of well-known, expensive, if not particularly good, actors, could bomb so quickly.

A few weeks before I'd spent several hours with James Wong Howe, the legendary Hollywood cinematographer who'd filmed the picture and who warned me not to expect much.

We'd had lunch together in an old (well, old for Los Angeles, twenty years) restaurant. Jimmy told me about his birth in the province of Kwang Tung, China, in 1899, and his arrival in the United States with his father in 1904. He spoke of his Hollywood career which began in 1915 when he was hired to sweep out Cecil B. De Mille's camera room, a job Jimmy asked for because of his interest in photography. He bought his first professional camera a year later and by 1922 he was M-G-M's chief cameraman.

From Mary Miles Minter on, Jimmy's been most stars' first choice and he has won more awards than any other cinematographer in the business. He's a warm, gracious host and despite his age and the dearth of jobs in the Industry, he's as busy as ever. He was off for Spain the following day, not on vacation, but to direct the photography for another film.

"I hope we'll make out better on this one than we did on *Molly Maguires*," he said. "That one isn't very good and I blame Walter Bernstein for much of its failure. His first script

261

was fair, but he kept changing it so much and so often the final one was pretty bad. I was bitterly disappointed; the picture has no heart; you never suffer with the people.

"And the salaries they paid were outrageous. A million dollars for Sean Connery, three hundred thousand for Richard Harris, and about a hundred thousand for Samantha Eggar; they weren't worth it."

Friends, too, who'd seen the movie when it opened advised me against going. I'd also read several poor reviews. What the hell, I said to myself, I've *got* to go. So I paid my buck, drove in, and parked. For the audience it was popcorn and hot-dog time not more than ten minutes after the picture was flashed on the screen. For me it was a depressing experience. I'd hoped for very little and got even less.

The film emerges with an almost deliberately myopic point of view, an unconvincing plot, characters who move around like puppets, a perversion of history, at least one stupid error in casting, and the injection of a silly love story. Worst of all, it committed a moving picture's cardinal sin—it was a bore. The only redeeming feature was Howe's photography which was magnificent, but this, the film's sole plus, wasn't sufficient to carry along his colleagues' ineptitude.

In my contract with Paramount, my agent, Paul Gitlin, made sure I received screen credit. When I drove out of that Lawrence County theater, I wished he hadn't.

Chapter Twenty-Six

WHERE I grew up in the hard-coal regions of Pennsylvania, our favorite childhood game was not "cops and robbers"; it was "Mollies and Modocs." When I was a member of John Noonan's gang of eighth graders, the legendary Molly Maguires were always the "goodies." We rode white horses and protected the downtrodden miner from his cruel, penny-pinching enemy, the Welsh colliery bosses. The reverse was true if I "served" under Llewellyn Davies; then it was Modocs to the rescue and the murderous Irish driven from the saloons and streets of Mahanoy City by the heroic Welsh patriots.

The strange part is that we were able to confine this bitterness to games; as far as I can recall, no internecine warfare ever occurred even though less than four decades elapsed since the last of twenty-one Mollies was hanged, an event witnessed by my own father. Birthday parties given by my friends, the Noonans and the Kellys, were attended not only by Roman Catholic communicants of St. Canicus, but also by the Davies sisters, Paul Tregellas, and other youthful worshippers at St. David's.

I make no claim that our lives in the anthracite area were ecumenical; God knows they weren't. Harsh words were exchanged from time to time between different ethnic groups and once in a while blood might flow. An aged, implacable priest who'd administered last rites to a Molly on the way to the gallows used to stir up latent anger among his parishioners with texts taken from the Old Testament, laying particular stress on that "eye for an eye" bit. Thereupon my neighbor, young Joe Toomey, would emerge from Mass just aching for some kid of Welsh ancestry to insult him.

Then there was a Schuylkill County Chief of Police, Gomer something or other, who had a reputation for using far more force than necessary to subdue Irish pay-day drunks. Naturally, in due time he was "attended to" but not nearly so violently as both his father and grandfather were handled under similar provocation. But, generally speaking, despite sporadic lapses from good behavior, we had learned to live with each other, pro-Molly or anti-Molly, because we understood the Molly Maguires; they were part of our heritage.

Ever since childhood, I'd hoped some movie maker with integrity, intelligence, and a sense of history would film the saga of this tiny, downtrodden, proud, cruel band of poverty-stricken, disillusioned Irishmen and follow its trail to the tragic, irreversible end of the gibbets of Pottsville, Bloomsburg, Sunbury, and Mauch Chunk, Pennsylvania.

A couple of years ago, when my wife and I were vacationing in Mexico, Paul Gitlin telephoned me with what sounded like good news; financially, I will admit, it was. Paramount, after lengthy negotiations, made what Paul considered a fair offer to buy film rights to my book *Lament for the Molly Maguires*. He urged me to accept and I did. There'd be no "artistic rights" in the contract, meaning I'd have nothing to say about what went into the picture, but since this is standard procedure, which I'd experienced previously, I wasn't disappointed.

This would not be the first film about coal miners, or even about the Molly Maguires for that matter. As far back as 1908, Kalem produced an eight-hundred-ninety-foot film titled *The Molly Maguires, or Labor Wars in the Coal Mines*. Over the years there were several more, although these had nothing to do with the Mollies. There were De Mille's *Dyna-*

mite, *Black Fury*, D. H. Lawrence's *Sons and Lovers*, and one I liked best of all, *How Green Was My Valley*, adapted for films from Richard Llewellyn's fine novel and magnificently directed by John Ford.

When we came back home I learned that Paramount had chosen Martin Ritt to direct the picture and Walter Bernstein to write the script, or it may be it was the pair who selected Paramount. Paul told me the allotted and already approved budget was three and a half million dollars, which in this era of Hollywood belt-tightening sounded like a lot of money to me and, I don't doubt, to stockholders of Paramount's new owners, The Gulf and Western Corporation. I'm sure the latter soon after must have wished they'd stayed in a business at which they'd always done quite well.

Recently I'd seen a couple of pictures which cost around a million dollars to make and which, incidentally, enjoyed excellent critical reviews and made money for their producers. I was happy to go along with the Hollywood movie mogul theory that if a picture that costs a million bucks to make is good, then one that costs three and a half times as much is, of necessity, three and one-half times as good. Q.E.D. That was *my* first error: Paramount's was the choice of the screen writer, Bernstein, who, when it came to knowledge of Molly Maguire history, did not seem to have too much background.

Yet, I suppose this is not of any real importance except to a few purists. People go to the movies to be entertained, not to attend lectures in history. It's only within the last few years, or since the release of "adult" Westerns, that we movie-goers, several generations of us, are becoming slightly suspicious about certain tenets we've been holding sacrosanct. To wit: all Texans are tall; justice on the plains invariably triumphs; and the only good Indian is a dead Indian.

It didn't matter in the slightest to me or to my fellow Americans that *High Noon* was a fairy tale, that *Dr. Ehrlich's Magic Bullet* had about as much real science in it as does the TV "naseograph ad," and that life in Atlanta, as seen in *Gone with the Wind*, is romantic horseshit. What did matter was

265

that these three films gripped their audiences from opening frame to "THE END." Paramount's *Molly Maguires* did not.

This probably is the moment to state that my purpose in devoting a whole chapter to *The Molly Maguires* is not to launch a diatribe against a single picture maker and a single movie. Rather, I use this film about which I know a great deal as an example of Hollywood's death wish, and, even more than just mere suicidal intent, there are symptoms of "over-kill" as well.

I speak now only of money, not artistic triumphs, when I ask where else in the world is failure regarded as a measure of success and so rewarded? And where else do heavy financial encumbrances reverse the law of gravity to fall up, not down? I have in mind Martin Ritt, the *Molly*'s producer-director.

Mr. Ritt's projected budget for completion of *The Molly Maguires* was, as I said before, three and a half million dollars, a tidy sum indeed. Then without apparent, or effective at any rate, protests from Paramount which lifted the tab, Ritt quadrupled the ante and produced a film that to date has returned less than ten of the fourteen million dollars it cost, and it was an artistic flop besides.

So what does the Industry do to Mr. Ritt? Why, the Industry rewards him generously with the directorship of a new big-budget film, *The Great White Hope*, another massive failure to be strung along with this gentleman's previous screen "credits." You'd think that Paramount, with nearly a hundred million dollars' worth of unreleased films so bad they lay gathering dust in the company warehouse, would have picked someone else.

Ritt's *The Spy Who Came in from the Cold* and *Hud*, both of which I saw and liked, were acceptable to most critics and made money for their backers. But, unfortunately for Paramount's reputation (and perhaps even survival), and Gulf and Western's stockholders' dough, many of his other films, in the eyes of *The New Republic*'s famed critic, were "pretentious duds."

I met Ritt for the first and last time shortly after he and

Bernstein bought *Lament* with Paramount's cash. Ritt was then making *The Brotherhood*, another step backward in Ritt's rise to success; the film, starring Kirk Douglas, was a near disaster.

Said Ernie Schier, the Philadelphia *Evening Bulletin*'s noted movie critic: "*The Brotherhood* is distinguished for one of the longest stranglings the screen has ever staged . . . and for some terrible acting."

Ritt is a charming guy; I liked him immediately. I don't know how old he is—he does not give his birthdate in the *Motion Picture Almanac*, but my guess is that he's in his early fifties. After an hour or so of pleasant conversation about the Mollies and my interest in them, I left with a feeling of confidence that he would make a great picture.

The picture, Ritt had told me, was to be made at Eckley, a coal-region village outside of Hazelton, Pennsylvania. I remembered the place well from childhood. There are exceptions, of course, but most extant hard-coal "patches" look just as depressingly grim as they did a hundred years ago during the reign of the Molly Maguires. Culm banks surround them, a tall abandoned colliery still casts its shadow over the village, and the narrow dirt street (its only one) is muddy in winter and dusty the rest of the year. The houses need paint; for more than a few it would be a first coat.

Eckley is one of the exceptions. As I recalled, it was a clean little town, not unlike those you'll see if you drive through Lancaster County's rich farmlands. Culm banks had been leveled, the colliery was razed, and trees had been planted on its site; the street was widened and paved, and houses with their new, modern fronts, were painted regularly. Something else I almost forgot. More than a few of the original patches are still lit by candles and kerosene lamps, but Eckley has electricity as evidenced from wires which stretch from pole to pole and house to house.

With a score of unrehabilitated patches within as many miles, why would Mr. Ritt choose Eckley where he had to reassemble huge piles of culm or facsimiles thereof, build a colliery, narrow the street, cover it with mud, rip down house fronts, chip off paint, and dismantle telephone poles and bury their wires? Whoever can come up with a rational answer to this question must be regarded as Hollywood's savior.

Three or four years ago I did a documentary for CBS-TV. It was called *The Miner's Story* and was shot on location. We needed an old breaker ("colliery" to you non-coalcrackers) which had stood the ravages of time. Not trusting to boyhood memories and not sure what was left in the region, I sought advice from an expert. I asked my friend Tom Barrett, editor of the Shenandoah *Evening Herald*, an authority on the Mollies, a former miner, and a lifelong resident of the area, where I could find what I was looking for.

"How many do you want?" Tom asked. "And do you need patches to go with them?"

I realize there must be times when movie makers are forced to simulate reality. I thought the 1935 version of *Mutiny on the Bounty* was great and I know it was made in a few feet of water on the M-G-M lot. On the other hand, if the Atlantic Ocean is handy, why would a producer, in the name of the *auteur* theory, demand that millions of gallons of water be pumped into an empty ditch three miles from the New Jersey shore?

The name for this film profligacy is known in Hollywood as a "runaway budget." As Herb Golden, an old pinochle player said, "The *Mollies* did it in spades. It's a classic example of what we used to call, over at Bankers Trust, 'progressive seduction' and I'll tell you how it works."

I think at this point I ought to say a few words about Herb Golden if only to show that for the past twenty-five years his words have carried considerable weight in the Industry. Although Herb's name is unknown to the general public, what he's said and done has often been responsible for the financing of many major Hollywood productions.

As I said earlier, I first met Herb when we were both police reporters in Philadelphia, each for rival morning newspapers, he on the now defunct *Record* and I on the *Inquirer*. He won a few, I won a few, and we became good friends. Herb did some local moonlighting for V*ariety*, then quit the *Record* to work full-time for the show biz bible in New York, winding up as the editor of the paper's motion picture section. Herb developed the uncanny ability to predict, with remarkable accuracy, the box-office future of nearly every film he reviewed (which was a lot easier than now, he admits). As you might well imagine, this talent, in a business where every venture is a gamble, could be as valuable as marked cards in a poker game. You might not win every hand but it would be nice to know that the next card you're tempted to draw won't fill that inside straight.

Herb left V*ariety* for Bankers Trust Company of New York, where he became its vice-president in charge of motion picture financing. He later became a vice-president of United Artists and some ten years ago formed his own Manhattan-based company, Lexington International, Inc., which, among other types of financing, arranges movie deals. *The Molly Maguires* was not among them.

"For this," Herb said with a smile, "I am indeed grateful. But you asked how come Paramount spent so much more than was planned without anybody blowing the whistle, and I'll explain.

"Ritt, as you know, was both producer and director of the picture. The budget of three and a half million dollars was high but not unusual for those days. And when you consider the scope of the undertaking, I could see where it would be approved.

"It's also not impossible, although it is probably unlikely, Ritt really believed he could shoot the picture for the budgeted figure. Producers then often didn't. They anticipated spending considerably more once they had the film company on the hook. You must remember every director and producer wants to turn out the best possible picture he can, artistically and financially. If this means reshooting a scene seven times because he believes it will turn out better that way, that's what he'll do—if he can get away with it.

"You mentioned that Marty practically had to turn a town upside down and build his own colliery when he could have had what *you* believe was just as good, or even better, by using a village and a breaker already there. But *you* weren't the director, Marty was, and that's a director's prerogative. He obviously thought he could catch some additional ambience or feeling and, if the picture had proved a vast success, the extra cost would have been worth it."

Herb relit his pipe and went on.

"Now you wonder why somebody at Paramount or G. & W. didn't blow the whistle when the costs kept climbing up and up. It's this way. When you have a production in operation and you discover it's going beyond the original budget, whoever is putting up the cash says to himself in exasperation, 'What am I going to do? I've already got three or four million in the pot, which I don't want to lose. I can't quit now, I'll have to go along.' And he does, sometimes on and on. It's a very serious matter to stop a production, replace the director, and have a new man pick up the pieces. It's been done, but not often.

"Well, that's the definition of 'progressive seduction.' It's the kind of reasoning which trapped Paramount into spending excess millions for *Darling Lili* and *Paint Your Wagon* or Metro on *Zabriskie Point*, or a dozen other studios on a hundred films that bombed. For every million dollars spent, the studio must take in, roughly speaking, two and a half times in film rental to make a profit. That's rule of thumb, but it's fairly accurate.

"In the good old days that Hollywood's always dreaming about and longing for, the majors could get back their original investment and turn in a fat profit with almost any kind of a picture they made. Those were the days of block-booking and when the majors owned their own theater chains and the star system still worked. There also wasn't any other cheap entertainment. But Hollywood's watershed year was 1948 when TV and its Milton Berle came along. People, allegedly ninety million of them every week, were staying home in droves."

He paused.

"I'm sure *somebody* at Paramount saw what was going on with the *Mollies* but obviously was in the normal dilemma on calling it quits. Damned few studio heads will, although I can give you an example of one who did."

I listened.

"When Jim Aubrey took over M-G-M, Fred Zinnemann was making a picture in England for the company. You know who Fred Zinnemann is, don't you?"

His wife, Trudy, broke in.

"Of course he knows. Zinnemann made Art's favorite film, *High Noon*."

Herb smiled and went on.

"Well, Fred's done a whole lot more good ones besides *High Noon*. He's made dozens of pictures, I can't tell you how many, and most of them were artistic and box-office successes, like *The Men*, which he did for Stanley Kramer. And *Member of the Wedding, From Here to Eternity, The Nun's Story,* and *A Man for All Seasons*. He's had a few failures, too, but he's gotten about every kind of award you can get. So when you're talking about Fred Zinneman, you're talking about one of the best, if not the very best.

"At any rate, the picture he was making in England for M-G-M was an adaptation of André Malraux's *Man's Fate*. The studio'd already sunk four million dollars into production which wasn't half finished. Aubrey asked how much more it would take for completion and the answer was at least another four million.

"Aubrey did a lot of checking and some heavy thinking, then came out with his decision. 'Kill it,' he told Zinnemann. 'We'll take a four-million-dollar loss now instead of maybe an eight-million-dollar one later.' That took guts. Maybe Aubrey will succeed in bringing back M-G-M to some of its former glory, or at least put the company on a paying basis, and maybe he won't. But at least he'll get an 'E' for that effort."

Herb sighed deeply and shook his head as I recalled to him the reviews on the *Mollies*.

Roger Greenspun said in the New York *Times*:

> *The Molly Maguires* is full of illustrations but quite without insight. The camera pans not so much to reveal action as to show off the mood and detail of a setting . . . even the dogs run out and bark on cue.
>
> Personally, I prefer the well-oiled mechanics of James Wong Howe's camera to the timid positions of Walter Bernstein's screenplay. In any case, both are subject to a directorial hand that mistakes effects for effectiveness and replaces complexity with confusion.

Getting closer to its source, here's what Ernest Schier wrote in the Philadelphia *Evening Bulletin*.

> *The Molly Maguires*, a story about rebellious Pennsylvania miners almost a century ago, might have been dubbed the spy who came in from the coal . . . with the aid of James Wong Howe's evocative photography, the soot-covered old mining town materializes on the screen. . . . The film suggests, rarely refines, and pursues its melodramatic tale weakly.
>
> That isn't dust on the faces of the actors, it is only grease paint.

I asked my friend Joe Davies, former city editor of the recently defunct Mahanoy City *Record-American* and a loyal Son of St. David, what he thought. Joe shook his head and smiled.

"It didn't make me mad at anybody, even James McParlan, and he's the Molly who's supposed to have sliced off my grandfather's ears and then ripped out his tongue."

I'll let Tom Barrett wrap it up for the prosecution. In

addition to his editorial responsibilities on the Shenandoah *Evening Herald*, Tom is author of *The Mollies Were Men* and a former president of Local Number 256, Ancient Order of Hibernians. Incidentally, his great uncle was a member of the Shenandoah branch of the Molly Maguires, the one infiltrated by James McParlan. I didn't like to question Tom on the probability that his uncle was hanged as a result of McParlan's "treachery." Instead, I asked him what he thought of the film. He grinned.

"Dull. I thought I'd get all excited and go out and kill a Welshman, maybe even our mutual friend Joe Davies. But I didn't get sore at anybody. I couldn't believe it was made by Paramount; to me it looked more like Walt Disney."

Chapter Twenty-Seven

WHEN Metro-Goldwyn-Mayer used to run studio tours, the guides, or so I'm told, always had trouble dragging customers away from a dressmaker's dummy of Joan Crawford. I saw it before it was sold to the highest bidder for the ridiculously low price of twelve hundred eighty dollars, and I, too, was pretty much impressed. I figured it would take one *hell* of a woman to occupy all that space; there was considerable expansion out in front and I do believe those shoulders would have been of interest to the late Knute Rockne.

Well, when I saw the original I didn't change my opinion. That *was* one hell of a woman pouring Pepsi-Cola for me in her apartment a couple of months later. Maybe Joan Crawford doesn't look as young as she did forty-five years ago when she broke into the movies, but at sixty-three, an age to which she admits without any hesitation, she's still one damned attractive broad.

I thought to myself beforehand, What in God's name can I talk about to a pro who's been interviewed thousands and thousands of times? With somebody of lesser stature I might start out with, "Well, what's new, kid?" but you don't treat *this* dame *that* way. Besides, practically everybody knows Joan Crawford was born Lucille Le Sueur in San Antonio, Texas, a long time ago; that she's starred in as many movies as John Wayne and even more than Bette Davis; that she's the recipient of all kinds of awards including the Academy's; that she was the Industry's top breadwinner; that she was married four times, twice to matinee idols and twice to multi-millionaires, and that currently she's head lady of a soft-drink business which is giving Number One a run for the money.

So what subject could we talk about that's always interesting and new? Sex, of course.

"Sex?" Miss Crawford raised heavy eyebrows in wonderment. "I'm all for it," she said reassuringly.

She went on.

"But dirty sex pictures, the kind they're making out in Hollywood these days? N.O.! They're disgusting and sick, and if you've seen one you've seen them all. I say sex is a private affair between one man and one woman, to be enjoyed in a bedroom with doors closed. *I* don't want an audience of *voyeurs*."

I'm sure her eyes must have flashed but I couldn't tell; she never once removed the huge, dark, tortoiseshell spectacles she wore and which have become one of her trademarks. The rest of her was clearly visible, a finely shaped head, long, straight, reddish-tinted hair, ivory skin, a slender neck resting upon those famed broad shoulders which dictated women's styles for several seasons, and, when she crossed them, legs as shapely as they looked back in 1929 when she starred in *Our Modern Maidens* with Douglas Fairbanks, Jr., whom she later married.

It's not easy to sit around making small talk with a legend although this legend did her best to put me at ease. Whiskey or a cocktail if I wanted one, but at eleven A.M. I'm happy to say nothing alcoholic sounds pleasant. Neither for that matter did Pepsi, which is what I settled for. However, Miss C. shared a bottle of the stuff with me so it didn't taste too bad. I mentioned to my hostess that I'd recently been seeing her product in far-off places where heretofore only her competitor's was available.

275

"It damned well better be," Miss Crawford said. "I'm all over the world plugging it. You ought to see my schedule."

My hostess turned to one of the two female secretaries on hand and asked for a copy of the current travel sheet. I took a look and gasped. During the next thirty days, beginning with a bottlers' convention in Chicago where she'd be the principal speaker, Pepsi's V.P., widow of Alfred Steele who ran the company, would make fifty or more other whistle stops to address Junior Chambers of Commerce and Junior Leagues, high school and college commencements, to judge beauty and pie-eating contests, to attend Little League ball games, Boy Scout and Girl Scout Jamborees and Bar Mitzvahs.

"Man," she said, when I returned the schedule, "you gotta be with it! I hope I am, our company's directed toward youth."

She smiled and tossed in a plug.

"The Pepsi generation, you know."

No matter whether Miss Crawford is making her pitch to kids or to their elders, you can be sure of one thing—wherever she goes she'll look and act like a movie queen. Forty years of being one at M-G-M under Howard Strickling's tutelage has proven to be good and enduring training. And everywhere Miss Crawford is seen, there'll be a lineup of admiring gents, even comparatively young ones, like say around forty years old, who'd be delighted to escort her any place the lady's heart desires, including the nearest Holiday Inn.

My date with Miss Crawford in her New York apartment was set up by her old director, George Cukor.

"There's a guy," commented my hostess, "who'll still be making pictures when the new crop of nudie and sex-film directors have faded into oblivion. There's always a place for a genius like George; he's one of the reasons why Hollywood isn't going to die."

I must have registered surprise; Miss Crawford shrugged her shoulders, the broad ones I told you about.

"Could be others differ with me, but I still think I'm right.

Of course, I believe the days of the very big-budget film are over. I have three good story ideas in mind and if I decide to make them, it'll be in Hollywood. These won't cost more than seven hundred thousand dollars, and if the first one goes O.K., I'll continue with the other pair.

"Tell you one thing, Hollywood's great because that's where the pros are and I like to work only with pros. They come to the lot on time, they put in a full day's work, they do their level best, and they have a sense of responsibility to their producers and studios. That's the way it ought to be; in fact, if it's my picture, that's the way it's *going* to be."

My hostess looked a bit grim.

"When I make *my* pictures, anybody who works for me and doesn't act like a pro, I'll kick them right in the ass and boot them out of the lot."

According to Cukor, Howard W. Koch, and a couple of other directors, Miss Crawford practiced what she preached and as Koch said, "Joan never missed a beat."

The last movie in which Miss Crawford starred, in fact the last one she acted in, was a low-budget film made in England. It was titled *Trog* and it was not a success although Miss Crawford, herself, drew good critical comments. We didn't talk about the film except in passing, but we did talk about an interview she'd had in London with a reporter from the New York *Times*. My hostess was annoyed at some of the conclusions her interviewer had drawn.

"It was unfair. The guy complained because he claimed he couldn't get an appointment with me for five weeks. What the hell! I was busy making a picture and that was my first responsibility. I had to be up at five-thirty A.M. to get to the studio on time. I'd put in a tough day and come back to my hotel late in the evening, dog-tired.

"No use bellyaching, though. Who gives a damn about retractions? Nobody! You know what they do with yesterday's newspapers."

I'd watched Miss Crawford appear on television a couple of

times as a guest on various talk shows. I asked her what she thought of that medium. She seemed somewhat less than enthusiastic.

"All right, I suppose. I've no objection. If you're willing to learn, you can get something out of it. But as a career, the answer is 'no.' "

She's also "guested" on a couple of TV dramas and starred in a Western, one of the late Dick Powell's. I hadn't seen any of these and so I was in no position to discuss them with Miss Crawford. I had the feeling she wouldn't have been interested anyway.

She once told George Gent of the New York *Times* she was a "bona fide, dues-paying, eye-straining, undisguised television fan." But this was shortly before NBC released an episode in its television series *The Virginian*. Miss Crawford had a starring role in it; maybe she really did like TV then. Who knows? This was back in 1961.

I couldn't think of anything else to ask my hostess and I was afraid I'd not be able to down another glass of the stuff I'd been drinking; perhaps it wasn't made for members of my generation. So I thanked her and got ready to take off.

Some wise man—Ben Franklin if I recollect, and I am about to paraphrase his words considerably to make my point —once said that if a female's got it at sixteen, she'll still have it at sixty. When I said good-bye to my hostess and looked her over once more, I thought to myself, How wise Poor Richard really was.

Chapter Twenty-Eight

THEY'RE BOTH gracious, lovely, intelligent women, so I'm sure neither Geraldine Fitzgerald nor Sylvia Sidney will be offended if I split this chapter between them. Actually, I can't imagine either of these still-attractive, middle-aged, soft-spoken, old-time movie stars, who now live full lives far removed from Hollywood, caring particularly what anybody has to say about them.

For each, the movie world is a thing of the remote past and neither has the slightest desire to return to it, although, of course, you can't be altogether *sure* of that. Even though they're different in so many ways, I'm tying this pair together because within an hour each used almost identical phrases to express her opinion about the "Beautiful People" who once lived in Hollywood.

I saw Miss Fitzgerald first. She lives in a good although not plush Manhattan apartment house. The view from her fifteenth-floor apartment is superb. You can see the Metropolitan Museum and a large, grassy clearing in Central Park where I watched a baseball game in progress.

"Kind of an anachronism in this jam-packed city, the way it's been for the last fifty years, I guess, to have so much open space for children to play in," my hostess commented. "Baseball now, although that season's just about over, but they'll be playing football soon, and then there'll be sledding, something for every season. They're all rich kids, I imagine, but from here you can't tell the difference and I sometimes sit where you're standing and look out for hours."

My wife and I had come back a few months before from a visit to friends in Ireland and when I closed my eyes momentarily and listened to Miss Fitzgerald's wonderful Gaelic lilt, I could easily imagine we were back in Dublin at a performance of the Abbey Players. It was in Eire's capital city that Miss Fitzgerald got her start on the stage.

"Not at the Abbey," she said, "but at the Gate Theater which was the alternate, maybe not so famous as the Abbey but quite good; my training there was superb. I spent a couple of seasons in Dublin. I was born there, you know."

I just couldn't help smiling at this totally superfluous information and my hostess joined me, only she actually laughed and her sharp, bright eyes lit up.

"Sticks out all over, doesn't it? I guess I've got the brogue worse than ever; my husband and I just got back from Eire a couple of days ago, or, rather I did; he's coming home later this afternoon."

We moved from the window to the center of the living room and sat in front of an open fireplace which fortunately wasn't lit; the day was excessively warm for October. My hostess took it for granted that my favorite beverage was tea (which I loathe) and poured a cup for each of us. I wish I'd have had the nerve to suggest Irish coffee, a far superior drink in my opinion, but I think I'd have swallowed camomile or anything my hostess suggested, she was so damned nice, and she kept our appointment on time.

In the past few days I'd had two unpleasant experiences, one sad, and the other merely annoying, with a couple of Miss F's erstwhile Hollywood colleagues. As a result I'd lost considerable confidence both in myself and the reliability of future interviewees and didn't know quite what to expect when I rang the Fitzgerald doorbell, or even if she'd respond.

The two women shall be nameless; I'll identify them only by stating that the first was once one of the most beautiful brunettes in filmdom, and the other a compatriot of Miss Fitzgerald, with a brogue quite as thick. I flew a good many miles in a southerly direction to keep a date with the brunette who had disappeared from everyone's sight some years before. Besides being a physical knockout, she was, or so I'd been told by a friend who did a series of newspaper articles on her, one of the most knowing actresses he'd ever talked to.

I thought the opinions of this particular Hollywood drop-out would be worth soliciting. And what's the use kidding myself, I wanted to see if she was just as alluring as ever, forgetting, of course, that twenty-five years had elapsed since I'd last seen her perform. She was fairly young then, even though she'd been a star in several films, and I figured she ought to be in her early fifties at the most.

I had a tough time finding out where she lived. A chance remark I heard in a talent agent's office (not hers) put me on the scent and finally I got her telephone number and address. We made a date for the following afternoon. She lived way out in the country on a small farm quite a distance from the airport and I was sure I'd never locate the place. But her directions were so specific I had no more than my usual amount of trouble finding it. But I'd planned for getting lost at least three times in my rented car so I still got to my appointment on time, actually a couple of minutes ahead of our date.

As directed, I turned off the main highway to follow a narrow, winding dirt road for several miles more, observing all the landmarks I'd been given. There wasn't anybody around to ask each time I strayed so I mushed along through the deserted countryside until I reached my destination. The house, a small, weather-beaten, white frame structure was in the middle of a dry, weed-filled garden.

I climbed up four shaky steps and rang the rusty doorbell. From somewhere deep inside I heard a faint tinkle and waited for the response which was not forthcoming. I pushed it again and again but still got no answer. The only thing I figured then was that my would-be date simply wasn't showing on time and assumed she'd been hung up somewhere and would arrive soon, full of apologies.

I waited for an hour; in that time only one vehicle, a noisy farm tractor, passed by. Finally I walked around to a side window and peered in. The husky voice I'd heard the day before should have aroused my suspicions but it didn't. She was in the classic drunkard's pose, seated on a chair, head lying between outstretched arms on the kitchen table, long straggly gray hair almost but not quite completely covering the ruined face, and a couple of bottles—dead soldiers, I was sure—by her side and a couple more on the floor.

I rapped my knuckles against the windowpane, if only to make sure the lady wasn't dead. She heard me, tried to look around, but didn't make it. The effort was just too much and that once lovely head fell back again, shoulders sagging. I got into my car and took off for the airport. When I arrived there I thought, just to make sure, I'll call her.

The phone rang a dozen times before she answered. Then came that same husky voice. "You got a wrong number, you ———'d up son-of-a-bitch, whoever you are."

Within twenty-four hours came my second letdown. I had a date which I'd confirmed in writing a week before with the lady herself; a carbon copy went to her agent. On the morning of our date I telephoned the actress just to be sure.

"Come for cockails at four," she said quite cordially, and promptly at four I pushed her doorbell. There was no response, I rang a couple of times more; still no one came. I'd have had to climb out the fire escape twenty stories above street level to peer into these windows and maybe be shot for my trouble. This was not rural America, it was Manhattan.

So I went downstairs and asked the doorman if he had any idea where the lady might have gone.

"Oh, I seen her take the dog out for a walk about a half-hour ago," he replied. "Was she expectin' you?" I nodded and he looked at me, I thought, in a rather commiserating fashion. "Why don't you sit over on that bench in the park opposite; you can see when she comes back."

Then he added enigmatically, "I wouldn't count on it, mister."

I sat and waited for almost an hour. Then I walked across the street to the apartment house. The doorman saw me coming.

"She didn't get back yet, mister. Do you want to leave a message?"

I did, with my telephone number on it, but she never called back. I talked to her agent who was sorry but otherwise non-committal. I knew this time that alcohol had nothing to do with it, a fact I confirmed with a producer for whom the actress used to work.

"She's not a drunk," he explained when I told him what had happened, "just unreliable."

I must say, except for these two exceptions, batting averages of the stars and those otherwise employed by the Industry, at least those I'd seen, was a thousand. And now back to Miss Fitzgerald, who'd answered the door seconds after I rang it.

For those with short memories, I'm listing a few of her credits, both screen and stage, past and present. What I remember best in the former category were *Wuthering Heights, Watch on the Rhine, Dark Victory*, the latter with Bette Davis. ("I fulfilled a lifetime ambition to play in a picture with Bette," Miss F told me.) Even when the pictures in which she appeared were given bad notices, the Irish actress seemed to come out well; I can't recall her getting anything but good reviews.

She's been in countless stage productions ever since she left Hollywood a good many years back. The last one I saw her in was Eugene O'Neill's *Long Day's Journey into Night*, in which she starred with Robert Ryan and Stacy Keach. The reviews were raves.

"I always seem to be acting in the sad ones," she said. "And for a while, when I was making movies all I seemed to be picked for were prison pictures. I got so I hated them. That's the trouble out there, or it was when I was on the scene. You had to take what they handed you. Bogie, whom I was crazy about, once told me that if you want to be a success, you conform; take what they give you and never rebel.

"We were like pawns in a game of chess; we were permitted to move in only one direction. Only queens could move in all directions.

"My trouble was that I did nothing but rebel and they didn't like me for it. I didn't like them either; they had a theory of 'anti-fun,' particularly the Warner brothers. I detested Hollywood from the moment I arrived and always had a mental bag packed to come back East. Which is not to say I didn't have lots of good friends. Bogie was one and so were Charles Lederer, Ben Hecht, Charles McArthur, John Houseman, and Henry Miller. Henry, by the way, was then living in a shack and we all brought him food like ravens. Most of my friends were writers; they were the only people I wanted to be with even though in Hollywood they're rated as third-class citizens."

She shook her head.

"I think they're getting better treatment now but I wouldn't know. I came to Hollywood in 1939 and left in 1946. While I've been back for short visits, I haven't really lived there since. It was a strange world, I had the feeling I was living during the last days of Pompeii. And I *knew*, like Cassandra, what the future was going to be, had to be.

"Yet, it was all so incredibly wonderful. Unless you were part of the scene you just can't believe it. But it was unreal and you knew it was going to come to an end shortly. The actors, those legendary beautiful people, surrounded you. They were the gods, nourished and cherished and protected, never exposed to public gaze unless they were watched over. The women were magnificent, the men suntanned and handsome.

"Everything that could be done to make them *more* magnificent and *more* beautiful was done. Their best features were emphasized; their noses straighter, their eyes larger, their foreheads higher. It was all a tremendous exaggeration. We were not real, we were dream people, carried on the palms of the hands of those who fed us and took care of us. We were trained race horses, manes plaited, silver bridles polished, we'd shine and sparkle and on order we'd kick in our stalls."

She sighed.

"To our 'owners' we were objects of tremendous value but there was no freedom and no *joie de vivre*. And even among the gods there was a caste system. There were just plain stars, then there were the superstars, and above them the super superstars. And, finally, the penultimate ruler of us all, the super, super superstar, Queen Joan Crawford."

Miss Fitzgerald refilled our cups. This time she observed my barely controlled shudder and asked me if I was sure I wouldn't like something else, perhaps a highball. I answered that I wouldn't mind a highball, and my hostess obliged. Then she went on.

"Please don't get the impression that some of these 'gods' and 'goddesses' weren't warm, wonderful men and women. Bette Davis, for instance. I had a good role but Bette never once tried to upstage me and she certainly could have, had she wanted to. I do hope you'll be able to talk to her; I'll call her later for you." (Miss Fitzgerald did call but Bette Davis wasn't seeing anyone.)

"Then Bogie was another; gentle, kind, and understanding. He was a true star; a pleasure to work with. And the most intelligent of all, David Niven, but he's living in England again. If you're going to be there I'll give you a note to take to him."

Miss Fitzgerald had to leave for the airport to pick up her husband, Stuart Scheftel, so we said good-bye. Something the doorman told me as I left the apartment house made me like Miss Fitzgerald even more than I had. He had a large smile on his face and his brogue was as thick as my hostess'.

"I see you got to Miss Fitzgerald, all right. She had to go

out for a bit right before you got here and she was so worried she might not be back in time. Told me to detain you, sir, and I was prepared to. [He was a pretty big guy and I wondered if he'd intended to use force.] But she returned about ten minutes before you arrived, all out of breath. That's a real lady for you, isn't she?"

I agreed heartily; then her doorman added the clincher.

"She's Irish, you know."

I hated to let the doorman down after that so I didn't say anything when he whistled a cab for me although it was only a few minutes' walk to the restaurant where I was meeting Sylvia Sidney. And now for the "department of coincidence." As usual I was early so I asked the driver to let me off a block away. He did, and I hadn't taken five steps when I saw Bennett Cerf stroll by. I didn't know him and I'm sure he didn't know me, but I wonder what he'd have said had I told him I was on my way to see his ex-wife who told me she hadn't seen Bennett for years.

At any rate, Miss Sidney was waiting for me in the company of her press agent, John Springer, who introduced us and left. Miss Sidney is sixty now and makes no effort to hide it. Her graying hair is pulled back and tied in a knot; she uses little makeup, but her figure is as trim as it ever was and her eyes as large and as lustrous as when I saw them in *An American Tragedy*, made in the late thirties. She starred in dozens of other films, *Ladies of the Big House*, *The Miracle Man*, *Trail of the Lonesome Pine*, *Violent Saturday*, and *Street Scene*, to mention a few.

But Miss Sidney, too, left Hollywood a long while ago and while her memories of the place are more pleasant than Miss Fitzgerald's, she never was fooled into believing life there was more than illusory.

"It was a dream world, a kind of Alice in Wonderland, with its kings and queens, princes and princesses, and our millions of loyal subjects. But it wasn't real and it couldn't last. They painted glamor on thick, but you had to know it was only

286

paint. True glamor comes from inside, not sprayed on the skin. I think Dietrich proves this point."

She sighed.

"But they made it all seem pretty wonderful at that and they all bent over backwards to make you happy—that is, the stars. If you had a headache, or a tummyache, or a toothache, they nursed you, and petted you, and pampered you like you were royalty. And everybody stopped working until you told them you felt better and would bravely carry on. They were all *so* sympathetic and *so* understanding. And it was all *so* damned phony. Those beautiful unreal people!

"You had your own private suite on location, you had your own dressers, your docile stand-in; your maid belonged to you *personally*, she was your adoring slave, and when you went out the red carpet was there waiting for you to step on. I will have to admit it was fun and it took a bit of getting used to when it was all over.

"Yet, during the whole time I was in Hollywood, I never *really* liked the life and never felt I was an integral part of it. I had a mental suitcase packed to take off anytime I felt I must. I suppose I was beguiled into believing the Hollywood world held the universe together and if it ever collapsed nothing else could survive."

Our waiter brought coffee for us. Miss Sidney continued.

"Even though I did very little partying, I wouldn't want you to believe there weren't a great many people I liked and respected out in Hollywood. I enjoyed both Walter Wanger's conversation as well as his abilities as a producer and I was fond of James Cagney and Spencer Tracy, not only to work with but to be with. I don't believe I'd ever go back again but . . ."

She shrugged her shoulders.

"Who knows? Maybe I wouldn't have the will power to resist if they offered me a good part with plenty of money. It was pretty wonderful when I think about it. I'm still acting though. I've just come back from a summer of stock which kept me in trim. I've a couple of new occupations going, as you may have heard."

Miss Sidney elaborated.

"First of all I raise dogs—pugs—and I've two champs, 'Captain' and 'The Kid.' A long while back I gave up my New York apartment and moved to Connecticut where I bought a few acres of land. I've got thirty dogs on it now in addition to my pair of champs. I've written several magazine articles about them, too.

"Now I'll tell you about my next activity. I do needlework. You may not know what I'm talking about but I think your wife will [she did], and recently I had a book published on the subject. I don't want you to think I did all the writing myself; I didn't. I had a collaborator named Allan Lewis. We did it together and I got a lot of pleasure out of it. Have you ever had an autograph party?"

I nodded. I've had several and they were all depressingly dismal affairs where I sat around in lonely silence surrounded by never diminishing piles of my "masterpiece" and tried to look occupied or at least uninterested in the people who passed by on their way to the corset department or gents' furnishings. Occasionally some woman would come 'round to tell me she's crazy about my work and can't wait until the current one I'm attempting to peddle is on the shelf of the local library. "I'm first on the list," she'll be sure to add.

I know a writer named Ed Love who turned out a couple of good books, one called *Subways Are for Sleeping* which was later made into a Broadway play. He told me Marshall Field of Chicago gave him an autograph party.

"For two hours I sat there on my ass," he told me, "and didn't sell one goddamned book. Finally I couldn't take it anymore and said to hell with it. I got up and started to leave. Just then a woman, all out of breath with excitement, ran up and grabbed my coat lapels and said, 'I just dropped a watch down the toilet bowl.'

"I didn't know what I was supposed to do except look sympathetic, which I did. After clinging to me for a couple of seconds she ran off but hadn't gotten more than three paces away when she turned around. 'It belonged to my daughter-in-law,' she said sadly. End of story."

So let this be a warning to writers who've not been through the ordeal. Avoid autograph parties unless you're a celebrity which, of course, Miss Sylvia Sidney still is.

The actress went on and her smile was beatific.

"Bloomingdale's gave me one and it was marvelous. Do you know how many books I autographed there in just a single afternoon?"

I had no idea what the figure would be except considerably more than I'd have been able to peddle.

"A hundred," I hazard, thinking big.

Miss Sidney smiled, and if she weren't such a sweet-natured person, I'd say she looked smug.

"We sold almost *two* hundred. By three o'clock that afternoon they actually ran out of books and had to send somebody over to the warehouse so they could replenish the supply."

I did some rapid mental calculations. Suppose Miss Sidney's book sold for ten dollars and her royalties had reached the fifteen percent status, which they do after the first ten thousand copies. She'd have made around three hundred dollars for five hours' work, which, for the ordinary writer would be an achievement of titanic proportions. However, this doesn't take into consideration that there were at least another four hundred hours previously of gathering material, collating it, doing the actual writing, then re-writing, editing, and finally reading proofs. Without a collaborator of Allan Lewis' caliber, the work load would have doubled.

So where are we? All I know is that according to my Hollywood correspondent, Mr. Ray Crossett, whom I hope you haven't forgotten already, Miss Sidney used to get paid three hundred thousand dollars a year for which she worked two-thirds of the time. I'll let anybody take it from there and develop his own figures, conclusions, and finally a moral if he can find one.

Miss Sidney talked about the young generation which is taking over the Industry and doing a good job of it although she's not sure how.

"Sometimes I think I understand them, but most of the time I don't. I must tell you about my young son, Jody; his father was Luther Adler, you know, a great talent. Jody and I often talk about the old days in Hollywood which, of course, he knows nothing about except second- or third-hand. I don't even know if he watches my films on the Late, Late Show. I know *I* don't. I don't ever even go to Sardi's anymore where I'd be bumping into people who'd want to talk about the old days; I've not the slightest desire to.

"Well, anyway, a couple of weeks ago they had a revival of movies made in the thirties and forties, and one of them was *Street Scene,* which really *was* my picture. Jody went and afterward came back to the house with a bunch of his friends who'd gone with him. I haven't any idea how they felt about *Street Scene* or what they said to each other when they were among themselves. They're an honest group of young people.

"I asked Jody what he thought of the movie. He's a very sweet boy and I could tell he wanted to let me down as little as possible and yet stick to the truth. He thought for a couple of seconds before answering.

" 'Don't you think, Mother, it's just a *little* bit dated?' "

Chapter Twenty-Nine

"STINSON, ESTELLE JUDY GEETING, if this should meet the eye of, you could help fill the blanks in your life and let the public know how your American Dream turned out."

I know something about you, Estelle. You were a twenty-three-year-old clerk (a "popular" one said the *Daily News*) in the F. O. Reed Shoe Store on Main Street in McKeesport, Pennsylvania, when your big chance to become a movie star arrived, so you'd be close to eighty now. Your first marriage, which ended in divorce, was to Robert I. Geeting, a fellow townsman with whom you had two children, both sons. One died shortly after birth and is buried in Lot Number 532 at the Richland Cemetery. The other, Raymond, survived and was adopted by your second husband, Eddie Stinson, the famous aviator and airplane designer, who was killed in a crash at Chicago years later.

I understand Eddie was in McKeesport looking over possible locations for a factory when he met you; that it was love at first sight, that your marriage to him was a happy one, and until his death you lived in the Detroit suburb of Dearborn. Nobody around your hometown of McKeesport seems to know what's happened to you since. Your sister-in-law, Mrs.

Joseph E. Judy, with whom you used to exchange Christmas cards, hasn't received one from you in over a quarter of a century, and your favorite niece, Delores Judy Trainor, who says you were very kind to her when she used to visit your Dearborn house, told me it's been more than thirty years since she last heard from you. Delores seems to think you may be living somewhere in southern California.

Your three brothers and two sisters plus their offspring have long since departed from the scene although I suppose that if I devoted time to it I could track them down and fill in a few of those blank spots myself. However, all I'd be doing then would be pandering to curiosity because, for the purposes of this story, I know all I need to know about you, Estelle. Yet, I can't help wondering how long it took you and the ten other "International Beauty and Brains Contest" winners to find out all of you were only glorified magazine subscription salesladies and that your chances for a promised fabulous movie career were never more than slim.

Photoplay's enormously popular contest—"The Chance of Chances for Half a Score of American Girls to Become Moving Picture Stars"—was by no means the first, nor was it the last, the Industry and its house organ, the fan mag, used to exploit Hollywood's vast appeal to the wide-eyed, gullible, movie-going public.

Almost thirty years after Estelle boarded that New York-bound express for movie fame and fortune in Fort Lee, New Jersey, and all points west, a Toledo, Ohio, chambermaid became a Hollywood "Cinderella for a Day."

On March 22, 1946, the Toledo *Blade* reported:

> For nineteen years little Mrs. Albina Malik . . . went about her duties at the Commodore Perry Hotel, working quietly, unobtrusively among the "unseen army" of those who serve hotel guests from all around the country.
>
> Then, the hand of Hollywood reached out to weave its magic—and motherly, bewildered Mrs. Malik was given a real-

life role about which she may have dreamed through the years as she watched the guests she served. For Mrs. Malik herself became a guest.

She had breakfast in bed, went shopping in Toledo stores, was whisked from restaurants to theaters in a shiny new car, and rested in a suite of rooms in the same hotel in which she worked.

And who was Mrs. Malik's fairy godmother, going around doing good deeds and plucking poor old ladies from their dirty jobs and giving them a taste of how the Beautiful People live? Read on.

The *Blade* continued:

. . . this shy little woman was the honored guest of United Artists, producer of the film, *The Diary of a Chambermaid*, and Ted Teacher, manager of Loew's Valentine at which the picture will be shown. The movie folk touched Mrs. Malik with their magic wand and gave her two days and nights of the life for which a Cinderella traditionally yearns.

. . . the movie wand had touched her and then had gone on.

Photoplay's "Beauty and Brains Contest" was announced in the October 1915 issue of that publication.

This contest was instituted for two purposes: to give ten unknown young American women a chance for stellar honors in the great field of motion pictures, and to provide one of the biggest of the producing companies with ten possible stars. . . .

It is only necessary that the contestants shall have *no previous stage or picture experience* [the italics are theirs]. Actresses either of the "legitimate" or photoplay stages will not be considered.

For the rest, send two photographs to The Judges, "Beauty and Brains Contest," *Photoplay* Magazine, 350 North Clark

Street, Chicago. Send a profile picture and a full-face study . . . also write a letter of not more than one hundred fifty words stating: "Why I would like to be a photoplay actress."

At first our nation was divided into five Grand Divisions. Later, perhaps at the insistence of the State Department, unwilling to offend our neighbor to the north, Canada was included and the number of potential winners expanded to eleven.

Photoplay went on with the contest details:

The girls from the Grand Divisions will be taken to New York in first-class trains, will be properly chaperoned in the metropolis, and will be lodged, expenses paid in full, at one of Manhattan's most celebrated hotels, and within two weeks at most after their arrival in New York, will be given photographic and dramatic trials at the Fort Lee, New Jersey, studios of the World Film Corporation . . . from each Grand Division will come a pair of 'Twins of Future Celebrity.'

Those contestants who pass the final photographic and acting requirements, under the tutelage of the World's most eminent directors, will be given contracts as World Film actresses for a period of not less than one year, at a regular salary.

. . . Thus, the winners will either have established futures at a single cast of the dice of chance—or, failing that, they will in any event have had one of the most interesting experiences and the greatest trip of their lives. The ten winners will be announced and their pictures and letters will be published in *Photoplay* Magazine for February 1916.

The pitch waxed literary. The Industry's "avarice for loveliness is like the avarice of Moloch for its old-time sacrifices of beauty and youth—except that this is a complimentary, beneficent avarice—an avarice which serves rather than consumes. . . . It wants young women. It must have—as the name of this contest implicitly implies—'Beauty and Brains.'

294

"No qualification is necessary beyond their possession."

The contest, with its promise of "instant stardom," caught on. Photographs of beautiful young hopefuls began pouring in from every state in the Union, and later from all of Canada's provinces. By the time judges were announced the following month, nearly three thousand entries had been snared.

I wouldn't want to leave an impression that the contest was rigged; I'm sure it wasn't. Otherwise, it's more than likely at least one of the eleven beauties, a previously selected ringer, would have achieved at least a modicum of fame in the Industry. None of the winners did, although several, including our Miss Judy, no doubt made excellent marriages as a result of their fleeting notoriety. The contest certainly provided conversation pieces for envious contemporaries and future offspring, and *their* offspring as well. So maybe the fact that the eleven young ladies, eventually chosen from more than fifteen thousand contestants, didn't go on to movie fame and fortune in *Photoplay*'s *bona fide* offer wasn't too important after all.

I keep wondering whether today's more sophisticated generation—those eighteens to twenty-eights who won't fork over three bucks to see Gregory Peck's or Doris Day's interpretation of life—really would believe *Photoplay* offered a shortcut to stardom. I doubt it, but as George Cukor said, you must consider the era before you scoff at the beliefs it propagated. And, in their day, the movies exerted an unbelievable influence over the aspirations of hundreds of millions of moviegoers who believed everything they saw on the silver screen and, what those who were literate, found in the fan mags. For nearly five decades these media perpetuated the American Dream.

One of the most intelligent actresses I spoke to was Lillian Gish, a survivor of the silents, a great lady, a highly perceptive woman, and an erstwhile favorite subject of fan-mag writers. Shortly before my date to see Miss Gish in her Manhattan apartment, I came across an interview which appeared in the selfsame magazine only a few months before the "Beauty and

Brains" contest was announced. It shouldn't take more than a couple of paragraphs excerpted from that piece to provide an example of the dreary drivel avidly swallowed and accepted by millions of its readers.

Richard Willis wrote in the December 1914 issue of *Photoplay:*

Most people don't like making calls, but I am one of those old-fashioned individuals who enjoy it. We had not met before, these delightful Gish girls and I, and there already existed between us the easy friendship of youth with middle-age, so it was with a light heart and a half-smile of pleased anticipation that I approached their house that sunny afternoon. Someone was playing the piano—not really playing, just strumming idly as though to fill a tedious interval when there was nothing to engage her attention.

I rang the bell and the strumming stopped abruptly, quick steps crossed the hall, and the door was thrown hospitably open by the very tall, very fair girl, with her blonde hair hanging down her back, who is Dorothy.

"Why, Mr. Willis, how good of you to come to see us," she cried, clasping my hand with the firm heartiness of a friendly boy. "Lillian, oh, Lillian, here's Mr. Willis," she called, raising her voice a little. In response to her call there entered another very tall, very fair girl, with color in her cheeks, a little more vivid than her sister's and with her very blonde hair piled high on her head.

"How do you do, Mr. Willis," she cried gaily, sweeping me a little curtsy and then sitting down beside her sister on the broad couch before the west window. As for me, I simply sat and beamed at them for the moment. Certainly two sisters never made a prettier picture than did Lillian and Dorothy Gish there in the west window on that quaint brocaded couch, Lillian in a delicate pink frock with a turquoise brooch at her throat and Dorothy in a dress of filmy white, with the sunlight that streamed through the window turning their blonde hair to gold.

Although Mr. Willis went on for several thousand words more, I rest my case. I didn't expect Miss Gish, who's now in her seventies, to remember an interview she granted when she was fourteen or thereabouts, but she seemed amused when I read that excerpt to her. I told her about the "Beauty and Brains" contest. She smiled.

"It wasn't quite that easy then, and I don't think it is now. I know I cannot recall a world in which I was not an actress, and that's true for most of us who've survived. Mary Martin, Charlie Chaplin, both dear friends of mine; the theater's been almost the whole of their existence. Hepburn is another great whose life's been the stage. She was playing Juliet and somebody asked her how old she *really* was. 'I'm fourteen,' was her answer, and it was true. She *was* fourteen when she played Juliet. So it was with Charles Laughton and my sister, Dorothy. It was hard work.

"These were true artists, professionals with understanding and empathy and even for them to get ahead and stay ahead was never easy."

She paused in thought.

"And sometimes their empathy led them into difficulties. I'm thinking of Charles Laughton, a man of enormous talents. I was doing *Night of the Hunter* which Mr. Laughton directed with Robert Mitchum. The film didn't turn out as well as it might have because Mr. Laughton liked Mitchum and refused to let him be all bad, which the part required. However, that's beside the point, I suppose, although Mr. Laughton told me he wanted to make his audiences sit up instead of slouching in their seats. But he didn't. That was all so long ago."

Miss Gish sighed, then continued.

"I don't think the current generation could be fooled easily, but then again you must remember the times. Today's young men and young women are smarter, to be sure. I find them a most perceptive lot and I do hope I understand them. I think they see through sham now, but perhaps they would not have in 1914."

What Miss Gish told me next has nothing to do with *Photoplay*'s talent search, but I'm including it anyway because I can't think of another place in which to use it. The subject was "nudies" and sexploitation films, and I didn't bring it up.

"I often go to the movies, matinees when the audience is small, to see dirty pictures," said this fragile, gentle woman, who much of the time I was with her didn't seem quite of this world. Her interest is not prurient. "Sex is beautiful and so is nudity, and I want to see what's happening to both these days."

And now we return to 1915 and the Contest. Hollywood then was not quite yet the capital of the movie world; other cities were in competition for the title and, strangely enough, Fort Lee, New Jersey, was one of them. Here, in this small New York suburb which now houses the Syndicate's hierarchy, were World Film Corporation's major studios, although the company made many of its products on location.

Contest winners would get their training and start at Fort Lee, where, claimed *Photoplay*, "[there] will be found, in daily work upon the architecture of future dramatic masterpieces, men like Maurice Tourneur, the famous Frenchman who staged such successes as *Alias Jimmy Valentine* and *Les Misérables*; Albert Capellani, who made the production of *The Face in the Moonlight*; Emile Chautard, who guided the famous actor Holbrook Blinn through *The Boss* which Blinn himself had put on as a play upon the legitimate stage—and perhaps better known than any of them to the public at large, James Young, whose *Hearts in Exile*, a Russian masterpiece, will remain one of the great dramatic pictures of 1915."

Judges were chosen the following month. These included Miss Lillian Russell, "the most famous beauty of modern times"; William A. Brady, "one of the most experienced, best-known and shrewdest of New York's theatrical managers"; Miss Kitty Kelly, photoplay editor of the Chicago *Tribune*; Lewis J. Selznick, vice-president and general manager "and all-around genius of World Film," and Julian Johnson, editor of

Photoplay. Later, Clara Kimball Young, another star of the silents, was added to the board.

All these hard-working professionals certainly knew the winners they would choose had little or no chance for success in the movie world. Nevertheless, they lent their names to the contest and gave it a semblance of honesty. The final letdown must have been tremendous. The contest rolled on, month after month, with photographs and letters pouring in to *Photoplay's* Chicago office. By April 1916, when *Photoplay* announced that the competition was over, more than twenty thousand (or so the magazine claimed) young American and Canadian beauties had offered evidence of their individual qualifications to become movie stars.

After several postponements, the eleven winners, together with brief biographies and pictures, were announced in the July 1916 issue of the magazine. Those who collect statistics might like to hear a few that *Photoplay* collected.

It is interesting to note that the average age of the winning eleven is twenty-one years and ten months—thus: the youngest nineteen, the oldest twenty-three. . . . Their average height is five feet and four and a half inches, the tallest being five feet and six, the shortest five feet and two. Their average weight is one hundred twenty-five pounds. . . . Four of them are hazel-eyed, two are blue, two gray, one brown, one gray-blue, and one gray-brown.

There is no mention of bust measurements. I attribute this failure to the fact that these statistics, so vital today, were then considered unmentionable. Number One was a Southern belle.

Lucille Satterthwaite, of Waynesville, North Carolina, was born and reared in that town. From her twelfth to her sixteenth year she spent the winters in Cuba. She was privately tutored by a governess . . . later winning a scholarship to Elizabeth College in Charlotte. She finished her class years at Sweet Briar, Virginia. She was voted the most beautiful girl in that school. At fifteen years of age she won the Southern beauty prize at Allenton, and at nineteen took the national beauty prize at Philadelphia. . . . She has a coat of arms on both sides of her family; her grandparents on her father's side came from Europe with William Penn, and the family of her mother is connected with British royalty.

I think Howard Strickling, who was to make his appearance in Hollywood three years later, would have been pleased with whoever did Miss Satterthwaite's bio.

Number Two was Florence Gray, of Seattle, Washington.

Her parents came here from Sweden; she excels as a swimmer. The beauties of Lake Washington are "all in her know" but she never has climbed the surf at Coney, or peered at the mysteries of life from the Woolworth Tower. . . .

Third in line was Claire Lois Butler Lee, of Wichita, Kansas, who

doesn't care to be rescued from a burning skyscraper and believes firmly that the hoyden who rides cross-saddle twenty miles to save her lover by shooting his neck-rope in two has no place in the better class of pictures. Marguerite Clark's manner of adorning the screen suits her better.

Miss Lee is followed by Peggy Bloom of Orlando, Florida.

Peggy has good red Irish blood in her veins and by that same token some of it at the roots of her hair, which is abundant and teases one into thinking it was kissed by the warm lips of an autumn afterglow.

Next comes another Lee, Mildred,

who hails from Kansas City, Missouri, and confides that "I am just a movie bug." As a millinery model her face has looked out from the pages of many catalogues under the shading of midsummer flares and the saucy precipices of December toques. She has a mezzo-soprano voice of real timbre, and has played in amateur theatricals in child parts.

Our own Estelle Clair Judy comes next and I quote her biography in full.

Not long ago she led all contestants in a beauty contest arranged by a newspaper in her city, and at a national convention of photographers her photograph won first prize for a McKeesport exhibitor. For several years she was chief operator of the Bell Telephone Company in her town. [No mention of the F. O. Reed Shoe Store on Main Street where she worked before becoming a "hello girl."] When she faces the camera at Fort Lee it will not be the first time that remorseless glass eye has surveyed her; she played the leading female part in a local photo-drama some time ago, and played it well. She confesses she was "terribly scared at first, but soon got over it."

One more telephone operator and another descendant of British nobility. The former is Dallas-born Alatia Marton,

who will plug in the "Busy" signal . . . when she quits her telephone desk in the office of the Portland Cement Company to travel thousands of miles to the Fort Lee studios of World Film Corporation to be tested for stardom. . . . She is a Texas girl, and Texas girls have a reputation for getting pretty nearly everything they go after. . . .

The other claimant to British aristocracy is Vivian Suckling of Winnipeg, Canada,

who can trace her ancestry back to English nobles. . . . Her father is dead; her stepfather is fighting "somewhere in France" . . . that Lord Nelson, whose heroic statue breathes patriotism through the vex of Trafalgar Square, was an ancestor . . . that Sir John Suckling, whose pen traced thoughts into the poetry of England, is niched among her father's fathers.

["Her feet beneath her petticoat,/Like little mice, stole in and out," according to my edition of *Bartlett's*.]
The ninth winner was Lucille Zintheo of Spokane, Washington,

a Diana in a cozy corner. She has a trick of stunning you with a rose-colored silk sweater against a background of coquettish hat and sun-shade to blend. The charm of her is so fresh. You catch yourself musing under your breath that if all girls were—ah—like this, Cupid would be after hiring himself a room in a wearyhouse. . . .

Next to the last is Phyliss E. Curl, of Roxbury, Massachusetts:

an accomplished horsewoman who shares with Billie Burke the delightful distinction of freckles which do neither fade nor mar, and she is blonde with wavy hair and dark blue eyes.

And finally we come to Helen Arnold of Louisville, Kentucky:

. . . It's a clumsy cast of the thinker's fly that fishes for brains where beauty is not, only [come again?] she is a graduate of Presentation Academy and Cross School. Horseback riding, tennis, and dancing are her favorite pastimes.

There they were, all eleven eager beauties, stashed away at "an exclusive New York hotel, every expense paid," waiting for that quick trip to stardom, which, of course, never came. *Photoplay* and World Film Corporation had other fish to fry and, except for brief mention, there is no further word on the movie careers of those ten American and one Canadian young ladies. The December 1916 issue of *Photoplay*, the one in which the winners were announced, did note that

> First in point of immediate and brilliant triumph is Miss Helen Arnold, of Louisville, Kentucky, an ingenue lead in one of the finest studios and under the tutelage of one of the foremost directors in New York City. . . . She was hired by William Sherrill, president of the Frohman Amusement Corporation . . . and is getting the ingenue role in August Thomas' great American play, *The Witching Hour.*
>
> Of equal interest, Miss Lucille Zintheo was hired by World Film Corporation. She is to appear in *The Price She Paid*, Norma Talmadge's first picture under her corporate name. Miss Zintheo will be directed by Allan Dwan.

There are a few words about Peggy Bloom and Lucille Satterthwaite being viewed for further consideration by several motion picture companies, but we are left wondering what these propositions were. The whole subject was dropped thereafter, at least as far as I could determine, except that in October 1917 Miss Zintheo's name appears for the last time.

> . . . after some very credible work in a number of pictures, Miss Zintheo found she preferred the stage. She made a genuine hit in *His Little Widow*, at the Astor Theater, New York. . . . You will remember Miss Zintheo was the young lady who brought Spokane into prominence.

It could prove an interesting chore to learn what happened to the prize winners subsequent to their realization that they just weren't going to make it at Fort Lee, Broadway, or Hollywood. Unless you have more trust than I in the truth of those idyllic biographies the young ladies themselves furnished, they probably went back home to become telephone operators, schoolteachers, clerks, and finally, mothers, grandmothers, and great-grandmothers.

I don't know how many of them are extant—they'd all be

in their mid- or late seventies by now—but I'd guess most of them satisfied histrionic desires by singing in church cantatas and playing the lead in hometown theatricals, and I'll bet at least one of them survived long enough to perform in *Springtime for Henry*.

However, I leave this monumental research project to others while I move on to a real survivor, the "Duke" himself, Mr. John Wayne, of Hollywood, California.

Chapter Thirty

ANY SON-OF-A-BITCH who says John Wayne is a good guy I'll punch right on his fat nose. John Wayne isn't a good guy— he's a *great* guy! I watched this huge, craggy-faced man pace restlessly around his studio office and try hard to concentrate on what he told me about the Industry. But all the while I kept daydreaming that "The Duke" and I were riding the range together on our way to fight off a mob of dirty, rotten cattle rustlers or maybe the pair of us were having a shootout with a bunch of sadistic renegades.

I'm a senior citizen and by now I should have learned that the Sixth Cavalry Division didn't always make it on time; that those tough, gun-totin' sheriffs frequently failed to remove their Stetsons in the presence of a lady; that the ladies themselves weren't always ladies, and that the baddies won just about as often as they lost.

But the very sight of John Wayne is sufficient to banish all such heretical thoughts. With the Duke around, you *know* the Sixth, colors flying, will be Johnny-on-the-spot; that the sheriff and the marshal are gentlemen at heart; that every woman, with the possible exception of those who hang around dance halls, is a virgin until she marries, and that in any shootout the survivors are those who are pure in heart.

The Duke's been making movies since 1931 and has starred in approximately two hundred ten major productions. The last one I saw him in was *True Grit* and I loved it as much as my eleven- and seven-year-old grandchildren did. In fact, over these past four decades, I can honestly say I never saw a John Wayne picture I didn't either like, or, as my friend Arthur Meyers would have phrased it, "didn't mind." And I have seen one *hell* of a lot of the Duke's films.

While I felt some were better than others, I'm not alone in thinking the Industry owes more to the Duke than it does to anyone else. Nor have I much respect for the opinions of Academy Award judges whose ideas of great acting are the wooden, stiff-kneed puppetry of Marlon Brando and Charlton Heston or the sickening, Graustarkian simpers of Miss Julie Andrews. You can keep 'em all; just give me John Wayne, and, if you want to toss in Wendell Corey, Barry Sullivan, and Robert Ryan, I won't object. I'm even willing to buy Rex Harrison. But for God's sakes, don't give me any Method School baccalaureates. I want to *believe* what I see on the silver screen.

You can't tell me (and a lot of professional reviewers as well) that Wayne's roles in *The Quiet Man, She Wore a Yellow Ribbon,* and *Wake of the Red Witch* don't belong in Hollywood's Hall of Fame. Well, it was a long time coming but the Duke finally made it as Rooster Cogburn, the grizzled, dirty, sow-bellied, one-eyed old U.S. marshal in *True Grit.* Don't take my word for it; here's what three critics with quite disparate readership said about John Wayne and *True Grit.*

Richard Schickel wrote in *Life:*

> Watching, one shouts, laughs and, unaccountably, feels tears beginning to tingle. For you feel you may be witnessing not just the beginning of a good movie's climax but a full-throated valedictory for a tradition. Here is Wayne, the last of a great generation of western heroes committing himself again to an action that at once affectionately parodies and joyously summarizes the hundreds—thousands—of similar mo-

ments that have preceded it in film history. And there is a tremendous sense of relief in the way he goes about it.

. . . the most important element in this very funny film's triumph is John Wayne. He has discovered what's funny about the character he has always played . . . and now he gives us a rich double vision of it. At his age and station in life it is a true and gritty and hilarious thing to do, the true climax of a great and well-loved career as an American institution.

Even the *New Republic*'s Stanley Kauffmann, who doesn't seem to like anything in the movies, had a few (not many, it's true) kind words of praise, if not of the film itself, at least for its star.

Wayne has *us* going for him after all this time, and we not only relish his continental body and sprawl as usual; we can relish his age and his new freedom to break taboos.

I must have read at least fifty more reviews from magazines and newspapers from all over the United States, every one saying something good about *True Grit* and John Wayne's performance. But I think what *America*, the Jesuit publication, reported pleased me most. This may be because I'm awfully tired of Fellini's pretentiousness, and when I go to the movies I like at least a modicum of entertainment inserted in those ponderous attempts to edify me.

The point is that *True Grit*, unlike *The Wild Bunch* and a distressing number of other recent films, allows its story to speak for itself without self-righteous editorial comment. As a result it is apparently going to be seen and enjoyed by vast numbers of people, which after all is the one ingredient without which no film communication is possible.

How do you get to a star like John Wayne who's always making a movie somewhere and doesn't live out on a ranch? I don't know if the following method will work all the time, but it did for me. I telephoned his office, which occupies a couple of modestly furnished rooms in a small building on the nearly deserted Paramount lot where the Duke runs his own production company, Batjac. I asked his secretary if it would be possible to set up a future date with the boss and her answer was, "Ask him yourself."

"Come on in tomorrow morning," the Duke answered, "nine o'clock, if that's not too early for you. I haven't a damned thing to do till noon."

At nine I was there. At three minutes past the hour his secretary handed me a cup of coffee and, shaking her head dolefully, said she was terribly sorry but she couldn't understand what had happened to Mr. Wayne who was always on time and she hoped I wasn't offended. Five minutes later I heard somebody pounding up the steps, taking at least two at a time, and then in strode the Duke, out of breath and full of apologies.

"I'm sorry," he said. "If there's anything I hate it's guys who think they're big shots and keep other people waiting to prove it. But this morning the goddamned whirlybird had some rough going coming in here from the farm. [He didn't say *my* whirlybird or *my* farm.] We hit a thirty-mile wind."

When Wayne isn't on location he commutes daily from home to the Gower Street lot which is about a half-hour flight, so I asked him if he wasn't used to a bumpy ride. He shook his head.

"Jesus, no! You never get used to that kind of roughness; it can scare the hell out of you."

Some of the Duke's colleagues out here in Hollywood say that while Wayne had a reputation for being considerate to others, he wasn't always quite so empathetic.

"He's never been other than decent to people whether or not he liked their politics—the Duke's on the far right, you know—" Ray Crossett told me. "But after that cancer operation he had a few years back, he's gotten to be one of the most understanding, decent persons you're ever likely to meet.

308

When you talk to him you get the feeling he's happy just to be alive."

Shortly before Christmas of 1964, Wayne went into the Scripps Clinic in La Jolla, California, for a routine checkup and was informed that he had a malignant growth on one of his lungs.

"That was really rough going," Wayne said. He took a few sips of his coffee, shook his head, and rubbed one of his huge hands over his chin.

"I was one of the lucky ones, that they discovered it so soon. The operation was completely successful. As you can see, I'm doing all right."

He grinned.

"That was seven years ago and I've been in great shape ever since. But it makes you think about those guys who aren't so lucky."

I recalled one of the less fortunate ones, Nat King Cole, and I remembered that the Duke had sent a telegram of hope and encouragement pointing to himself as an example when the great entertainer was faced with an operation similar to the Duke's.

Immediately after Wayne's operation at Good Samaritan Hospital in Los Angeles, the actor's studio announced that only a benign abscess was removed from one lung and news of the malignancy was withheld.

"My advisors all thought it would destroy my image," he told the Associated Press. "I thought to myself: 'I was saved by early detection. Movie image or not, I think I should tell my story so that other people can be saved by getting annual checkups.'"

He did. Obviously the Duke's image was in no way harmed by the revelation and since that melancholy Christmas of 1964 he's been in excellent health, a fact he thinks about much of the time. After our second cup of coffee, Wayne stood up and walked around the room.

"If this annoys you I'll sit down again," he offered. "But I have a hell of a time sitting still; I'm kind of restless."

While occasionally he gropes for the right word, his voice is strong and clear and I had no trouble hearing what he had to say about Hollywood, its future and his own. On one of his walks around the room he paused for a few seconds to glance out a window which overlooks the empty Paramount lot.

"It's just a goddamned shame," he said. "What's happened to Paramount and all the other majors? There's nobody around here anymore who knows how to tend store. They're all in trouble. They keep bringing in people who don't know a damned thing about the Industry. Maybe they know how to sell Canada Dry Ginger Ale, but they *don't* know how to make moving pictures.

"They come out here and put their dough in the majors. Because of the land grabs of real estate, they figure they can pick up cheap and sell at a big profit. I have no objections to real estate operators, but don't send them, or oil company executives either, to run a business they don't know a goddamned thing about.

"The stupid jerks have a hard time making their minds up about anything, and when they finally do they haven't got the guts to stick to their decisions. Fellows like Jack Warner or L. B. Mayer, and even Harry Cohn whom I didn't like but who *did* know his business, made plenty of mistakes. But they made plenty of successful pictures, too, and when they decided on something that was it. But the studio heads out here now, they vacillate all the time. I'll give you an example, an expensive one for Paramount, of what I mean."

He sat down briefly to refill our coffee cups and went on to pace and to talk.

"*Green Berets* was part of a two-picture deal, the other was a Western, I had with Paramount a couple years back. Everything was all settled; the deal was closed and they *still* couldn't make up their minds about anything—script, location, and so on—and kept me waiting and waiting and waiting until I couldn't stand it anymore.

"Finally we went over to the Warners lot where everything looked O.K. because Jack Warner was in charge. But Jack had just about had it himself and was leaving the company with somebody else taking over. Well, to make a long story short, the new man—I won't mention his name—kept questioning me about everything I was doing every second. He forgot I'd put nearly forty years into the Industry and he hadn't put in forty weeks.

"I was so goddamned disgusted I told them I was ready to call off the deal unless they could get somebody in to straighten out the mess. After a lot of inaction, they brought in Mervyn LeRoy, who knows what movie making's all about. He came out here even before *I* did, and it didn't take him more than a few hours to get everything back on the track."

The Duke walked over to the desk where I was struggling with my notes trying desperately to keep up with the rapid flow of his conversation. He smiled apologetically.

"I'm sorry I've been going so fast, but I get wound up every time I think of what they're doing to a great Industry. Yell out if I get too far ahead of you."

I promised I would and Wayne continued, slowing down slightly.

"This business requires integrity and it's not here today. There's no dedication anymore and then the idiotic mistakes they keep on making, one after the other. Experience means nothing; no wonder everybody says Hollywood is dead, and I'm inclined to agree. Let's talk about budgets for a couple of minutes. We had some mighty big ones in those days and we had plenty of small ones, too. But whatever they were, we stuck pretty close to what was allotted in shooting time and cash and did the best we could. There weren't many so-called runaway budgets in those days. You think Jack Warner or Adolph Zukor and the others would permit spending twice and sometimes five times as much as they were told to spend? Hell, no! Somebody'd get his head chopped off if he did. But today!"

He whistled.

"Do you know what movie really knocked Hollywood on its ass? Believe it or not, it was *The Sound of Music*, and do you

311

know why I say this even though the picture grossed a hundred million bucks or so?"

I shook my head.

"Because the majors thought they'd discovered the formula for success. All they had to do was spend money; the more they spent, the more they'd make. It was as simple as that. The *hell* it was! Everybody started to make pictures with multi-million dollar budgets like *Paint Your Wagon,* and you know what happened to most of them. They didn't nearly bring in production costs, let alone profits.

"Let me tell you something else they did, which is almost unbelievable. They found a real star in Julie Andrews and she could have had a long successful career ahead of her. She created a wonderfully sympathetic, simple role, a lovable girl everybody liked and proved it by shelling out their dough at the box office. Julie was a marvelous contrast to the characters they'd been doing out here in those X-rated films.

"So how do they handle Miss Julie Andrews and her future?"

The question was rhetorical; I just kept on making notes.

"Why, they put her into an expensive picture, *Star,* tried to make her into a sexy, sophisticated dame which, believe me, she isn't, and disappointed the millions of fans who came to see her as they remembered her in *Sound.* So *Star* became a costly failure, not only for Julie and the studio which made it, but for the whole damned Industry."

The Duke waited a couple of minutes until I caught up. Actually I was hoping he'd get a telephone call or two so I could take a breather, but they never came. Only later did I find out the Duke rarely ever permits any interruptions to his interviews. ("Mr. Wayne has too much respect for writers trying to talk to him," his secretary told me.)

The Duke continued.

"You know something, I've been in all types of movies, not all Westerns, believe me, but I try to be an essentially decent person in every one."

He chuckled.

312

"Even when I'm playing the drunk—there are nice drunks, too; I know a few of them. But I've never played a cruel, harsh character, and I never will. Once, a while back, I was contemplating doing a different kind of film with a different kind of hero, something offered to me. Fortunately I talked it over first with John Ford. You can tell how long ago that was when I tell you the example John gave me.

" 'Duke,' he said, 'take a look over at Harry Carey and watch him work. Stand like he does, if you can, and play your roles so that people can look upon you as a friend.' And that's what I think I've always done."

I'd been waiting, not eagerly but expectantly, for the patriotic pitch I'd been told was inevitable. It came, albeit in abbreviated form.

"This is a great country," the Duke said, "with great traditions and great folklore. I just hope nobody's going to mess us up."

He paused to look at a large autographed picture of our vice-president hanging in a prominent spot on the wall.

"If there were more guys around like that one, it'll never happen. He's got the guts to stand up and speak out. As far as this new generation of 'Americans' is concerned, I'm damned glad their courage doesn't equal their rhetoric."

I withheld comment; this was an interview, not a debate, and besides, I *like* John Wayne and while I may not agree with many of his political philosophies, I can't deny his patriotism.

"Speaking of folklore," he went on, changing the subject, "one of the goddamnedest things happened with *The Quiet Man*. Did you see it?"

I nodded.

"Over here in America, of course, we all get a bang about our own traditions. You know, the winning of the West, tall Texans, cowboys, Indians, sheriffs, U.S. marshals and other lawmen, but who the hell ever figured we could get an audience to pay to see the folklore of Ireland? But by God we did!

"When I saw the script for that one I told John [Ford]

we'd be up the creek if we did *The Quiet Man*. He didn't agree and he was right. That picture made money; John was producer-director and he knew what it was all about; people flocked into theaters to see what they were doing in Ireland. He took a gamble I don't believe I'd have taken."

He sighed.

"Well, that's the way it is around here now as I said before, little guts and little vision. There's still plenty of talent around, although, if you know where to look for it and it doesn't get misdirected. Ever see Paul Newman?"

I said I had.

"Now *there's* an actor who's got it if he'd stop hurting himself playing those anti-hero roles. The man has real talent and you know what I'd do if I were as young as Newman? I'd form my own television producing company and get ready for pay-TV. Because that's what's coming soon, sooner than most of us think, and that's what's going to save the Industry, even though it's all over for Hollywood itself.

"Who needs Hollywood anymore? What's the use of shooting a New York street scene on a lot out here when you can do one for far less right on location in New York. Or, for that matter, if you're doing a movie in England, Mexico, or Italy. Maybe they don't quite have all of Hollywood's skills, but they're learning fast."

He shook his head.

"It's not that union costs are much lower elsewhere; it's simply that they give you a kind of freshness and cooperation you don't get here anymore. In Hollywood, it's 'I'll get mine and to hell with you.' You know that old story about the greenhouse man and the cut-glass vase, that's the famous example. But goddamn it, it's true in some form or other in every studio out here, and that's one of the main reasons we're dead.

"But we were talking about commercial TV. What we have now on TV is controlled by Madison Avenue, but I don't think they'll hang onto the same hold on pay-TV. They can't without their fifteen or twenty percent collected from the commercials. I see pay-TV in the not-so-distant future and this, I think, is how it will work as far as those who make it are concerned.

"At the moment when we're making a picture for both media, we know our feature films will show in theaters for from one to a couple of years and then, after quite a while, they go on the air. But pay-TV is going to work differently. We'll do the feature film, all right, but we'll pull them out of the theaters in three to six months, hold them for another three months, then show them on pay-TV. And it won't be the tiny screens we show them on now."

The Duke glanced at his watch; it was almost noon.

"Sorry," he said, "but I've got a twelve o'clock date with an AP guy. Why don't you come along? I'd be pleased to have you as my guest."

I figured I'd be about as welcome to the AP man as he would have been to me the last couple of hours, so I declined politely.

"O.K.," Wayne said. "But before you go I want to show you something. See that over there?"

He pointed to a highly decorative wall screen which I judged was about three by five feet in size.

"That's what's coming, you mark my words, and it'll be the death blow of dirty X-rated pictures which have just about run their cycle anyway. What you're looking at is a family-size screen and it will show family-type movies."

He grinned.

"I just hope I'm around long enough to act in them."

I hope you are, too, Duke. I'll ride the plains with you anytime. You name it.

Chapter Thirty-One

THE M-G-M Lion no longer roars. On a quiet day, if you listen hard, you might hear Leo emit a mouselike squeak as Jim Aubrey twists the poor, forlorn beast's tail. But the glory that once was Metro's is gone forever; the great American dream machine which ground out our foolish fancies at the rate of fifty-two a year has rusted beyond repair and its once-lustrous components are scattered from Culver City to Capetown.

Metro-Goldwyn-Mayer, at least the Metro-Goldwyn-Mayer I knew for nearly five decades—the studio which turned out *Ben-Hur*, *The Big Parade*, *Broadway Melody*, *Good-Bye Mr. Chips*, *Grand Hotel*, *The Good Earth*, *Gone with the Wind*, *The Great Ziegfeld*, *Andy Hardy*, *Mutiny on the Bounty*, *Showboat*, *The Wizard of Oz*—is dead. I attended the wake although they called it an auction sale.

While I shed no tears, I couldn't hold back a sentimental gulp that smoggy May morning when a slick auctioneer mounted the platform on Stage Number Twenty-seven and offered a pair of Marie Dressler's petticoats—the ones she wore in *Tugboat Annie*—to the highest bidder. I don't know where or how the well-dressed, elderly gentleman planned to use Miss Dressler's oversize undergarments, but he had a cheerful (or it could have been sheepish) grin on his smooth-shaven face when he upped his offer to one hundred twenty-three dollars, and, amidst cheers from the gallery, claimed his prize.

I should hate to leave anyone under the impression that such trivia were all that Mr. David Weisz, the "international auctioneer," and his colleagues offered for sale on M-G-M's one hundred-eighty-acre Culver City lot where they disposed of millions of items which had been gathering dust in the studio's warehouses. Apparently M-G-M never threw any-thing away. Far more important merchandise was put on the block, as, for example, the Louis XVI Aubusson and Beauvais salon sets used in the Norma Shearer–Tyrone Power version of *Marie Antoinette*.

They sold the one-hundred-seventy-five-foot boat *Cotton Blossom*, a steamwheeler used in *Showboat*, an antique rail-road engine, The Reno, and four coaches she pulled along in countless horse operas and in Jimmy Stewart's classic *How the West Was Won*. If you had the dough you could have bought a Dutch village where Katherine Grayson sang "Tulip Time," the tiny French town M-G-M built for *The Singing Nun*, the Philadelphia street Katharine Hepburn trod upon in *The Philadelphia Story*, and a segment of New York's China-town.

Mr. Weisz's minions sold the stable where Elizabeth Taylor—then only twelve years old—quartered Pirate, the great black stallion she rode to a protested victory in *National Velvet*. There were bidders for the house where Eddie Cantor lived in *Forty Thieves* and the porticoed Tara of *Gone with the Wind*, any number of Conestoga wagons, one with a once blazing arrrow still embedded in the tattered canvas, a World War One "Jennie," the bed Debbie Reynolds slumbered on in *The Unsinkable Molly Brown*, Mickey Rooney's 1931 Model-A he drove in the *Andy Hardy* series, a Locomobile, a Stanley Steamer ridden in by Lionel Barrymore and Wallace Beery when they made O'Neill's *Ah Wilderness*, a Sherman tank and Judy Garland's slippers, the ones she wore in *The*

Wizard of Oz, bought by a sentimental California millionaire for fifteen thousand dollars. I can only hope there was enough magic left in poor Miss Garland's footgear to give the gentleman his money's worth.

A Des Moines, Iowa, lady bought the Chinese wedding carrying chair upon which Luise Rainer sat in *The Good Earth*, and a Canadian youth was the highest bidder for the clothing Paul Muni wore in this movie adaptation of Pearl Buck's bestseller. There was a complete arsenal from muskets to machine guns plus remnants of a "typical" frontier town including saloon, blacksmith shop, marshal's office, general store, and post office. There were slave ships and a model of the *Mayflower*. The chariot Charlton Heston rode in *Ben-Hur* went for twenty-six hundred dollars. Item No. 11624 was the table Freddie Bartholomew used in George Cukor's 1935 version of Dickens' *David Copperfield*.

It would take reams of paper to list all the memorabilia; it took months to dispose of everything. Figures were not released but experts believe the amount realized from the sale was slightly more than thirteen million dollars, or a gross profit of nine million dollars since the price the auctioneers reportedly paid M-G-M was four million dollars. Even four million dollars was a lot more money than the studio had made on any of its films in a hell of a long while.

Bill Golden, a big, friendly ex-newspaperman who's been handling M-G-M's p.r. since the departure of Howard Strickling, for whom he worked, says the sale was the best thing that could have happened to M-G-M. A week before the auction I talked to Bill in his almost abandoned office, which in Strickling's day housed half a hundred employees.

"This way we cleared out all the sentimental trappings of the past which were holding us back from concentrating on the future. Jim Aubrey's had the guts to streamline our operations and after floundering around at last we know where we're headed. Let the past bury its dead!

"There's no longer any need for the huge lot we always operated on. Jim says we're going to hang on to about twenty-

318

five acres and sell off the rest. We'll make some pictures ourselves, of course, not nearly as many as we used to, possibly twenty or twenty-five a year. And about half of these will be made in the United States although not necessarily in Hollywood. The rest we'll probably make abroad. I doubt if *any* budget will be over two million dollars.

"M-G-M's always been ahead of the other majors and I think we're going to keep the lead. We know where we're going and they're still trying to figure it out. Movie-making will be a completely different operation in the future."

He shook his head and sighed.

"But Jesus! It was fun while it lasted. This lot crawled with stars and they all showed up at lunch time and sat together at a huge round table. Taylor, Tracy, Allyson, Turner, Crawford, Pidgeon, Grable, Montgomery, Katie Hepburn, Rooney, Garland, Garson, Errol Flynn, Lionel and Ethel Barrymore, Garbo. I could go on and on. We *were* the glamor capital of the world."

Bill looked at me.

"Well, that's that. You're going to the sale, aren't you?"

I told him that Marcy Rothman, a slick little blonde (an ex-Philadelphian by the way) who handled the sale's enormous public relations job, had invited me to a working press preview of the auction.

"Would you like a pre-preview?" Bill asked, and although I didn't quite know what he meant it sounded interesting. So he arranged for his assistant, Dore Freeman, to give me a chauffeur-driven tour of the lots. Most of the items had already been removed to the huge, barnlike studios where they'd be auctioned off, but there were quite a few immovable objects that would have to be disposed of, if at all, where they stood.

Esther Williams' Olympic pool was an example of the latter. While I've never had the pleasure of meeting Miss Williams in person, so I'm not really qualified to make a comparison, I'm still sure the lady has held up better than her pool from which weeds grew out of deep wall crevices and where a green scum had settled on puddles of rain water covering the neglected bottom.

We drove by another swimmer's idyl, this a tiny copse of woods where Tarzan, in the person of Johnny Weissmuller, swung from limb to limb with the great apes until he became Lord Greystoke. There was also a fifty-foot-high façade of a railroad station and a half-acre lake upon which so many sea dramas were shot. I forgot to ask Marcy if anybody bought these items, but I wouldn't be surprised if they were sold.

We wound up in the wardrobe and sewing rooms from which porters were removing dressmaker's dummies. Pete, our chauffeur, came along with us for this part of the tour.

"Whose was this, Twiggy's?" he asked, looking at a flat-chested model. The porter stopped and Dore smiled. "I think it's Hepburn's," and according to the tag he was right. Another dummy caught Pete's eyes but for a completely opposite reason.

"I don't have to look," Freeman answered before the question was asked. "It's Judy Holliday's."

Pete whistled, then reverently removed his chauffeur's cap. "May she rest in peace."

I guess that also sums it up for Hollywood.